Praise for Ross Brewitt's Previous
... LAST MINUTE OF PLAY

". . . a unique look at our hockey heroes through the eyes of a man who has been there to see it all. Wry, witty, and hilariously funny. . . . *Last Minute of Play* is a gem."
— **Teresa Hergert,** *TSN*

". . . he scores the hat trick with this one. Blue and I loved it!"
— **Don Cherry**

". . . Brewitt does it with the honesty and sincerity you'd find from an old friend sitting across the rec room, enjoying a cold one on a frosty Canadian night."
— **Bob Feaver,** *PETERBOROUGH EXAMINER*

". . . he's done what I thought impossible — come up with a host of fresh anecdotes. Excellent hockey book? Ross Brewitt's memoirs."
— **Jim Proudfoot,** *TORONTO STAR*

"Just what I always wanted to do. Sit down in my living room with Dave Keon and Eddie Shack and Phil Esposito and Chico Maki . . . *my* hockey heroes. Thanks a puckload!"
— **Dan Blakely,** *CHUM FM, Toronto*

"Brewitt sure isn't heaven-bent when he writes about the NHL's people, but there's too much affection in the telling for him to be hell-bent. Ross passed on a lot of kiss-and-tell, and instead chose to kick-and-yell about the game he loves so much!"
— **Paul Wieland,** *Buffalo Sabres TV Director*

"From the close checking of Chico Maki, to the scoring touch of Phil Esposito. From the quiet grace of Dave Keon, to the loud and boorish behaviour of Harold Ballard — Brewitt's tales of hockey's enduring personalities are a joy to read."
— **Frank Rupnik,** *SUDBURY STAR*

"The boys of our best winters open up to Ross as they never would to us, exposing their hearts and their hurts. Luckily, for the reader, we can eavesdrop. It's the best!"
— **Wayne Stevens,** *800 CKLW, Windsor*

"Most hockey books are like the regular season — this is a playoff book."
— **Dennis Hull**

INTO THE EMPTY NET

Ross Brewitt with the NHL Old Stars.

INTO THE EMPTY NET

Tales of Big League Hockey

ROSS BREWITT

First published in 1994 by
Stoddart Publishing Co. Limited
34 Lesmill Road
Toronto, Canada
M3B 2T6
(416) 445-3333

Canadian Cataloguing in Publication Data

Brewitt, Ross, 1936–
Into the empty net

ISBN 0-7737-5674-4

1. National Hockey League.   2. Hockey — Canada.   I. Title.

GV847.8.N3B74 1994   796.962′64   C94-931329-7

Cover design: Brant Cowie/ArtPlus Limited
Typesetting: Tony Gordon Ltd.
Printed in Canada

Stoddart Publishing gratefully acknowledges the support of the Canada Council, the Ontario Ministry of Culture, Tourism and Recreation, Ontario Arts Council, and Ontario Publishing Centre in the development of writing and publishing in Canada.

To the wit and candor of the players.
And, to Angel and Mike,
who kept me pointed in the right direction.

Contents

Prologue

ED SHACK AND I SAT in a coffee shop at the Regina airport. We had just endured a two-hour drive after speaking the night before at the Estevan Bruins' celebrity dinner. To say we looked tired would be redundant. We were talked out, burned out, and washed out. The usually unrestrained Mr. Shack sat spread-legged, pants stuffed into his black cowboy boots, his 12-litre straw hat pushed back, moustache drooping, staring balefully at all the "varmints and galoots" scattered around the other chairs and tables. A real-life Yosemite Sam.

A lady who had been fixedly watching Eddie, hushing her table partners several times, finally screwed up enough courage to approach him and ask guardedly, "Are you Eddie Shack, the hockey player?"

"I'm Eddie Shack, the *old* hockey player," he boomed back, startling her into a flinch, loud enough to cow a couple of Air Canada workers at the cash register. One instinctively reached for his ear protectors. The woman reached into her large handbag and withdrew a copy of . . . *Last Minute of Play* for Ed to sign, turning to look gleefully at her group, as if to say, "See! Who's a dummy now?"

"Where am I, Roscoe?" Shackie asked, handing me the book to flip open to his picture.

"Page 41, Eddie." I handed the open book back, and he scrawled the usual

"Ed Shack — #23." Meanwhile the once-cautious and tight-lipped woman was yapping a mile a minute, trying to get her life story *and* the reason for being in Regina in one serpentine sentence. ". . . and we're from Ontario, but we've got these relatives on my husband's side — that's him over there in the red jacket, glasses — they moved out here for business, he's a geologist — not my husband, his nephew, and . . ."

"You better get him to sign it, too," Eddie ordered, interrupting and pointing at me slouched comfortably in my chair.

"Who's he?" she asked disapprovingly, as if I were in a line-up behind bulletproof glass.

"He wrote the book," Eddie said, still pointing like a dog trainer, urging the woman to "fetch." She grudgingly came around the table and reluctantly offered the pen and book, looking down her nose at me through large round glasses.

"Who do you want me to sign it to?" I asked, flipping to the front pages.

"To me. No, make it to him," she said, wavering between choices but staring at Shack, who was busily preening his moustache with a large thumb and index finger.

"To Eddie? He's already got one."

"No, to the other guy, him . . ." she said, now peering intently at the book, trying to compare my picture with the real thing.

"The guy in the red jacket or the geologist?" I asked, pen poised. Satisfied with my photo ID, she ignored my question and sailed into a story about buying the book: "The clerk in the store had suggested it if I liked hockey, and I *love* hockey, ask anybody, they'll tell you I've been watching hockey all my life. Every Saturday night we'd have a bath and my . . ." I shifted a look over to Shackie for relief, but his eyes had glazed over. So I signed the book.

"To Him: Nice to accidentally meet somebody who accidentally bought the book by accident. Hope your ears don't fall off!" I penned my name with a flourish.

"Do *you* really know all these people?" she asked, glancing over the list of chapters, ignoring the autograph but giving me a second, uncertain, once-over.

I recalled the question after the manuscript for this book was almost finished. I recognized belatedly how very fortunate I was to be able to answer her in the affirmative. I had followed a direct route in a lifetime of sports beginning from my hometown of Thunder Bay, through hockey and baseball, as a player and coach, into radio, on to a once-in-a-lifetime job with the promotion arm of the group who ran *Hockey Night in Canada,* working with the Leafs and Maple Leaf Gardens, then on to the Buffalo Sabres with Punch Imlach. Soon after that came the opportunity to work with the Toronto Maple Leaf players in the formation and direction of the Molson ProStars, a fastball team hatched by Darryl Sittler that toured Ontario for five summers in the mid-1970s. Then came the NHL Old Stars, soon to be the Labatt's Original Six oldtimers, touring North America for another five years beginning in 1980.

And all this was intertwined and laced together by speaking engagements, story writing, notes and memos, golf games, press-box visits, and late-night gab sessions. I had the rare opportunity to be on the inside, rubbing shoulders with owners, managers, coaches, and the players, God bless 'em. Every damn funny one of them.

The stories that follow are as close to my memory, research, and interview talents as a man can get, because if you hang around dressing rooms, practices, and game-day skates, as well as in the endless repetition of lobbies and at airport gates, you'll hear a lot of comments and evaluations of the players, coaches, and management.

Hang around the media and you'll hear even more discussion about who's hot and who's not. Conversely, the players, coaches, and management can give you chapter and verse on the media. It's a never-ending dialogue, biased and slanted, which one side rarely hears face-to-face from the other.

As an illustration I'll relay a little story I was able to witness first hand. I won't mention the names or the teams so as not to create a wide rift between two people now in management positions.

Punch Imlach made a trade, as he often did, but this one was not a popular one, to say the least. Come to think of it, most of Imlach's trades were unpopular, which should say something about the man's supreme confidence in his talent for swapping talent.

One of the players in the trade was considered a particularly distasteful acquisition by a venerable member of the media, who could be heard denigrating the player from the press box at any opportunity. The media type, an outspoken and supremely confident man on his own, lurched out of his seat one night when the player in question gave the puck away and was circling with his head down after the resulting goal-against.

"That asshole plays like I screw," the man roared, standing with fists balled on the countertop. "Not very good, and not very often," he seethed, red-faced, looking up and down press row, making sure we had all heard. Another crusty old scribbler took in the scene then yelled back, "Get outta here. Nobody could possibly play *that* bad!"

Today the two gentlemen in question talk without reservations, but I'm sure the hackles would rise if the remark was repeated between them.

Press boxes can be the most interesting places, as in that incident. Except when they're boring, which happens a lot. To relieve the tedium there's often a discussion-du-jour between the scribes and talking heads. I remember an unfunny one in the media room where the accredited gathered to eat for free. The subject was the hypothetical aftermath of a plane crash involving one of the NHL's top teams. The newsies concocted mock-obituaries and the stark results of such a horrendous accident. There was a moment of sad reflection tempered with relief that the tragedy was imaginary. Then one of the group wondered what would happen if the ceiling were to cave in on the cream of the city's media.

"Nothing," said an unsympathetic visiting scout at the doorway, taking a snapping, crunchy bite out of an apple before wandering off to the press box on high. We all agreed.

The press-box incident I recall most fondly was the night we made an airtight case for hockey over every other known athletic endeavour. The question was, what's the biggest gamble in North American team sport?

Baseball? Intentionally walking a batter to fill an empty first base, taking the chance on turning a double play or giving up a three-run homer? Was it one manager removing a regular and bringing in a cold pinch hitter to go with the best percentage, or the other manager going with a fireballing reliever to throw it past the other team's big hitter? Maybe a squeeze bunt that even the guys in the washroom can see coming? Baseball is too slow. Dramatic, but not second-by-agonizing-second, piss-pants scary, like hockey.

Football? Opting not to punt and going for broke on the last down? Could be, but it's still planned. Throwing a "Hail-Mary" pass into an end-zone melee that resembles a Roman orgy? For a game that lives and breathes tendencies, stats, percentages, and execution hinging on nths of seconds, that's sheer desperation. Putting all the money into a field goal by a sparrow-legged, mallard-necked geek in an oversize helmet? From 52 yards out? Now we're gettin' close.

Basketball? Tossing a ball from one end of a court to the other for a three-pointer is not a gamble. It's got all the thrill of watching a lottery draw when you don't have a ticket. It's the kind of last-chance logic that compares favourably with astrology, reading tea leaves, and the faithful belief that patronage will be scourged from the political agenda by the incoming new guys.

Soccer? The only gamble in the world's most popular game is whether there will be a riot, a stampede, an insurrection, or simply a community sing-along.

Volleyball? Right up there with indoor soccer, rowing teams, bowling teams, tag teams, and team knitting. Swimming teams? As comedian George Carlin succinctly put it, "Swimming is not a sport, but merely a way to keep from drowning."

The biggest gamble of all is in the great game of hockey. Not ice hockey, as people from the American networks are often heard to exclaim, feeling it's necessary to differentiate between roller, field, ball, table, floor, or road. Nope. Hockey is the game where the coach pulls his goaltender, leaving nothing but naked netting. This manoeuvre is done with only one thought in mind. *To draw even.* All the eggs in one basket. There is no turning back, no half-in half-out, no fudging, no cheating. It's the ultimate bet, unique in sports. Everything is wagered on this last-ditch storming of the gates to have even a chance of getting a tie, in order to eventually win. The very decision to take out the goalie in order to add another player on the attack says it all. There is bald-faced commitment, the pure confidence of a coach to call on a strategy that will take the game out of his tenuous control, delivered without recall, leaving the outcome to the talent and ability of the players. Their job is to function, literally, like tightrope walkers without a net. Everything is wagered on a quick grin from Lady Luck, a blind trust in the bounce of a little rubber puck, and the inevitable laws of physics.

No other major sport allows for this kind of substitution. No other contest condones this type of risk or one-sided advantage. Because it can work both ways. The team pulling the goaltender is the one with the worse odds. They can fail to score and remain exactly where they started. Losers. They can be scored upon and lose by two. Or they can score and, at best, only draw even.

Back when I was with the Buffalo Sabres organization and shared car rides and conversation with GM and coach Punch Imlach, we often talked about the game and its unforgiving, but fair, playing surface.

"Anything can happen on the ice," he said one night after a regular-season game, sitting in the confines of his office in the Auditorium. The team had salvaged a tie with the extra attacker and sent the hometown fans out of the building in a festive mood. Now, after the hubbub outside and inside the dressing room, after the thrust-and-parry of the media, he sat tilted back in his office chair, scrubbing a tired face with his hand, trying to massage some energy back to the surface. On this night, though drained and drawn, he was feeling reasonable, almost charitable, about the extra attacker.

"It's somethin' you gotta do. You can't pass up the opportunity. See them goddamn Russians?" he added cryptically, pointing behind me. I almost swivelled in my chair, fully expecting to get a glimpse of the Red Army Chorus, until it dawned on me he was referring to the eighth game of the '72 Canada-Soviet series. "Those bastards wouldn't take Tretiak out of the net when Henderson got the goal. They just sat back and played out the string. Know how long you'd last pulling that shit in the NHL? Not very." He looked over to a framed colour photo of the first Sabre team, and snorted, "Forget that strategy crap, that's for the newspapers."

"Tonight, then, was just building the legend," I offered into the lapse of conversation.

"Yeah, I suppose. Told our guys the only thing I could. First, get the goddamn draw. Don't have to be a genius, yuh know. Even these guys gotta understand *that*. Move it in, move the puck around, and take high-percentage shots. Get it to Rick Martin, get it back to Rene (Robert). Take a chance. Yer losers right now, so you got nothin' to lose." He threw up his hands in a gesture of finality. "I told them — she's all yours." Still charged up, he absently moved items around the desk top like a chess player, then stood, jamming hands into his pockets.

"What happens? Their dumb defenceman drops in front of the net. I mean, you gotta be stupid to drop in front of a shot comin' from that far out. Who the hell did he think he was? Tony Esposito? Ticks off his damn arm and it's in. Yeah, so now I look like a PhD. Hell, it was them that made a mistake."

It was simply a time the good guys won, according to Punch.

It also underlined how fickle hockey can be. As often as I watched games, either from the press box or the stands, when an empty netter was scored I invariably looked toward the losers. Television rarely shows the losers until after that instant of abject loss has passed, the split-second sense of defeat that has such finality trailing it. Instead they seem to gravitate to the celebration of the winners, the ones who have it sewn up, the ones who know they have a lock on the game.

If you look through the high fives, past the hugging and back pounding, you'll see the losers' head-down skate to the bench, and their coaches' inscrutable glance up at the clock, for no discernible reason. They wait, stricken, abandoned, standing alone, naked in the eyes of the celebrants.

The feeling out there is akin to the aftermath of a slapshot off the foot. A hot stinging that grows and grows in intensity as the first numbing coverup recedes. There's no use whining, and there is no comeback. It's over.

Much like the careers you are about to be introduced to, some famous, some only notable among their family and friends. To them the NHL is buried, like a dead-centre slapshot into the empty net.

*   *   *

In . . . *Last Minute of Play* I dealt with those who had reached the ends of their careers. In this collection I have added some more of the people I had a chance to deal with over the years in hockey, their observations on and remembrances of a space in their lives that's important to them, if only for the memories.

As before, I have had each of the people profiled select six players called the "90-Second All-Star Team" — one goaltender, two defencemen, a centre, and two wingers he would feel confident sending over the boards to score but not be scored upon. The only string attached was that the players had to be people he either played with or against over his time in the NHL.

Their choices are listed at the end of each profile.

7

The Old Stars

Gone to Join
the Circus

I'VE BEEN ASKED MANY TIMES who started the Old Stars, and I never neglect to list the parents as Ed Shack and Bill May.

May was the reigning idea-guru of Pop Shoppe International, a quiltwork of soda-pop licensees around Canada and the U.S. who rose to public prominence on the idea that people would buy soft drinks directly from the bottler, and return their own heavy plastic cases full of empties. Distributors followed and soon corner stores and gas stations were part of the marketing empire. They all owed their ready public acceptance to the ample beak and outrageously growled claims of Eddie Shack. He delivered "I got a nose for value" in a latter-day Jimmy Durante style on radio and television, and his countenance grinned off signboards and in newspaper ads.

May wasn't the first to employ the considerable talents and appeal of Mr. Shack, but he was the first one with enough temerity to stick with him. The cowboy hat, walrus moustache, and prodigious proboscis, which had weathered 17 seasons in the NHL, were to become the focal points for a successful ad campaign. But in his off time, he still loved to play hockey and, had it not been for Shackie's disgruntlement at playing with the NHL Oldtimers, the Old Stars would have had to surface in another way, at another time. In spring 1979 Eddie was looking for a change.

"Some of them old bastards smoke goddamn pipes in the dressing room —

Aiming for a change-on-the-go. Shack handled the on-ice humour with the Old Stars.

Trainer Joe Sgro with the author at the Original Six television shoot in Markham, Ontario. His sense of humour was second to none.

Larry Cahan, one of the "All-Star" comics to play in the NHL: a 6'2", 225-pound defenceman, with tremendous strength but no mean streak.

between periods — and talk about their grandchildren, fer Christ's sake," he growled at an afternoon meeting in May's office in Etobicoke.

He went on to bridle at the slow pace of the games played by the Oldtimers, and the travel, mostly in their own cars, never knowing if weather or "babysitting" chores might cut the roster down to ten skaters. Shack also refused to believe the only teams they could line up against were other sets of oldtimers, radio station "celebrity" teams, the local firefighters, or the industrial league all-star squad.

May spun a great story about taking the show on the road and playing the big cities against bigger and better teams. While he had me mesmerized for a while with his practised spin doctor's skill, I noticed he hadn't mentioned anything about *him* being involved with these bigger and better teams. He also failed to mention how this project would be mounted — until he slid in the thought that I was "the only guy who can get a decent sponsor and pull this whole thing into a saleable package." He added, as icing, that he and Eddie had come to this momentous decision about two minutes before calling me to the meeting.

"Roscoe . . . you're the guy who put the Molson ProStars on the map, stickhandled them through five seasons, and you can do it with the NHL Old Stars, too." Which should answer the question of where the name came from. Billy May, again.

As the seasons went by I was constantly asked how come it was the Labatt's NHL Old Stars and not Molson's, and I always had the same answer. I explained how I took the line of least resistance, showing up on Molson's Fleet Street doorstep with an outline and a first-year budget. Molson's sponsored the ProStars. Molson's sponsored the NHL telecasts. Who else, I reasoned. But Molson's was lukewarm at best, and they were offered two weeks to think it over. After the allotted time I called. And called.

With time running short I took the plan to Labatt's, dropping it on the desk of an old pal, Dick Bradbeer. At the time he was everything Labatt's stood for in the promotion field. He moved me to Betty Verkuil, who was the new Ontario promotions manager. In ten days we had a deal, but it wasn't without some burning questions being raised. For that meeting I enlisted the support of Bob Nevin and Norm Ullman, two of the players committed to the proposal. Shackie couldn't make the meeting — which may have been a plus, in the light of what happened, because it came down to one concern.

"How can we be sure you guys won't get out there and trash a few hotel rooms, or get into something — say a fight with the locals?" Betty asked the three of us sitting around the tiny cubicle of an office.

"It won't happen," I offered lamely, mildly offended she would link me with such shenanigans, doubly miffed that such a thought would ever cross her mind, but really distressed because the possibility had crossed my mind more than once. For support, I turned to the two gentlemen who were obviously there representing the players, expecting at the very least matching pained expressions. They only managed to look unconcerned.

"Why not? What guarantees do we have?" Verkuil persisted. It seemed to me that it was impossible to provide guarantees — and even if you had them, who's to say some clown won't mess it up? I was about to say, "Well, shit happens," but instantly recognized that as a career-altering phrase.

"We'd be out there representing Labatt's, and we understand the concerns," I countered, trying to instill a picture of responsible professionals doing a job. "The rules are spelled out, and we'll stick to them — as a team," I added, realizing that this was a pretty flimsy guarantee from a business standpoint.

"And who would a goof-off answer to if the situation comes up?" Ms. Verkuil wanted to know. Norm Ullman, the quiet, unassuming listener, Hockey Hall of Famer, carried the day.

"He'll have to answer to us," he said, pointing to himself, Nevvie, and me. I've never been sure what convinced Betty that day, and I probably never will. I do know if she had looked into the grinning eyes of Eddie Shack, we'd have been out of there in a minute. Whatever she heard in our remarks gave her the fortitude to recommend that the new and improved Old Stars become the Labatt's Old Stars.

We toured the United States and Canada for five years, 147 games in all, and while personnel changed from trip to trip, the nucleus of the team remained intact.

Along with Nevin, Shack, and Ullman, there was Jim Pappin, Dennis Hull, Pit Martin, Fred Stanfield, Tom Williams, Pat Stapleton, Bill White, Dale Tallon, Errol Thompson, Dallas Smith, Darryl Edestrand, Marv Edwards,

Mike Pelyk, Pierre Pilote, Chico Maki, Jack Valiquette, Jim McKenny, Mike Walton, Larry Mickey, Dean Prentice, Derek Sanderson, and Brian Glennie.

In addition, we had single and two-game performances or bits and pieces of seasons played by Frank Mahovlich, Carl Brewer, Bob Wall, Don Luce, Gerry Meehan, Hilliard Graves, Keith McCreary, Stan Mikita, Doug Favell, Gerry Desjardins, Billy Harris, Al "Junior" Langlois, and Noel Price.

It would be nice to say the transition from Oldtimers to Old Stars was easy, but it wasn't. There were those on the Oldtimers who despite being outfitted with new gloves, pants, and uniforms, plus having their practice time paid for, still wanted it to remain the way it was. As I recruited new and younger players, including Dennis Hull, Pat Stapleton, Fred Stanfield, and Pit Martin, it was obvious animosity was stirring and a split was in the offing. Some of the players — Ullman, Nevin, and Shack, for starters — always believed the compromises we had worked out would suffice. For them it was difficult to play on both sides of the fence, and soon it came down to making a choice. By the end of the first season I was making my reports to Mike Buist of Labatt's and was surprised when he called one day and said, "Do you know anything about a meeting I'm attending with some of the players?"

When I said it was a mystery to me, he explained that a four-man delegation was coming to the Labatt offices to discuss the coming season. It didn't take long to find out who the four were, or who was behind it. On the Tuesday of the meeting Buist called again.

"Seems they want to stay sponsored by us, and they want to have 'players' in charge of the team. I told them in that case the meeting would be short, that if you weren't running the Old Stars there would be no Labatt sponsorship. I closed up my notepad and that was that."

The people behind the "coup" never played with us again, with the exception of two, who steadfastly claimed to have been uninformed, ignorant, or both. It was the only time it was player against player on the Old Stars, because for the most part, the team was a happy group.

Eddie Shack was the leader of the fun part. When he was on the trips, there was always something going on. Like the time in Vancouver when he ordered an omelette. With instructions. As he had done countless times before.

The Hotel Vancouver has been home to kings and dignitaries from around the world. Eddie didn't care, and when the uniformed waitress paused at our table to take the orders, she noted everything on her pad until Eddie spoke up.

"Yeah. I want orange juice, and toast, them little potatoes, and a cheese omelette. Now, make sure you tell the guy," he admonished her, holding up two bear-like hands to indicate caution, "tell him I don't want it hard, you know. I want it runny in the middle. Like snot."

The waitress gasped, put a hand to her mouth, and headed briskly for the kitchen. Eddie said the eggs were perfect. Message received, thank you.

On our first trip to Sydney, Nova Scotia, we played in the old arena, the biggest Cape-Cod-style building I had ever seen. It was all wood, inside and out. There we played against our old buddies from the NHL, Paul "Jigger" Andrea and Norm Ferguson. After the game we were paid a visit by two more notables. John Hanna, an old teammate of Shackie's on the Rangers, and the Lord Mayor. I mentioned to His Worship that the building was old and should there be a fire my considered opinion was that the only thing left standing would be the sprinklers. He gave me a lecture on the state of the union and the prudence of fiscal responsibility. However, he harrumphed, be assured that on our next visit, a new edifice would be in place.

Eddie, who had listened to the entire speech with widening eyes, guffawed, and wearing a big old grin and a large towel uttered his response to hogwash. "It's easier to slide through shit than sand, big boy!" Barefooting his way to the shower, he left the Mayor and me to ruminate quietly about this profound adage over our post-game beer.

In Yarmouth we were walking back to our hotel after lunch when Ed spotted some lobster traps piled on the docks. He split from the group and we could soon hear his "haw haw haw" ringing across the waterfront and see him shaking hands with some of the dockworkers. He marched away with a lobster trap on his shoulder, waving his thanks to the men in the boats. "I told them I needed one for my bar" was all he said to us, giggling as he walked through the hotel lobby.

The next day, there was Eddie, lobster trap on a leash, dragging it through the Halifax airport. Believe me, a trap isn't something you can safely store under the seat, but he was reluctant to turn it in to the baggage check before we boarded. His eyes lit up when it appeared on the baggage carousel in Toronto. The last I saw of him that trip was when he walked out of "Arrivals" dragging it behind him. People stopped to gawk — as if he needed the attention! To one startled woman who was staring at this celebrity in cowboy boots and hat, dragging a lobster trap, he only growled, "Have yah ever bin to sea, Billy," leaving her blinking in puzzlement.

I only bring these few "Shackie's" up as an indication of the antics that were the daily fare on any Old Star excursion. But Eddie Shack didn't have to carry the whole load as far as humour went. We had people who did very well in their own way, and on their own time.

For instance, there was Joe Sgro, the first man I recruited when the Old Stars team was conceived. He was the long-time trainer of the Toronto Maple Leafs, the trainer for Team Canada '72, and one of the pitchers on the Molson ProStars as well. He was the first recruit because, as I had explained to the people of Labatt's, "if we want to have a first-class show, we're going to need Joe." The idea was that the players would be treated in a professional manner: class-A uniforms, gloves and accessories that matched, new skate laces, white and blue tape, sticks, the works. And Joe made it happen.

The first time Dale Tallon played a game with us he glanced into the dressing room in Niagara Falls and saw the uniforms hung up, names and numbers out, the skates neatly placed under the seats, shin pads, gloves, and elbow pads stashed above, shoulder pads, jocks, and socks hanging from hooks over the neatly folded equipment bags lying on each seat. Two rolls of tape, one white, one blue, were also on the bench for each player. Sticks were lined against a wall, and the medical kits and extra gear were stowed neatly in a corner. The hair dryers were plugged in, ready to go, disposable razors, shaving foam, deodorants, shampoo, towels, and soap were perched on the shelves in the shower room, gum sticks were on an equipment case in the middle of the room, and beer was iced down in one plastic tub, cans of pop in another.

"Shit," Dale said, looking from side to side, "this is better than Pittsburgh!"

But that was Joe. The million-and-one things a professional trainer knows, and does, were something I knew we were missing, and all those problems were solved when he agreed to join us. Still, in the back of my mind, one other thing was almost as important as gum and tape. As I said to Joe on our first meeting at a Leaf practice, "What am I gonna do if one of these guys goes tits up? Call 911? Joe, I don't know mouth to mouth, I don't know where to put an ice pack, I don't know about taping, and I don't even own a pair of rubber gloves, let alone a suture remover. Please . . . join us." On that whiny note he agreed to be our one and only trainer. And he brought more than first-aid and equipment-repair knowledge to the team: in his own special way his sense of humour was second to none.

For instance, we had a referee for the first couple of years named Ron Ego, an ex-NHL linesman who went on to be a WHA referee. Experience had taught us we needed our own referee, for show-business purposes. Ego was a big man, over six feet tall, and growing to similar measurements in the waistline. A jolly guy, he used his wonderful laugh with careless abandon. Like most officials he was very un-officious. On road trips I paired him with Joe Sgro and more unlikely roommates weren't to be found anywhere else on the team. Sgro was into jogging and physical fitness. Ego shunned exercise. Sgro was up and at 'em early, Ego liked his sleep. Sgro had the occasional brew, back then Ego was into Canadian Club, *and* the occasional beer.

We had played in Dawson Creek on a Saturday night and were lolling around the hotel Sunday morning awaiting a one-hour evening bus trip to a place called Chetwynd for our third of a four-game Northern Alberta trip. On the top floor of the hotel we had a string of adjoining rooms and had gathered in Ego's room to watch a televangelist pleading for understanding, and money, on the only channel available on TV. Five or six of us were discussing the previous night's game with Ego, who was lounging in his pajamas, under a pile of bedsheets. Sgro came through the door, bright-eyed and alert as one can only be when returning from a five-mile morning jog in the cold October air. He was wearing a Maple Leaf toque, a nylon tracksuit over sweats, and was beginning to perspire fiercely in the indoor warmth. He paced the large room, "cooling down" as he put it, wiping his face from time to time with a towel, while Ego lay in bed, droopy-eyed and less than awake.

"What the hell are we gonna do all day around here?" Larry Mickey sighed.

"You ought'a know. Aren't you from one of these burgs?" Brian Glennie muttered, referring to the *NHL Guide,* which listed Lacombe as Mickey's birthplace.

Ego groped around for a moment under the bed or under the covers, I couldn't tell, but came up with a new bottle of Canadian Club. "I got a forty-pounder," he said sleepily, brandishing the bottle overhead. "Let's get a hooker, and have a party."

Now before anyone gets upset, it was only a joke, a carry-over from the lines we had used on the bus the day before.

"How small is Chetwynd?" was yelled in unison, followed by one of the many small-town jokes.

"It's so small they have sex and driver education in the same car."

"How small is Dawson Creek?" by the choir.

"It's so small the town hooker has to work part time at Mr. Muffler."

Sgro, still hot-walking himself, stopped sharply, raised a threatening finger, and barked, *"Bad sidewalks."* That was it, leaving even the befuddled Ego looking at the ceiling, squinting, trying to grasp a relationship.

"Joe," I said, looking into the incensed eyes of our trainer, who was obviously angry, "what about bad sidewalks?" I put my hands out to the sides and shrugged. He whirled back to me and stuck the finger in my face.

"Listen, coach. I've been out there running through this town, up streets, down streets, zigzagging, out to the highway and back, crisscrossing the main drag, all on the damn sidewalks — hurdling the concrete, stubbing my toes all over the goddamn place. It looks like a bloody rock garden out there . . ." The last part was delivered as he put his hands on his hips in exasperation.

"So, what's the —." I never got a chance to finish, before he stuck his sweaty face almost nose to nose with mine and said, "You clowns don't get it, do you? *Bad sidewalks means bad hookers!*" he roared at us like a demented teacher, yanking off his toque and revealing the worst bad-hair day in hockey history, glaring at us like we were students who refused to do their homework, and stomping into the bathroom, slamming the door while we all broke up at his performance.

The next morning he shifted gears. Rising early, I was shaving while my roomie, Marv Edwards, an even earlier riser, read a two-day old newspaper. I could hear Sgro in the next room rummaging around and getting ready. We always left the adjoining doors open and although I couldn't see him, his voice was as clear as a bell.

"All right Ronald," he was saying to his roommate, "I realize you're awake, but if you could just give me an indication — let me see you move your left foot." There was a momentary pause. "Good boy — now, if you could wiggle the toes of your right foot. No, no . . . see Ron you're not listening. The right foot." Again the pause. "Beautiful! Now, I want you to put your right thumb in the up position. *Outstanding!* Next, I want to see you sit up, and touch your toes — index fingers are fine." Pause. *"Perfect,"* Joe yelped sharply, as if a new height had been reached.

By this time, curiosity getting the better of me, I stepped out of the washroom, face soaped and razor in hand, to see this intriguing spectacle. If Ego could touch his toes, from any angle or position, I wanted to be the second person to see it. Edwards was already in the doorway and as I looked over his shoulder, there was Sgro, absently packing his suitbag with his back to Ego, not even looking at him. Without so much as a backward glance, Sgro stuffed a pair of shoes into the pocket of his suit bag and continued, blissfully unaware anyone was watching, which made the scene almost hysterical.

"All right, Ronnie, you're doin' real good. Now if you could just do this one last trick — I want you to blink your eyes — first the left . . . good, and now the right one. *Atta boy, Ronnie,*" Sgro growled, jabbing the air in an "alllll-right" sign.

I looked over at Ego as Edwards dropped to his knees laughing. Ron, mouth open, tangled in a mass of bedsheets, oblivious to everything, had not moved a muscle. Even our howling together with the pop-eyed, giggling Sgro couldn't wake the referee from his sleep.

It was like that on the road. A place to have laughs, to be in a group with inside jokes, and to be a support group for ourselves. Players who were once sworn enemies joined and appreciated the humour, the pranks, and the characters in a whole new setting. I recall a game we played in Chicago at the Circle Arena on the campus of Illinois U. For this game we gathered together extra players and split the squad, although we all dressed in one large dressing room. The promoter of the event, which set a Circle attendance record of more than 9,500 — there to see Bobby Hull and Stan Mikita reunited for the first time since 1972 — came in to warn us about the rules. "There'll be no body contact, no boarding, and absolutely no fighting," he admonished all, then left the room, which had grown silent at the ludicrous announcement.

Reggie Leach, one of the milder members of the "Broad Street Bullies" from Philadelphia's heyday, broke the ice and broke up the room by drawling, "What seems to be the fuckin' problem? I played that way my whole career."

Another game in Vancouver, this one against the Canuck Oldtimers, found a group of us gathered around a hospitality suite (courtesy of Labatt's) listening to my old Thunder Bay compadre, Larry Cahan, expound on his days with the also-ran New York Rangers and the wily ways of his coach, Phil Watson. Cahan, another East Ender from Fort William, was a 6'2" 225-pound defenceman, with tremendous strength but no mean streak. He played 13 years in the NHL, none of them easy, none of them winners, but he made up for it with his comic touch and a flair for what made people laugh.

"So, I go into Watson's office and I know he's gonna stiff me. He says, 'Tell you what, Cahan. I can't give you a raise this year. It's out of the question.'" Cahan waved a cigar expansively, imitating Watson and setting up the punch line. "'But, here's the big picture . . . Cahan. If we make the playoffs I'll make sure you get a cool 2G's in your pocket.'" Cahan sat back for a moment, then leaned forward again, assuming his own role. "'Well that's real good, Mr. Watson, but if it's all the same to you, why don't you just buy me a fuckin' sweepstakes ticket.'"

In the Old Stars years and during the Original Six television shoots in Toronto, I heard Larry tell that story again and again, and it never failed to bust up a crowd of hockey players.

Then there were the trips to The Rock, Newfoundland, where we were "screeched in" several different times. It's a quaint little custom the locals have to introduce visitors to the wonder of Screech and coated baloney, which as far as I could tell are native staples. In Clarenville Bob Nevin and I were approached by two burly gents, one with a bottle, the other with a loaf of baloney covered in the printed outer layer, dripping oily juice on the floor — and onto Bobby's shoe. No novice when it came to knocking back Screech, Nevvie only had one question before the ritual. "Is the Screech to wash down the baloney, or the baloney to wash down the Screech?"

It's the one time we almost didn't make it.

Once an elderly garage attendant in Stephenville gave Pat Stapleton and me directions, knowing full well we were tourists. "Don't go down dis road too far, boys," he cautioned, jerking his head toward the main street.

"Why not?" we asked in unison.

"Well, she goes all da way t'England, but she's washed out at da light-house," he said gravely. We could still hear him cackling as we drove off.

One of my fondest memories of the Old Stars days was a trip we took to Humboldt, Saskatchewan. Flying into Saskatoon we were met by a large bus, the sales manager for Labatt's, Gary Mitchell, and five guys who billed themselves as the University of Saskatchewan Marching Band.

"Who got tricked into this?" I said quietly to Mitchell as we got under way, nodding my head to the fresh young faces of the band.

"Don't worry," he replied nervously, "you're gonna love 'em." I can remember having my doubts. I was wrong.

At the end of the first period the U of S Marching Band took to the ice. Huge sunglasses, fright wigs, old-style bathing suits (the ones with the hole in the knee), makeup, big clown feet, red ball noses, fully loaded brassieres, plus the trumpet player in combat boots and a white tutu were a sight to see. The five-man band was comprised of King Tutu on trumpet, twin kazoos, a trombone player, a bass drummer with knee-mounted cymbals, and a baggy-pants guy who doubled as the hum-a-tune player and baton twirler. First cabin, all the way. I can remember thinking, "What the hell would Betty Verkuil say to this ridiculous shit?"

According to the PA announcer, who was obviously following a script, they performed intricate marching manoeuvres, serpentine steps, formed the letters "I" and "L" for no apparent reason, and then they lifted the crowd into a standing ovation when they did a perfectly timed split around the Zamboni, which was bearing down on them, all to the tune of "This Ain't Dallas." In short, they almost stole the show.

They won our hearts as well. Coming into our dressing room at the end of their stint they were treated to cold beers. Shackie, unable to resist, hiked the tutu up with the blade of his stick to reveal nothing on underneath. The applause and cheering emanating from our room must have puzzled the fans in the rink awaiting our return. It was simply five young guys being welcomed into the Old Stars family.

As we rode the bus back to Saskatoon, the traffic ground to a halt at the scene of a semitrailer tilted off the shoulder of the road. It was surrounded by the flashing lights of three RCMP patrol cars and a pair of giant tow trucks. Mitchell left the bus, returned from the frigid night air in minutes, rubbing his hands and advising us that no one was hurt, but the trailer was going to be a write-off. A few donned coats and left the bus to see for themselves. Suddenly the piercing cry of a trumpet playing "Taps" reverberated through the arctic air of the Saskatchewan night, pissing off every Mountie and anyone wearing coveralls for miles. We were waved through the mishap, at 2:00 a.m., on a rocking bus, trailing the strains of "Six Days on the Road" played Sally Ann style. Lots of bass drum.

Those are just a few moments that spring to mind when the Old Stars are mentioned. When the alumni get together, as often happens in arenas around the country, the stories flow, retold and refurbished all over again.

You're going to read a lot more of them as the profiles of those who have experienced "empty-netters" unfold.

Pit Martin

Cadillac Jack's and
the MPH Line

MARCH. WINDSOR, ONTARIO.

"The Rose City" was not at its best the day Bob Kolari, the ex-WHA referee, and I arrived to meet with Pit Martin. We'd driven into the border city fighting wind-driven sleet and snow all the way from London.

So Cadillac Jack's was a welcome sight, at least from the outside. Inside it seemed cavernous, and definitely devoid of patrons, although we had to admit it looked more like a nighttime haunt than a place to meet at three o'clock on a Wednesday afternoon.

We walked up to the empty bar and a politically incorrect bartender named "Butch" greeted us as if we were lucky to get in ahead of the rush. Kolari was wearing a Blue Jay jacket, I wasn't, so I introduced us just for laughs.

"Hey, Butch. This here is Todd Stottlemyre," I said, pointing to the bigger-than-life Kolari, "and I'm Dave Stewart. We're here to discuss the cover charge." Dead, unrecognizing silence, although the grin stayed in place. This in spite of a colour photo of the two wayward Blue Jays on the front page of a newspaper on the bar.

"OK, Dave, what can I get you fellows to drink?" he said with an even bigger smile. Definitely not a Jays fan, and as it turned out, not a hockey fan either.

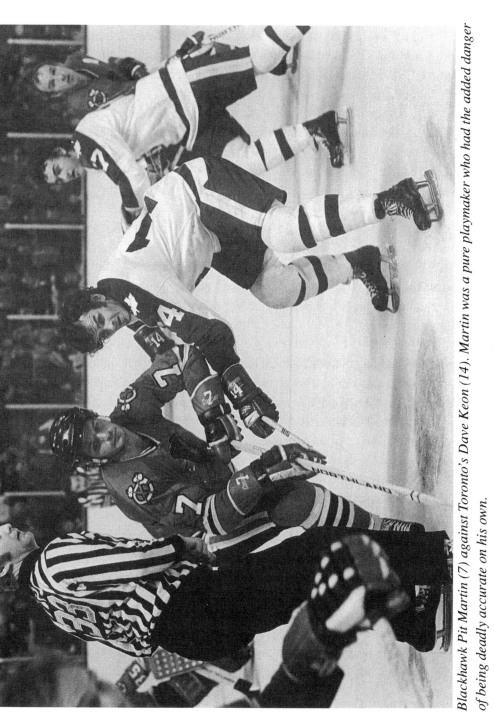

Blackhawk Pit Martin (7) against Toronto's Dave Keon (14). Martin was a pure playmaker who had the added danger of being deadly accurate on his own.

"Have the mixed couples luge runs started yet?" I asked, trying to determine how far afield I could go with this guy. He looked at me blankly, so I pointed to the Olympic coverage silently playing on three TV screens around the barnlike room.

"Oh, not that I know of. I don't think there's any skiing today anyway." That was far enough, which was just as well, for at that moment in walked Pit Martin.

We had the advantage of seeing him without being seen, and it gave me a chance to compare the real thing with the memory. A few years had passed since we had been in each other's company, and as he searched us out I couldn't help but think how little he resembled a hockey player. The guide book always said 5′9″ but most would dispute that as being the club PR guy's idea of building up the team. We used to call that kind of fudging "print muscles." The 170 pounds I could go for, because the intervening years had been thin ones for Pit. Though he hadn't stretched an inch, his weight hadn't changed much either.

The greetings out of the way we moved to a table by the large front windows looking out on Chatham Street, which was a wall-to-wall mess of snow, slush, and cars. As we settled in I ran his final stats through my mind and wondered about fleeting fame. Here was a guy with over 1,100 regular-season games and an even-100 Stanley Cup contests under his belt. In 17 years in the NHL, he had scored 324 goals. So how come he was mainly remembered as a downside member of the Deal of the Century?

Raised in Noranda, Quebec, he had apprenticed with the Hamilton Red Wings juniors before splitting parts of three seasons with Detroit and Pittsburgh of the American Hockey League. On December 30, 1965, he was dealt to Boston for Parker McDonald and in 41 games scored 16 goals for the fifth-place Bruins. This was back in the days of the six-team NHL, when a 20-goal season spelled success for any forward. The next year, his first full NHL season, he was the only Boston player to reach 20 goals in 70 games. It was also the start of a career for a guy named Orr. Despite Martin and Orr, the Bruins sank to sixth.

The Bruins were looking for something, anything, to get help for Bobby Orr. They already had Ted Green, Johnny "Pie" McKenzie, Ed Westfall, and John Bucyk, but they were missing the integral pieces up front. Meanwhile, the Hawks were still trying to find the elusive centre for Bobby Hull and felt the man they needed was the smooth, slick Martin, an easy skater with darting speed, a playmaker and a young 20-goal scorer who could keep pace with the Golden Jet.

As in most trades, you give some to get some. According to a telephone poll almost 25 years later on a Toronto radio station, the deal that saw Martin, defenceman Gil Marotte, and goaltender Jack Norris vacate Beantown to make room for centres Phil Esposito and Fred Stanfield, plus giant winger Ken Hodge, was the Deal of the Century. As the years went by, the Bruins won two Stanley Cups, while the Hawks, though division champions for four straight years, only made it as bridesmaids in the finals a couple of times. Some called it the Steal of the Century. Those are the surface facts, but how did that deal affect one of the principals?

Sitting across from Pit Martin I glanced at the large club ring on a smallish hand, a big diamond dead centre, and reasoned it must be a divisional championship. Although the Hawks were close, there were no cigars except for the one in the hand with the ring on it. He was dressed typically. Tan slacks, ivory turtleneck, with a beige, quilted ski vest deferring to the inclement weather. A touch of grey fringed the sideburns, but otherwise it was the Pit Martin I remembered. Off the top I asked the question about the trade. The hand and cigar made a "so-so" motion.

"Welllllll . . . ," he started with a tone that was a familiar cross between a singsong and a whine. "At Boston we finished out of the playoffs, but I felt pretty good about myself. I played every game — 70 — 20 goals — just getting comfortable, you might say. Things are looking good, and I'm thinking positive about the contract talks to come up when (GM Harry) Sinden says he wants to see me in his office. Hell, when the general manager asks for a meeting, you go. But I might as well have stayed home, I never got to say two words. How's this for an opening? He said, 'How can I describe your year?' and I sit back to listen. 'Mediocre' is the word he used to sum up my season, and that was the end of the discussion. Yeah — mediocre. When the trade came on May 15 I was happy to get out of Boston and over to Chicago. I was so high I held out for 18 days at the training camp." He took a drag on the cigar, and squinted through the blue haze that followed.

"Whatever you're paying for stogies, Pitunia, isn't enough. Buy good ones," I said, stifling a cough. He smiled and reminded me I was the only one who had ever called him by that nickname.

"Anyway, I get to Chicago for training camp and there was a group of us, unsigned, who weren't going to go on the ice without a contract. You know, you go out there, get injured, and it's goodbye Charlie. Easy for them, right? Let's see — Pierre Pilote, Marotte, Ken Wharram, and me, we were all gonna sit it out. Pierre caves in first, says he's going to skate with the boys, Marotte goes into the office and signs right there, and I can't remember what happened with Wharram, but it leaves me and Tommy Ivan (Chicago GM) in a meeting.

"I've turned down their offer, and I'm holding out for a raise of $1,500 based on my season in Boston, which ain't that bad. So Tommy says, 'We've got an arbitrator for cases like this.' Guess who? Clarence Campbell, yeah, the president of the NHL. This is the guy who's gonna look at this case impartially. Tommy calls Campbell up and says, 'I have Mr. Martin here, and we've made him an offer but he has a higher figure in mind.' Then he hands me the phone and Clarence says, 'Now, Mr. Martin, you are a third-echelon player, at best. What the Blackhawks have offered you is fair, and there's no reason why you shouldn't sign.'

"I hand the phone back. Naturally I don't agree, but he talks to Ivan for a few moments longer, and Tommy hangs up the phone saying, 'Well now, I'll have the contract drawn up for you to sign.' That's when I got mad. I told him either pay me the raise or forget it. I made my way to the airport and went back to Windsor. These two guys believed if they said it, that's the way it was gonna be. It was like that back then. Take it or leave it."

Except for the intervention of Jack Adams, the long-time Red Wing GM, who had watched Martin develop both as a junior and in the American Hockey League, Pit's career may well have been somewhat shorter than 17 years.

"Jack called me and said, 'I hate to see you out of the game, kid. Look, Chicago is playing an exhibition game in London. Why don't you meet me at the Windsor Tunnel, bring your skates, and let's go up and see the boys play, maybe chat with Tommy and see if we can't resolve this situation.' All I said to Adams was that the chat could be short. It would only take 1,500."

The two drove to London and ran across Ivan in the dining room of the Holiday Inn on Wellington Street. Small talk was the order of the day, but

Ivan eventually got around to setting up a meeting in the arena manager's office for 6:30 p.m. And the real cards came out on the table.

"Tommy hemmed and hawed for a while before saying, 'Pit, it's not so much the money. Campbell is the arbitrator, and for me to go your way, well, it would cause us some embarrassment, if you get the idea. Can't you see that?' So I just said, 'You pay me the $1,500 in a separate package and I'll sign your contract. Only you and I know, and nobody gets upset.' 'Deal,' Ivan says, and I played the next game in Montreal, with Bobby Hull on the left side. I scored 10 seconds into our first shift, too — on Gump Worsley. But that was it for a while. Boy, was I out of shape."

Another blue cloud of smoke hung over a grin. "I always liked Tommy Ivan," he added, to no one in particular.

If he liked Tommy Ivan, he loved Billy Reay, a no-fooling coach who had the audacity to treat the Hawks like men, letting them do their thing within certain guidelines. Billy Reay walked that fine line between being one of them and on his own at the same time.

"The first year Bobby Hull scored 44 goals with me at centre and Chico Maki on the right side. The year before, with Esposito, he had scored 52. I took a certain amount of heat over it, but hell, I honestly believe Bobby could score 50 with Paul Terbenche (a defenceman) at centre. We were just different styles, different players, different thinking. Bobby came from behind, and waited for you to give him the puck, and he was everywhere, on his off wing, coming up centre, half the time we were bumping into each other. He didn't need a fancy centre. Bobby could do it on his own. As far as I was concerned, it was obvious we didn't belong together, but you do what you have to do. The next season Billy put Jim Pappin, Dennis Hull, and me together at training camp and it was just like one of those Road Runner cartoons. Acme Instant Line. Just add water and, zoooooooommmmmm . . ."

Off the ice, the three were as unalike as it was possible to get, yet each brought a special talent to the line. In a game Dennis Hull was the loose cannon, the one who could explode in a burst of speed and fire one of his patented bombs from anywhere on the ice. He was truly one of the most feared shooters in the league. Pappin brought an analytical mind, a great touch around the net, and a sense of defence carried over from his Maple Leaf background. Martin was a quick, buzzing centreman who could pass to either side, forehand or backhand. Despite his size, he was constantly in and out of the opposition goalmouth for rebounds and loose pucks. He was a pure playmaker who had the added danger of being deadly accurate on his own.

The proof was in the stats. All three had been in the teens for goal production in the season before they formed a trio. Martin had 16 and Dennis Hull 18 with Chicago, while Pappin scored 13 in 58 games with Toronto. They all had identical 30-goal seasons their first year as a line. For seven years (1968–69 to 1974–75) Billy Reay had one-third fewer worries in filling out the game sheet, as far as front lines were concerned. They were a lock on all but a few nights, because all three had durability, collectively missing only 104 of the 544 Chicago games in the seven years they played together. Meanwhile, they put in 601 goals for the Blackhawks.

"We didn't know that from the start, eh?" Again Pit waved the smouldering stub of the cigar between index finger and thumb, looking at it studiously for a moment, gauging how much enjoyment was left. "That first season Billy Reay came to me and asked why Dennis had never scored a hat trick. He could shoot a puck through a wall, scared the living shit out of our own guys in practice, but like Billy said, he'd get two and then forget how to play the game. He'd be all over the goddamn place. Usually you could rely on Dennis to go up and down his side, like Rick Martin, because he was one of the best positional wingers in the game, but then he'd get two goals and next thing I know he'd be like Bobby, coming from behind, crisscrossing, getting on the other side. I'd be looking for him here, and he'd be way the hell over there," and he pointed from a "Bud" sign behind us to another one back of the bar. Butch, being an attentive bartender, thought we had ordered another and in jig time there were two more beside the ones we were working on.

"Back then, people were down on Dennis because of the comparison between him and Bobby. There were letters to the editor complaining that he should be better. But you couldn't mistake the talent, and that's when I noticed the goalies flinching. Any time he banged one toward the net, they'd jerk a little, so we worked it out, and as soon as he got open I'd try to slip him the puck. That's how he got the extra space to shoot. Like I say, we just clicked, and gradually he became confident in himself. Dennis deserved everything he ever got — the All-Star selections, Team Canada."

The subject of Dennis Hull was completed, as was the cigar, which he regretfully deposited in the ashtray to smoulder. I poured some beer on it as the *coup de grâce*.

"Pappin was another case altogether," he sighed, crackling the wrapper off another mosquito-mover. "The only ex-Leaf I had anything to do with before 'Bird' was Ronnie Stewart. In Boston. He was a critical son-of-a-bitch, too," he wheezed, teeth clamped on the new Corona, diligently searching through an array of vest pockets for the matches to fire it up. As he became visible through the haze once more, he began talking.

"Roscoe, I don't know whether the rest of the Leafs were like that, you know, Nevin, Pulford, Horton, or any of those guys from the Stanley Cup teams, but hell, every time you made a move Pappin or Stewart could tell you how to do it better. Pains in the ass, the two of them. Honest! I never had coaches who had as many answers for anything and everything. I told Dennis shortly after we hooked up with Jimmy that the Maple Leafs were all alike, giving everybody shit all the time. We'd just never been exposed to it before."

He paused for a moment, and we turned to stare through the window behind me at a car whose tires were screaming in protest. A disgruntled Windsorite in a black sports car was fighting six inches of slush in a spot big enough for a Brink's truck. The slush won.

"It wasn't as if Pappy was without faults, fer Christ's sake," he muttered, dismissing the sports car wizard. I turned back on the high stool and mentioned that we northerners would never have a thing like that happen to us, jacking my thumb toward the window. The only acknowledgement I got was Butch bringing us two more.

"Jimmy was nearsighted as hell," Pit went on. "Couldn't see worth a shit, and didn't wear contacts. If it was a 30-foot pass, he never saw the puck leave your stick. If you didn't put it on his stick, he'd skate right over it, to hell with it. He wanted all passes on the tape." He jabbed the cigar to the side and downward. I fully expected Butch to show up again with yet another round.

"One road trip we had played in Vancouver and the next day we hit Oakland. He never stopped getting on my case. Then we moved to L.A. with a day off, and I'm sitting in a bar near the hotel with a double in front of me, really feelin' miserable. In comes Bobby Hull. 'Pit, what's the problem?' he asks. I told him, 'Goddamn Pappin has driven me to drink.'" I ducked under another rolling cloud of Havana smog.

"See, we didn't look at the game the way Pappy did. He picked out things about the other team, how we could do things better against them, what their tendencies were, what certain players would do in certain situations. Looking back, I suppose all of us like to think we know the game, but Jimmy was a guy who took it apart. He was a real sports fan, and I don't just mean hockey. All sports. Baseball, golf, boxing, everything. Man, he could eat up a newspaper, get all the stats, changes in standings, the whole works. Me, I never even watched hockey games when I was at home. Yeah, 'Bird' was a very astute observer of the game."

Behind me the tires were spinning with an even more insistent squeal. The door opened and a line of business types trekked toward a centre table, and for a brief time the roar of the sports car filled the big bar. Butch, ever watchful, hustled to their table, and I could only surmise that we'd be able to wave and point with impunity for a while.

"But then we started to get it together and the MHP line (Martin-Pappin-Dennis Hull) was born. We had patience, had a feel where the other guy was at all times, and we stopped trying to fit ourselves in. Instead we let the other team adjust to us. Pappin had a lot to do with that, and so did Billy Reay."

Once again the name of the Chicago coach surfaced, as it always seemed to when Blackhawks of that era spoke of the team. Sort of a Windy City Mutual Admiration Society.

"Billy never wanted to hear anything bad. He was a liberal with a difference," Martin said, waving through his own fog without seeming to notice it. "My very best years in hockey were with the MHP line, and Billy was responsible for that. He rarely told us what to do, or how to do it, just let us go out and perform. He was at his best in the February games, when the doldrums hit. February is such an unpredictable month. In March you can see the playoffs, you get your ears up then, but in February, that's when a coach has to be watchful, kick a little ass, get a few guys to perk up. Billy Reay was good at it. Hell, even then our practices were only 45 minutes, never those two-a-days you get from some of the slave drivers. When we went on the road there wasn't any entourage like you saw with some of the other clubs. It was Billy, two trainers, and the players, that was it."

Pit smiled as the dawn of a memory peaked over the horizon. He hunched over, his head down near the tabletop, like a school kid laughing when he wasn't supposed to.

"We were in Philly. They had that goon team then, and we had tied — 5–5, I think — ah, what the hell, it doesn't matter, it was a moral victory anyway. It was Wednesday night, and we didn't play again until Saturday is what I remember for a fact. Billy had extended the curfew after the game and we descended on the hotel bar like a cloud of locusts. Man, we're all pumped up, tying the Broad Street Bullies in their own building. Our line did well, even by Pappin's standards, and we plow right through all the name-brand beer. About a half-hour after curfew we're still poundin' 'em back but now we're down to the local crap." He waved the cigar over his head searching for the names. "Pingencrap, Schlotzendip, shit like that, really acting up, too, when suddenly somebody says, 'Here comes Billy.'"

Pit looked surprised when Butch put down two name brands again. "The guy really pushes, doesn't he?" he asked, looking over his shoulder at the retreating bartender.

"Where was I . . . oh yeah . . . There's a couple of doorways off this bar and the guys are diving behind tables, crawling out to the kitchens like goddamn commandos, and through fire exits, anything to get away from the place without being seen by Billy. But Dennis and I are boxed in at the end of the bar with no way to leave, so we duck behind this latticework partition where all the dirty linen is piled, you know, napkins, tablecloths, towels, plus there's a little closet, full of stuff. Now we're trapped." He takes a look around, like someone might be eavesdropping, but there's only the eight accountants, and the ever-alert Butch.

"Is this the one when Dennis tried to stuff you in a dumbwaiter?" I asked, recognizing some of the story from Dennis Hull's account. Martin actually looked offended and the cigar stopped dead, in mid-gesture.

"Naw — that was all bullshit, really. We had a better plan," he replied, realizing this was a new story even I hadn't heard.

"We were gonna get in the laundry wagon and pull the dirty linen over us, and soon as Billy left we'd sneak back to the room." I had to agree it was a much better plan.

"But we started laughing and couldn't get enough linen to cover us, which only made us laugh louder. Then we could hear Billy, and we had to stay down behind the partition, almost ready to piss ourselves. We waited and waited and I whispered maybe I should take a look — you know, see if he was gone. So, I rise up, just a little, and there he is, standing patiently, looking straight at me from about ten feet away." Pit sat there shaking with laughter and only rubbed his fingers together to indicate another speeding ticket on the highway of hockey.

By 1976–77 Pappin had been gone for two years, banished to California and Cleveland. Martin had 17 goals, Dennis Hull 16, and the MPH line was no more, the laughs a thing of the past. The Blackhawks traded Martin to the Vancouver Canucks seven games into the season, although he still had the touch, scoring 15 goals and 31 assists in 67 games. The following year would be his last. In 1979 he retired, outlasting both his MPH linemates.

"I'll never forget that Canuck training camp somewhere on Vancouver Island — Comox I think. We had Harry Neale, his first year as an NHL coach. We went through land training, two or three miles of running through the bush every morning, then back in the gym, on the ice, gym, back on the ice. Jesus, I'm 34 by this time, and I figure my career is over, or I'm dead, one of the two. About then they started showing us the colour swatches for the new team. Hey, the colours weren't bad, still aren't — but the goddamn uniforms! We played an exhibition game with them. New gloves, new pants, new everything, breaking them in during a game, and you know how tough new pants are to form up. But everybody was talking about the uniforms, everybody but us. Hell, we were all trying to make the team while trying to pretend we didn't notice. But the people everywhere in hockey and around the league were saying it anyway." He sighed, and shook his head almost imperceptibly. There was a tinge of embarrassment and it showed. "Some psychologist in California said the colours and shapes were aggressive." We let that one hang.

"Next year, I went back to training camp, still ready to play. The desire was there. Nobody could outskate me, and goddammit, I made the land training, made the plays on the ice, but they didn't renew me. I left there a free agent, and came home to Windsor. As far as I'm concerned, *they* retired me. I wasn't ready to go. Couple of phone calls, but . . ." and it seemed fitting that the cigar had gone out, too.

By the time we left Cadillac Jack's that afternoon, the accountants had loosened up a bit, Pit had gone through another cheroot, Butch still had no idea who Pit Martin was, or Todd Stottlemyer, either, and the sports car remained hard against the curb.

Later, I was left to remember the Pit Martin I knew. The Original Sixer was reunited with Jim Pappin and Dennis Hull on many occasions, but proved he could be every bit as fleet and graceful with less-familiar linemates, and could still make those deft moves and sneaky passes to anyone who wanted to play.

But with the exception of the notoriety of the big trade, he never received the recognition he deserved, and it made me wonder why. The MPH line played seven great years together. Pit Martin played 16 seasons in the NHL.

You figure it out.

90-SECOND ALL-STARS

G — **Tony Esposito** *". . . night after night, a solid performance."*

D — **Bobby Orr** *". . . how could you pick anyone else."*

D — **Bill White** *". . . mobile, moved the puck, best defensive man."*

C — **Stan Mikita** *". . . intuition . . . he'd get you off the hook."*

RW — **Gordie Howe** *". . . he was always given room . . . explosive."*

LW — **Bobby Hull** *". . . geez, I almost forgot about him!"*

Pat Stapleton

Bring on the Clowns

I'VE NEVER SUBSCRIBED TO THE THEORY that anyone can be described in a single word. Occasionally there are those who become so entrenched in their ways that one word can sometimes be enough, but it's never complimentary, if you get my drift. Don Cherry comes to mind. Most people in this country have a one-word description of Grapes. Sometimes the word is "great," sometimes it's "fabulous," occasionally it falls into the doughnut shop creativity of "sour." It becomes a matter of personal perspective, but most people are complex enough that once you get to know them, a longer description is usually necessary.

It's the same with Pat Stapleton. Only until you get to know him is one word sufficient.

Once, on an Old Stars bus travelling between Bridgewater and Halifax, I proposed a word-association test, the kind where you respond with the first thing that comes to mind. The word I tossed out was "Stapleton." The answers came from front and back, thick and fast.

"Bullshit."

"Asshole."

"Short."

But the one that stuck out like a sore thumb was *"run!"*

For me it had more credibility than all the others. You have to remember,

NHL All-Star defencemen Pat Stapleton and Bill White (background) with Team Canada '72. With a skating style that looked a lot better going backward, Stapleton was an adept puckhandler and a superior passer.

to hockey players, a test like this is a licence to sully and besmirch. With this particular group, I might have heard the same answers had I yelled out "Mother Theresa."

Whoever yelled out "run" could have added flee, leave, or scram, all with the same intent and purpose because, innocent as he appears, Pat Stapleton was, and is, a gold-medal practical joker. Nothing and no one is safe around his inventive mind.

At 5′8″ he was a bit of a practical joke himself as far as hockey was concerned. Born and raised in Sarnia, he graduated from St. Catharines, the Southern Ontario team that sent the likes of Bobby and Dennis Hull, Phil Esposito, Wayne Hillman, Stan Mikita, Pierre Pilote, Vic Hadfield, Fred Stanfield, Chico Maki, and Dick Redmond, among many others, to the National Hockey League. The strange part was that he was a defenceman. A short, stocky defenceman. Packing 185 pounds and with a skating style that looked a lot better going backward than forward, he had great anticipation for the play, was an adept puckhandler, and a superior passer.

He turned pro with Chicago in 1960, playing his first year with Sault Ste. Marie in the Eastern Pro league. In the summer of 1961 he was drafted from Chicago to Boston, playing a full rookie season with the Bruins, who had finished last in the Original Six NHL the year before. With Stapleton joining the club, Boston nailed down sixth even earlier in the 1962 season, but it wasn't his fault.

He barely hung around with Boston in '63, spending 49 games with Kingston of the Eastern Professional Hockey League, and for the next two he played back-to-back 70-game seasons for the Portland Buckaroos of the Western league. But though he was beginning to mature as a player, the Bruins continued to exert a firm stranglehold on sixth place. In his second season he started to show NHL offensive skills and for a long part of the 64–65 season he battled the legendary Guyle Fielder, an MVP and crown prince of scoring in the Western league on numerous occasions. Stapleton scored 29 goals and 57 assists as a part-time centre, playing 10 games at either end of the schedule on defence, while Fielder would put up 17 goals and a league-leading 85 assists over the year. The signal had been sent.

In the summer of 1965 he found himself on the paper roster of the Toronto Maple Leafs for 24 hours before being drafted by Chicago the next day, back where he should have started in the first place. To underline the point, Stapleton would be named to the second-team All-Star defence in his debut year with the Hawks and continued along those lines through eight NHL seasons with the Blackhawks.

In Chicago he would eventually pair up with Bill White as a defence partner — and straight man. It was 1970 when White joined the Hawks, and by the 71–72 season the two were a regular tandem. The marriage was successful, both being selected as second-team All-Stars. It was the intro they needed to be named to Team Canada '72, and as chance would have it, the only game they missed in that historic series was the opener in Montreal, a shocking 7–3 loss. Installed on the blue line for the second game against the Soviets in Toronto, they played in all the remaining games in the series and were the steadiest blue-liners for the winning side.

On the '72 trip, Stapleton and White also teamed up on the flight from Moscow to Prague. It was a time of camaraderie and reflection on what they had accomplished. Many of the players had openly spoken about writing a book, as is the case with most people who have gone through a tramatic and deeply moving experience. But Stapleton simply saw it as a chance to sucker some poor soul, so with plan already in mind, he made sure he and White sat directly in front of one of the team doctors. Once they were cruising along toward Prague they began a discussion on the inner workings of *their* book, agreeing how Phil Esposito had to be a chapter, and so did Paul Henderson. In stage whispers, they discussed the subjects that would be covered in detail: Sweden was a definite, considering the stuff they had to put up with there, and of course there were the Canadian games, a disaster by anyone's standards, plus the fickleness of the Canadian public.

"We gotta tell it all, brother," Stapleton enthused. "Put it right out there in the open, no holds barred. Then we'll talk about the drugs. How the guys were taking all that shit. Who knows what the hell the doctors and trainers were passing out back there?"

The good doctor bolted out of his seat like he'd been reamed with a plumber's snake.

"What are you talking about? Drugs? What drugs?" the Doc asked in a hushed but urgent tone of voice. "All we ever prescribed or dispensed were vitamins, antihistamines, aspirin. Maybe a few tablets to get to sleep . . . the occasional pain killers . . ." he ended weakly, sensing something ominous ahead.

"Not what we heard," was Stapleton's reply, along with a snort from White. "That's what you're saying now, but it's definitely not what we heard. Hey, we're not into that stuff, but if other guys were, well, I gotta wonder where they were gettin' it. Let's face it, Doc, some of our guys played so far over their heads they must'a bin on somethin'." White, ever the "Mr. Interlocketer," concurred.

After much-guarded discussion, the doctor agreed to write a chapter himself, based on the medical "facts" and extensive records, and submit it to Stapleton for inclusion in "the book." A thick envelope was delivered to Stapleton's home in Strathroy, Ontario, within days of Team Canada's return.

Another prank concerned one of the other doctors in the entourage, who also shall go nameless. On hearing the group would be greeted by the Prime Minister upon touchdown in Montreal, the doctor was almost beside himself with glee. A staunch Liberal and fervent admirer of Pierre Trudeau, he could hardly wait to shake the hand of the Canadian leader. He learned of this momentous event while crossing the Atlantic, and somewhere between the cruel sea and Dorval airport he fell asleep.

A sharp knife was involved, possibly a razor blade. Others said it was a scalpel filched either from trainer Joe Sgro's extensive medical trunk or one of the doctors' cases. Either way, the sleeves of the ardent Liberal's coat were cut away from the shoulders except for a few strands of thread, enough to keep the jacket presentable but easy to pull apart.

In the bustle of meeting the PM, the doctor was jostled and bumped enough by those in the know to have him meet Trudeau pulling up his coat-sleeves like a high-school deb tugging at loose bra straps. It was an old trick in the right place.

Years later, touring with the Old Stars, we were in Dartmouth, Nova Scotia, to play the local junior team, and Pat had become chummy with the team coach and manager, who doubled as the arena manager. From this acquaintance our boy Paddy learned that there had been concerns over a creep who occasionally visited the wrong washrooms in the arena and had scared the hell out of women in their cubicles. I have to mention at this point that there was never any confrontation, according to the women, just a male voice in the washroom asking them provocative questions. Naturally, this matter was of particular concern to the arena manager. Was this a goofball out for thrills or a pervert with more on his mind?

The morning of game day, the manager was visited by two "detectives" from the "morality squad" in the persons of our own Tom Williams and Claire Alexander. You can imagine his surprise when two six-footers in leather trenchcoats walked into his cubbyhole of an office, brandishing their wallets with ID and badges. In fact the "badges" were cheap money clips with the seal of the City of Timmins, a gift from an earlier game that year, which they had snapped onto their wallets beside their Ontario photo-ID driver's licences.

They announced they had reason to believe, based on confidential but circumstantial evidence, that the culprit was none other than the junior team's assistant coach. Incredulous, he protested that he'd known the man and his family for years, trusted him implicitly. The officers assured him this was not an arrest — yet — only an investigation, and proceeded to take out notebooks and put the manager through a grilling worthy of an axe murderer, making up questions as they went along and taking copious notes. When they left they offered the advice that he and his assistant would do well to have their stories and his alibi straight within the very near future.

He was a sputtering, red-faced, if not relieved spectator at the game as "Inspector Williams and Sergeant Alexander" skated in the warm-up, waving and laughing. Stapleton, the instigator, fixed by the stony stare of the manager as he skated by, only mustered a shrug, wondering how the manager could make such a ludicrous connection.

But it wasn't always laughs and chuckles playing hockey. There were the times in the minors, the times when they were favoured to win the Stanley Cup and fell short, as in 70–71 when they lost to the Canadiens in seven on the last-minute heroics of Henri Richard. In 71–72 they watched from the sidelines, out of the final as the Bruins topped the Rangers. Once more, in 72–73, they battled into the last round, only to lose to Montreal again. And then the opportunities were gone. Not many players get two or three kicks at the cat in a career. Unless you are Henri Richard.

For Stapleton the NHL was history after the spring of 1973, fading into the fog of the WHA, with the Chicago Cougars and Indianapolis. He was a player, a player-coach, and a part owner, but that, too, would evaporate into retirement at the farm in Strathroy.

Then came the Old Stars, a resurrection, and a whole new cast of characters to prey upon. One member of the team who felt the sting of a Stapleton "sting" was another alumnus of the WHA, referee Bob "Bobo" Kolari.

Kolari had contributed mightily to the Old Stars' on-ice show and was a respected, full-status member of the group. Still, he was as vulnerable to Stapleton's stunts as anyone. Although he was a long-time official, making him more suspicious than the rest of us, he fell victim to a late-night caper in Smiths Falls, Ontario.

We had played the Junior B team there and as was the custom following the game and post-game festivities our door was open. Being the last to say goodnight to our hosts, I made my way up to the sixth floor in the elevator. When the doors slid back, there before me was the gaping entrance of Stapleton and Pierre Pilote's suite. The time was 1:00 a.m. and the crowd scattered around the chairs and beds included Bill White, Fred Stanfield, Tommy Williams, Jim Pappin, Bob Nevin, plus our hosts.

"Did I miss anything?" I asked, accepting a cold one.

"Naw, too early," was Pappin's answer, glancing at his watch. Stapleton was watching Johnny Carson, completely bored. It was obviously a dog night. It appeared nothing had tripped up these Eastern Ontarians, certainly nothing to be worthy of a next-day anecdote. The check-in clerk had not fallen for the palm-reading ploy, nor had there been any success with a room service cart full of empty dishes being rolled up to the room of Jim McKenny and Darryl Edestrand. There a "waiter" with a distinct Oriental accent had announced their delivery was ready. McKenny and Edestrand told the "waiter" to try something distinctly unique. Three times. That night at the reception, a local tow truck operator who moonlighted as a linesman during our game had failed to fall for the police emergency call reporting that the Old Stars' bus had collided head-on with the Zamboni.

After some desultory chitchat, and some disparaging remarks about the Carson show, Stapleton suddenly brightened.

"Are you with Bobo?" he inquired. I nodded and he asked, "What room?" Phone in hand he dialled quickly and we all waited.

"Is this Clownee, the referee?" he yelled excitedly. "Never mind. This is

Percy, at the front desk. You better get down here real quick, yer coach is in a fight with the whole hockey team. Gettin' the shit beat out of him, too. Better get your ass down here." The phone was slammed into its cradle.

Within seconds we heard the sound of a door being yanked open, then pounding on doors and bare feet running down the carpeted hallway. "C'mon guys, Brewitt's in a fight in the goddamn lobby," he roared. Then, as Kolari came into our open-door view of the elevator, we saw he was in his shorts, one leg in his pants, hopping around in circles trying to insert his other foot into the remaining pant leg, all the while jabbing his finger like a jackhammer into the elevator call button.

Our howls of laughter were genuine, as was the sleep-interrupted, bleary-eyed glare Kolari laid on Stapleton when he told him to attempt something *really* unique. At least I knew I had a true buddy in my roomie.

But if any one incident epitomized Pat Stapleton, it's the story of "the foot race." I had heard parts of it before from some truthful eyewitnesses, as well as those who only repeated it as legend. It was the application of a play on words, but it caught a big fish who should have known better.

His name was Johhny Morris, a speedy former wide receiver and NFL great with the Chicago Bears who was now a network sports commentator and colour man. Back in his college days in the Big Ten, he had held several NCAA track records.

The local Chicago network affiliate wanted Johnny to expand his horizons, suggesting he get closer to hockey in Chicago, so he found himself included at the "wake" in the Hawks' basement dressing room. The end of a season is not the happiest of times in any sport, and with the Blackhawks out of the playoffs the traditional locker cleaning was in progress with the usual Stadium farewell party. Security guards, clubhouse attendants, gatekeepers, a few cops, and some front-office people were on hand, along with the full range of the media.

In the spring of 1969 Chicago finished dead last in the East Division. This party was also a goodbye for Ken Wharram, the one-time member of the "Scooter Line" of Wharram, Mohns, and Mikita. Wharram had always had the great wheels, and the fact wasn't lost on Morris.

"The way he skates, he could have been a great track man," Morris enthused to a group sitting randomly at their cubicles, shuffling fan mail. Some say you could see the light click on over Stapleton's head.

"Wharram? I'm a faster runner than Wharram'll ever be," he said, stuffing skates into an equipment bag. Morris looked at the stumpy build of the defenceman and laughed. The short stubby legs might have helped the snicker, too. Stapleton seemed stung, so Morris eased up, unsure and wary.

"What's so funny?" the Blackhawk asked, sitting up from his bag-stuffing. "Are you supposed to be fast? Some kind of Jesse Owens?" Stapleton added a snort of his own and went back to selecting a pair of gloves from his stall. Morris was now put in the position of explaining himself to a group of Canadian athletes he had to assume had no idea who he was or what he had been. Besides, none of the other hockey players — Stan Mikita, Bobby Hull, Chico Maki, or Wharram, for that matter — acted as if Stapleton was joking. Did they know something he didn't?

"Well, I've done some track in my time," Morris replied, carefully, to the question.

"So?" The hockey player's flippant answer wasn't what the ex-Bear expected, nor were the baleful stares of the other players, which may have nettled him into a blunder.

"So how fast are you?" Morris ventured, still unsure of his footing, looking around the room at the group who were becoming interested in the exchange.

"I'll race yuh," Stapleton replied without hesitation, not even glancing up from the equipment bag. "I'll race you anytime, anywhere, for any amount."

The hook was in.

Flustered at being challenged so quickly, Morris also had to listen to a couple of the Hawks say "I'll take some of that action." His confusion grew as members of the more knowledgeable Chicago media began to dip into their pockets to cover those bets. Knowing that the cynical, hard-core press rarely delve into their pockets for anything only added to his consternation.

"Wait a minute," he ordered. "Where are we gonna hold this track meet?" It was his second mistake. As the bets began to mount, the security men suggested they could block off one lane of traffic alongside the block-square stadium, and one of the lounging, pistol-toting policemen volunteered to be the official starter. Things were moving along quickly and side bets were now the latest development between the players, media, and civilians.

"This is crazy," Morris said, waving off the argument that had spilled into the Blackhawk players' rec room, where the pool table was now being covered with wagers. Sucked in by pride, he challenged Stapleton into one last consideration.

"Let's see you start out of the blocks," he dared Stapleton, now jogging in place, bouncing around like a fighter before a big bout. After a consultation with Maki, Mikita, and others as to what "starting out of the blocks" meant, Stapleton slipped down to a four-point lineman's stance, feet wedged evenly against the dressing room wall, and with a roar rocketed out of the pose and through the doorway leading to the outer hall, surprising even himself. The watching Hawks cheered lustily and offered to press the bet.

Now convinced he had a problem on his hands, but still intrigued by the challenge, Morris asked if Stapleton had sneakers or was he going to run in his street shoes.

"Doesn't matter to me. I said I'd race you anywhere, anytime, pal. I'm ready." With that, the entire mob — players, security, cops, media, and civilians — climbed the stairs to the street level and out into the Windy City sunshine. The lane was blocked off on Washington Street, and as Stapleton continued to bounce up and down like an oversize pogo stick, Morris loped easily over to his car and returned wearing a pair of low-cut turf shoes, the kind football players use.

Then, with much jockeying for advantage and heckling from the sidelines, the cop finally roared *go* and the two bolted down the track.

Morris, dirt and cinders spraying backward from the force of his takeoff, sped down the pavement like a monkey with turpentine on his butt. Stapleton, almost exhausted from all the running in place, merely lurched out of his stance, danced a few steps forward, ran a few more backwards, did a couple of toe-loops for the benefit of his teammates, then pranced back into the Stadium and down the stairs followed by the cheers of his peers. The media were left upstairs in a muddle watching Morris greyhound himself farther and farther down the avenue, blindly straining for the distant street barrier.

By the time the ex-wide receiver made it back to his supporters and they had returned to the pool table, the Blackhawks were counting their winnings.

"I said I'd race yuh, John. Never once said I'd beat you. Now I've raced you, and you lose," Stapleton beamed.

For the record, the money was returned by the dupers to the dupees, but not until the take had been counted and duly noted for posterity. Stapleton had won $1,200, plus the respectful wariness of a new batch of people. Had the story ended there it might have been just another time-proven prank that clicked. But it was to come back to haunt ol' John in the early 1980s.

After the Blackhawks had recovered from their petulance over losing Bobby Hull to the upstart WHA, and realizing a good PR move might be what the club needed during a slow stretch, they decided to retire the Golden Jet's jersey just before a Christmas home game against the then-lowly Pittsburgh Penguins. Among the out-of-town invitees for a couple of great freebie days in Chicago were Fred Stanfield, Chico Maki, Pierre Pilote, Bill White, and Pit Martin, and as luck would have it, yours truly. Together with our wives we took part in the lavish social functions surrounding the event leading to game night and the actual retiring of the jersey. At the gala cocktail party in the Stadium Directors' Lounge, a cross section of Chicago's upper crust was there, along with a host of players including Keith Magnuson, Stan Mikita, Cliff Koroll, Eric Nesterenko, Jim Pappin, Dale Tallon, and Elmer Vasko. So was Johnny Morris.

Although he was now a part of hockey lore and I knew him through "racing circles," to this point I had never met the man, and when Pit Martin offered to introduce me I was looking forward to it.

"John, this is a friend of the boys from Toronto. We have a hockey team that tours the country . . ." The outline went on until I had been established as a bona-fide person to meet. We shook hands. I remember him as a trim, tall man, obviously still in excellent condition. After we had exchanged pleasantries I innocently asked if he "ever raced around the Stadium anymore."

His face darkened, and he glanced around wildly for a moment. "Is that little sonofabitch here? That little bastard . . ."

Fortunately the room was wall-to-wall with people and it was easy for Pit and me to melt into the throng, while Morris searched wildly for a glimpse of his tormentor.

Hook, line, and sinker after all those years.

So in the event you run into Patrick James Stapleton, be forewarned and do like the man in the word-association test advises.

RUN!

(Pat Stapleton declined to select a 90-SECOND ALL-STAR TEAM.)

Bob Nevin

Straight Priorities

THE PLACE IS CALLED "SOUPY'S," a street-level "Cheers" with an attitude, in downtown Toronto. The name is derived from Jerry "Soupy" Campbell, a former Ottawa Rough Rider middle linebacker who used to dispense rectum-shrivelling jolts around the CFL like a politician handing out campaign promises. On this day he stands behind the bar dispensing draft beer, odds, point spreads, and advice on the Stanley Cup playoffs.

Interesting as "Soupy" may be, he isn't the object of my meeting. Waiting for me is a guy who knows all about the rush and crush of the playoffs. From the inside. Today my main man is Bob Nevin. Golfer, tennis player, connoisseur of vintage ales, and sometime bartender at the establishment in question.

Nevin sits on one of a few metal bar stools, the usual bemused look on his face. Over a long period of time, I can't ever recall seeing him upset at anyone or anything. In fact, I've never seen Bob Nevin angry, never seen him demonstrative, good or bad, never seen him get flag-waving wild about a win, or chin-on-the-curb down at a loss. If he comes out on the good side of a situation, he's likely to acknowledge the fact with nothing more than a smile, perhaps a chuckle, interspersed with nods of agreement in all the right places. If it goes against him, then it's merely philosophical murmuring, with

New York Ranger captain Bob Nevin against former Toronto teammate Bob Baun. Nevin was a cagey specialist who lulled you to sleep and then made you pay for your attention to flashier players.

even-tempered shrugs for punctuation. The man is unflappable, which is probably the reason he's considered a consummate pro. By other pros.

Nevin had lots of reasons over 17 years to be up or down, to be ecstatic or forlorn, to thank The Man for being in the right place, or curse the whimsical notions of those who would tinker with careers.

Once, while sitting in another of an unending string of boarding gates, he confided to me a bit of trivia, that he had been the first player to make the journey through the entire Maple Leaf minor system to the NHL.

"Yep," he enthused from behind a newspaper, "right from Shopsy's Peewees, to the Weston Dukes, to the Marlies." He paused for a moment to let this jewel of wisdom sink in, snapped and refolded the paper to a new page, and added, "to the Maple Leafs. Then I got traded."

I have no idea what brought on this tidbit of news, for on one hand he can be private and guarded, and on the other can contribute to any conversation. Any conversation, on any subject. However, whether he chooses to partici-pate or not is his own call, and in that regard he can be as capricious as anyone I know.

Another time, listening to a couple of teammates discuss the thorny problem of what to do when hockey was over, specifically how to go about making a living, he admitted with a touch of pride that his last known job was as an eight-year-old *Globe and Mail* carrier, and therefore he had been seriously considering a personal career retraining program. The line was delivered in a low-intensity deadpan, producing much laughter and comment, but it underlined his approach to most real-life topics, an almost Alfred E. Newman "what, me worry" syndrome.

Underneath the veneer of nonchalance is a person well aware of the goings on around him, observant and tuned in. That's the way he played the game, too — not showy or presumptuous, nothing flashy or head-turning, only a player very much aware of his place, very much concerned with the details of his assignment. After Alex Delvecchio, he may have been the most underrated forward in the game. His hockey career is a study of making the utmost of the hand dealt.

When I first met him I was aware of all his major career moves. He started with the Leafs, had been on back-to-back Stanley Cup winners there (1962 and 1963), then was traded to the Rangers (where he was named captain), shuffled off to Minnesota and the Kings, eventually ending his career with Edmonton of the WHA in 1977. Those are the superficial facts.

The first thing you notice about his stat sheet is the decided lack of asterisks and abc's, which is the NHL's way of indicating All-Star selections, trophies, and awards. The figures are steady and consistent, but the story isn't in the numbers until you get near the end of his NHL career, and even then it's up to the reader to discern the true value of the player.

At six feet and 190 pounds, he was also a contradiction in appearance, both on and off the ice, in that he looked taller but not as heavy. Lanky was the descriptive word. Yet over his career he averaged 70 games a season. He played in every regular season game in three years, and all of those were after he was 30. Given the nature of the game, he was durable by anyone's standards.

After spending two seasons in the minors, he jumped to the Leafs in grand style, teaming up with another rookie in the person of centre Dave Keon. The two would impress the Original Six crowd by starting with 20-goal seasons, the benchmark of the day, and ending one-two in the Calder Cup voting as rookie of the year. Though Nevin scored 21 goals to Keon's 20, and led in total points 58 to 45, Keon won the trophy.

Not once in our travels did I hear him mention that — no casually dropped comment, no "by the way" — when I brought up Dave Keon, as I did on numerous occasions. In fact he never made conversation out of any of the interesting points I was left to eventually discover for myself.

His considerable ability, and his attitude, allowed him to change with the needs of the team and lead younger players by example. As I got to know him better, I came to understand that even as a young player in his 20s, Nevvie was considered by teammates, including some with a few years on them, to be a veteran, the prototype of a professional player.

Though not possessing a great gun as a shooter, he relied on the accuracy of an adequate wrist shot, a great pair of deft hands, and a puck sense that not only made him a dangerous player around the net, but a gifted defensive skater who could position himself quickly. In a word, he was reliable. In any situation.

In his fourth season with the Leafs, he expected to chase a third straight Stanley Cup as a member of Punch Imlach's defending champions. So did Dick Duff. On February 22, 1964, Nevin received a call from King Clancy.

"All he said was, 'When you go to the game tonight, don't come into our dressing room, turn right. You've been traded to New York.'" Nevin, Duff, and two up-and-coming young defencemen, Arnie Brown and Rod Seiling, were dealt away for what Imlach felt was the missing link in another Cup win. An all-star on the power play. He got his man in the person of Andy Bathgate, and Toronto went on to spring from third place to a third straight championship.

Nevin stepped onto a team that had only mouthed occasional burps of playoff aspirations for years, and the situation would not turn around over-night. The Rangers finished fifth in his first full season. Still, his unassuming leadership quality saw him made captain of the Rangers' derelict ship almost from the day he arrived. It was the beginning of an eight-year relationship with Emile "The Cat" Francis, the diminutive ex-goaltender turned coach/GM and the guy Nevin remembers fondly as his best coach.

"He turned us around. He wanted the players to stick together, live in the same area, and go out socially, during the season and after, too. With the Cat, it was all spelled out: what each guy was supposed to do, what was expected of him, how we were going to grow in the same direction. Imlach . . . well, looking back, Punch was a motivator, I suppose, and he respected what you could do for him, but in the end it was 'I won, you lost' — that kind of feeling."

Although the Rangers sank ignominiously to sixth place in the spring of 1966, Nevin's 29 goals and 62 total points were not the reason. He cracked the top ten scorers, placing eighth, but it was obvious the Rangers needed to concentrate on their defence to change their fortunes, so the emphasis and roles were redefined.

In 66–67 New York finished a solid fourth, scoring almost the same number of goals as their cellar-dwelling year before, but dropping the goals scored on them by a whopping 72. For the next five seasons they would be in the playoffs, never once going above 200 goals against.

Despite having one of the premier teams in the late 1960s and early 1970s, there was no Stanley Cup in Manhattan. Changes were made. Most of them were dictated from "upstairs" rather than from the office of Francis. The captain was traded again, to Minnesota. After two nondescript, routine seasons with a routine, nondescript team, an old playmate came calling. Bob

Pulford, now coaching in Los Angeles, picked Nevin off the reverse draft and he became a King.

In L.A., Nevin contributed a workmanlike 20 goals and 30 assists the first time around. In 1974 he was lined up with Butch Goring and Dan Maloney and things began to happen.

The Kings finished second in the division, fourth overall, with their first and only century mark, 105 points. The team set club records for most points, most ties, fewest losses, fewest goals against, most shutouts, longest road-winning streak, and longest undefeated streak.

At the age of 37, Nevin had a career year.

If anything, the recollection of that season showed the priorities of the man. He never mentioned that it was his best personal mark.

"Pully put us together at training camp, and we just went from there. We were out against the best in the league: the French Connection in Buffalo (Perreault, Robert, Martin); Bucyk's line in Boston; Lemaire, Shutt, and LaFleur in Montreal. That was our job, to shut down the big lines, and we had a lot of success. The Kings had the second lowest GA in the NHL. Only Philly was better, but while we were checking them, they forgot about us. Goring and Maloney scored 27 each. Our line got 85 goals that year, almost a third of the team total."

Somewhere in the mathematics of the remark I found 31 goals Nevin had contributed. It matched his previous all-time high, back with the Rangers in 68–69 when he was with an arguably better team. Coupled with 41 assists, the 72 total points was his best mark in the NHL, good for a tenth-place tie with Buffalo's Rick Martin in the overall point standings. But the reward of that banner year wasn't in the scoring race.

"Our line was a plus 38 — *plus 38* — against the toughest guys in the league. That was the most satisfying thing about the whole season," he said quietly, turning back to the paper. The hockey lesson was over. Then he had a small laugh and offered an add-on.

"Butch was the wheels, Danny was the brawn," and he bobbed his head and snorted into a chuckle as I anticipated the last remaining piece, "that's right, and I was the brains."

But the following year, the goal production dropped to 13, although his assists were on the money at 42. He was now in the 300-goal club at 307, a productive player at the age of 38, still a cagey specialist who lulled you to sleep and then made you pay for your attention to flashier players. He was the same 6′ 190-pounder he had been when he came into the league, and over three seasons had only missed eight games out of 240 played by the Kings, and he was still checking the best left wingers in the league.

But hockey, like all professional sports, is unforgiving. Despite the contributions, both on the ice and in the dressing room, training camp in the fall of 1976 came and went without a deal. Pulford wanted him back, and according to GM Jake Milford he was of the same mind, but no contract was forthcoming from "the Big Guy," owner Jack Kent Cooke. The official story line was "we're working on it." Meanwhile, Nevin sat out the first few weeks of the season. Finally, with some regret but still wanting to play, he took up an offer from Edmonton of the WHA, where an injury-riddled season rang up a 17-year pro career.

Nevvie doesn't look at the world through misfortune, even though there are legitimate areas for reflection. He tends to toss off "could-have-beens" with statements of fact, the kind that don't leave room for regret, for instance on his first trade from what may have been a dynasty to an also-ran in New York.

"If Punch hadn't been so hung up on trading for the right guy on the power play — hell, I believe we could have won four or five Cups in a row with the guys we had. Maybe all the way through to '67. But it was his call." The statement is made without rancour, or irony, or ill-feeling. Just a statement of fact.

Even more of a clue to where he's at came with the answer to my question about what personal memorable incidents he recalled about the two Stanley Cup victories in Toronto.

"The first one we played against the Hawks," came the answer. I sat back smugly, thinking I was going to hear a tale about a big goal, maybe a winner. This final series was a homer's dream, both teams winning two games in their own arenas to tie the set, then the Leafs scored a big 8–4 win, again at Maple Leaf Gardens, sending the series back to Chicago for the sixth contest. If the pattern was going to hold true, all the Leafs had to do was outwait the Hawks to a seventh game.

The two teams battled back and forth, the wide-open play of the fifth game a thing of the past, in an anxious and tense affair until Dick Duff, trying to get out of his own end, lost the puck and Bobby Hull slapped the miscue into the first goal near the five-minute mark of the third period. The Leafs were forced to stand around for at least ten minutes as the raucous, celebrating Chicago fans littered the ice with programs and debris in a tribute to the Golden Jet.

When play resumed Nevin took the wind out of the Windy City with a goal to tie it up moments later. Then Duff, making up for his mistake, took the fans out of the game entirely with a goal that would add to his growing legend as a clutch player, and prove to be the winner.

But the drama was far from over. Toronto took a penalty with 1:30 to go in the third period, an unpardonable sin in hockey strategy, but understandable for a visiting team clinging to a one-goal lead over a home team facing elimination. Imlach, hat pushed back in exasperation, had one thing going for him. He could look down his bench for veterans in this kind of situation. Captain George Armstrong, crusty old hands like Bert Olmstead, Eddie Litzenberger, not to forget Bob Pulford, Ron Stewart, Billy Harris, and Frank Mahovlich. But in typical Imlach fashion, brash and bold, he tapped on two other players to kill the penalty.

"I heard Punch call out Davey Keon's name, then mine. We went out for the face-off with Carl Brewer and Bobby Baun. I recall looking up at the clock; I can still see the numbers — 2–1 — and the time left against the Blackhawk power play. Hull, with Red Hay, and Murray Balfour. I think they had Stan Mikita on the point with Pierre Pilote. On top of that, they pulled Glen Hall for the sixth guy. Anyway, we won the Cup." Plain and simple. No qualifier, no Toronto window dressing. I sat there waiting for the punch line, at least some explanation other than the obvious victory, as to why this was a moment to remember.

"It was the single most important moment of my career. Dave and I — second-year players, rookies basically — being trusted out there in that situation. I've never forgotten the moment and what it meant to me."

What about other memories? Who was the most difficult winger to check?

"Bobby Hull was the toughest package of all. He was so physical, and he had getaway speed whenever he wanted to turn it on. All you could do was try to stay with him and hope he ran into some sand traps or something." He paused for a moment in thought.

"Big M. Frank Mahovlich was another guy I never tried to get into the game. You know, you didn't want to agitate him, or get him pissed off in any way. Just go to the face-off and ask about Marie, and the kids. The big guys like Bobby or Frank — all you could hope for was to keep them somewhere below a hat trick. Then you were doing your job. I believe I treated every guy I was out against with some respect. How the hell would he have gotten there if he couldn't play? Especially the rookies — I never trusted the rookies."

Today, in Soupy's, still looking for some weakness in his unflappable outlook, I asked if he had ever hated any of his opponents. No. Did he hold any grudges for dirty play, perhaps an attempted spearing somewhere along the way? Nope. How about an inadvertent butt-end? Bad language? He just shook his head. Suddenly he brightened, eyebrows going up as if a thought had just popped into view.

"I hate Dean Prentice," he said helpfully and nodding agreeably, as if he should have thought of it before.

Dean Prentice? One of the all-time good guys in hockey? The man who typified clean play, who was a skating advertisement for the Lady Byng Trophy yet never won it? A 22-year NHL veteran who took under 500 minutes in penalties?

"Why?" I asked, only mustering a confused shrug.

"We played together in Minnesota," Nevin offered, mysteriously.

"So?"

"That's when he quit drinkin'," Nevin said, a touch petulant.

I looked at him then, trying to keep a straight face, his moustache a-twitch, yet attempting to look righteous in his offended state. I knew Nevvie could hold up his end in any post-game "thirst-quenching contest," but to be angry with another player for abstaining was a little bizarre, even for him.

"So?" I repeated.

"So when he quit he took all his booze, all the vodka, all the rye, all the beers, and poured them down the sink."

I decided to wait him out.

"Geez, I was only living two minutes away. He could have called and let me rescue the stuff."

Theatrically, he crossed his arms and looked away in mock exasperation, sulky and suitably miffed.

And not so imperturbable after all.

90-SECOND ALL-STARS

G — **Johnny Bower**

D — **Tim Horton**

D — **Bobby Orr**

C — **Stan Mikita**

RW — **Gordie Howe**

LW — **Bobby Hull**

". . . everything you need on a team is right there."

Pat Quinn

Clockwork Oranges

PAT QUINN'S DANCE CARD READ 6′3″, 215 pounds, but the only thing they came close to was the height. He is a grizzly bear of a man. Ever see a friendly grizzly? Or how about a Heavyweight Champion of the NHL?

It's a title attributed to ex-referee Bruce Hood, who saw a few dust-ups in his day.

"We were in Minnesota, early '70s," Hood squinted, trying to recall the telltale colours of uniforms. "Quinnie was with Atlanta Flames. So was Billy Plager, a real aggravating little bugger, and he started some shit with big Ted Harris. Now Harris was one of my candidates for champ, but when Pat stepped in to take up the size difference from Plager, and those two giants started beating on each other . . . Christ, you could feel the punches landing through the ice. It was something to see. Pat won."

Hence the heavyweight championship.

Mention the name Pat Quinn and most hockey fans remember the night he almost put Bobby Orr in Row M at the Boston Garden. A clean check, too. What most hockey fans don't recall is that a month later, in Toronto, Quinn caught Bobby again. Orr was motoring through centre with Paul Henderson on his tail. Henderson was trying to clutch and hamper, all the while flailing away with his stick, attempting to dislodge the puck. To say Orr had his hands

Pat Quinn: most hockey fans remember the night he almost put Bobby Orr in Row M of the Boston Garden.

full was an understatement. Sensing a heavy hit, Pat, as most defencemen not known for their speed afoot are wont to do, lined up Number 4 and drilled him as he crossed the blue line.

Orr would have been seriously hurt except for Henderson, trailing stride for stride, who also went down under the check, keeping Orr's helmetless head from hitting the ice. Dazed and understandably shaken, both Orr and Henderson left for the benches. Pat stayed on to finish his shift. Instead of the harsh booing he had received in Boston, Quinn was treated to the cheering of the Leaf fans. He had this odd habit of slapping his shoulder pads into place before face-offs, like a dowager adjusting her bra straps, and he was doing it double time that evening, absorbing the plaudits of the crowd.

After the game, Red Burnett of the *Star* said he asked Orr in the dressing room, "How's it feel to get hit by that dummy again?" casting a little salt on Orr's open mental sores.

"Only been hit twice like that in my life, Red. He can't be that dumb," Bobby answered carefully.

And therein lies the common incorrect assumption. Watching him play, people assumed Quinn was big, lumbering, and lead-footed. So far, OK, but when they cast aspersions on his intellect, when the fans and the public assumed he was a primary school dropout, that's when they made their mistake.

From a junior career starting in Hamilton, he arrived at Edmonton in time to win a Memorial Cup with the Oil Kings. Then he meandered through a series of teams down south, such as Knoxville, Memphis, and Tulsa, but he continued to pursue his education in a patchwork quilt of colleges and universities: McMaster, University of Tennessee, Tulsa University, and York, where he eventually left with a Bachelor of Arts in Economics. Hitting the books didn't end with his playing days, either. Through his coaching career in Philadelphia, he eventually surfaced out of a job with the Flyers but with a Doctorate in Law from Delaware Law School. Orr was right, this was no dummy.

Case in point. We had invited a large group in for a barbecue when we lived in Rexdale, Ontario. Several Leaf couples were included, as well as personal friends and some neighbours. As we reached the mid-evening part, a local politician and his mate dropped in to pay their respects and possibly scare up some votes for the coming November election. His was a courtesy invite only. It was rooted in the premise that each year our crescent was blocked off for a street party and the annual "Open Garage Bar Crawl." For that little favour you need to know somebody at city hall.

His name escapes me, but he was an alderman, typical of those born-for-politics types, the ones who gladhand anybody, never listen to what is said, and always pretend to be on close terms with whomever's hand they're attached to at the time.

He waded through our crowd like a bad rumour. "Nice to see you, how's the wife and kids?", which struck me as odd since "the wife" was standing right beside me. He barnstormed the party. "Always a fan of the Leafs. Yes sirree. No need for introductions, hahahaha." He leaned back to whisper, "Who is this one?" and I slyly said, "McKenny."

"Having a good year, Ken . . ." he boomed. "Yes . . . I thought so . . . hahahahaha."

You know the type, I'm sure.

By some strange mixing, Mr. Alderman gravitated to where Quinn was sitting and they began to talk in earnest. For three hours. I'm sure he recognized Pat (although Jim McKenny went into a blue funk for a week) and I know they got into a political discussion, because I heard the term "metro form of government" at least ten times. But three hours?

Sir Alderman sent me a letter two weeks later, addressed to Mr. Roy Brevett, reiterating he only meant to stay a few minutes, and to express his thanks for a most entertaining and enlightening evening, and how he especially enjoyed "Pat Quinn, a most interesting man." Which I thought was quite remarkable, considering he got half the names wrong.

Now that I've established (for any doubters) Mr. Quinn's intellectual credentials, let me take you back to my favourite Pat Quinn anecdote. The fact he played nine years in the NHL establishes journeyman status as a minimum, and his size and toughness are a given. What we haven't dealt with was his Irish temper and a great sense of humour.

When he was playing with the Canucks, the team was returning home on a charter from Oakland following a two-game road trip to California. The cards were being dealt, newspapers and magazines popped up like daisies, while some of the passengers dropped off. There were others up to no good.

Quinn, picking out a pair of seats for his large frame at the rear of the plane, neatly folded a new blazer he had picked up in an exclusive men's shop in L.A., placed it carefully in the overhead rack, and proceeded to join the sleepers. On arrival, the usual rush was made for customs and the waiting team bus to the arena where the players' cars sat waiting. Sleepy-eyed and still a bit groggy, Quinn took the blazer from his arm and donned it as they made their way through the terminal. Suddenly, he felt dampness in the area of his pants pockets and discovered two freshly squashed oranges had been placed in the pockets of the new jacket. In the short walk they had seeped through the coat, and managed to soak his slacks as well.

Retrieving the offending mush, he boarded the almost filled bus, completely livid and snarling. The only mark dividing his apoplectic face were the black eyebrows, joined together in a straight line, resembling a railway tie. Standing like a human threat in the bus stairwell, he surveyed the now-quiet passengers and roared, "Which one of you dirty mother-fuckers did this?" He held up the two oranges overhead in one large hand. There were no takers.

"Stand up like a man, you bastard," he bellowed, sliding from a pink- to a white-faced rage.

Again the busload was cowed into bug-eyed silence. "Whoever did this," he rasped, holding up the hem of the stained, mottled jacket, "is gonna be one sorry son of a bitch." Whereupon he wound up and fired the two oranges toward the ducking passengers. One hit the floor about ten feet down the aisle, the last remaining drops of juice, pulp, peel, and seeds spattering pant cuffs and shoes for another 20 feet. The other hummed ominously through the air like a Nolan Ryan fastball and mashed into the rear window, above two media tag-alongs, who clutched their briefcases in cringing apprehension.

Quinn loomed like a Stanley garage door. Still no response. He almost gargled in frustration, saying, "I don't have to take any of this bullshit," except it came out embarrassingly close to "burr-shit." More than a few lips were bitten to suppress the urge to laugh.

Reading down the rows of faces, he touched on everyone trying to sense guilt in the dim light, then said, "Whichever of you lowlife assholes ruined my jacket can meet me at the dressing room tomorrow at 11 o'clock." He walked belligerently to an unoccupied double seat and jammed his large frame straight down with force.

Normally the Canucks, like most teams at home, practise between 10:30 and 11:00 a.m. After this particular road trip, however, the itinerary specifically stipulated that on the day of the return, practice would be at 1:00 p.m. A couple of hours' leeway to re-meet the wife and kiddies. A thoughtful touch from management.

That night, when a suitably subdued Quinn arrived home, he began to see the humour in the stunt. He remembered the ones he'd instigated over the years, the fact it would cost him nothing more than a little drycleaning, and maybe he shouldn't have drawn attention to his new, stylishly exclusive duds. Being the kind of person who couldn't hold a grudge over a prank, he got over it, had a chuckle himself, and went to sleep. He also recalled the practice was for 1:00 p.m.

The next day, arriving at the dressing room, he was sitting in his stall pulling off shoes, when a pair of bare feet came into view. As he raised his eyes there stood Andre Boudrias, all 5'8", clad only in an inner jockstrap, hands on hips, a sneer curling his lips as he said, "I was here at 11, asshole. Where the fuck were you?" After an instant of silence, the room burst into hoots and laughter.

For that story alone I have the feeling Quinn is a player's coach, a guy who hasn't forgotten those platinum days when you are a part of the young world of sport. Whether he's a player's GM, whether he's a player's president, I have my doubts. I know he's a businessman, and somewhere, somehow, the distinction has to be made. It isn't always easy. I don't envy him his three hats.

Often, when I recall the story about the oranges, which he told to me many years ago, I can still see him laughing, the eyes almost disappearing into the big grin, and I compare it to a scene I saw on TV during the playoffs. It was of the grizzly bear Quinn, eyebrows in the lock position, standing at the bench, frustrated as his team left the ice. He took his overworked gum out of his mouth and forcefully overhanded it toward the referee. It reminded me of the oranges, and I couldn't help but wonder, despite the respect of his peers in management, the Coach of the Year honours, the rewards of responsibility, if he doesn't wish for those simple days when he just played the game.

And went to school.

90-SECOND ALL-STARS

G — **Johnny Bower**

D — **Bobby Orr**

D — **Tim Horton**

C — **Jean Beliveau**

RW — **Gordie Howe**

LW — **Bobby Hull**

". . . you could put those six out there, without a care in the world."

Peter Mahovlich

Just Another Sweater

THE FIRST ITEM THAT STRIKES a person who has met Frank Mahovlich, then meets brother Pete, is not the difference in size, although it is quite startling. Frank played at 6', 205 pounds, Peter at a towering 6'5" and 205. Frank had a skating style that featured a fluid, straight ahead long stride, free arm working in fine-tuned synchronization, a threatening sight to any goaltender in the other end. Hence the nickname "the Big M." Pete, as his opposite, looked like a phone booth sporting knees and elbows, with a pair of pants large enough to protect Vancouver's Cliff Ronning from armpit to ankle.

No, the first impression is not size but the differences in personality. Frank, the elder by eight years, has a mature aura, a sense of what he is and where he is. In most instances a quiet, sometimes aloof, private person, one who is approached with deference.

Peter is personable, garrulous, an open and friendly extorvert, and the kind of guy who more often than not appears to be ready to create mischief. Pete is the adult who when walking down a street could join in a kids' road hockey game. And win! Frank would probably stand to the side, smiling benignly, interested but distant nevertheless.

Pete trails the Big M in every statistical category. Frank played 18 seasons,

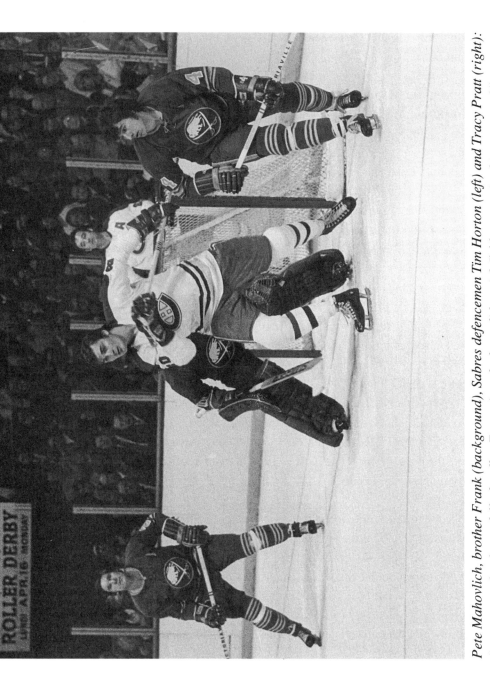

Pete Mahovlich, brother Frank (background), Sabres defencemen Tim Horton (left) and Tracy Pratt (right):
" . . . a water bottle . . . full of vodka. Every time the bear did a trick I'd have to give him a reward."

17 to be realistic. *The NHL Guide* considers 56–57, when he was brought up on a three-game "lend-lease-take-a-peak" basis from the St. Michael's juniors, a "season."

Peter, to be generous, played 16 seasons. He, too, was good enough for a three-game "look," brought up from the Hamilton Red Wings to the big boys in Detroit. Unlike Frank, who never spent a night in a minor-league hotel, Pete split parts of his next three pro seasons between the Wings and their minor-league affiliates in Pittsburgh and Fort Worth. He experienced his first trade a lot earlier, too, moving from part-time duty with Detroit to a split-shift job with the Halifax Voyageurs and the Montreal Canadiens in 69–70.

In 70–71, Frank, who had been his brother's teammate in Detroit, followed Pete to the Canadiens. The Big M checked into Montreal for 38 games. It was Peter's first full season in the NHL, and the Brothers Mahovlich did something few brother acts have ever accomplished. They won a Stanley Cup together, Frank setting a record with 14 goals and 27 total points. It was Pete's first, Frank's fifth.

Although knocked out in the first round the next year, they would be the second set of brothers on Team Canada '72 that fateful fall, joining Tony and Phil Esposito. Team Canada brought Peter Mahovlich to my attention, and to a lofty position in my own "Hall of Fame."

Pete Mahovlich stood out in the second game of the Canada–Russia series in Maple Leaf Gardens, September 4, 1972, when everything was on the line for the Canucks. Reputation, national pride, and the myth that we were the best on the face of the earth was only a tattered remnant of a flag after the humiliating 7–3 loss the Soviets had hung on the boys of winter in the Montreal opener.

Saving the reputation didn't come easily either. Sitting in the northeast corner golds, I had the angle on seeing a classical moment in Canadian sport. In the third period, with the score 2–1 in Canada's favour, killing a penalty to defenceman Pat Stapleton, Mahovlich first faked a Russian rearguard to his knees at the blue line, then stickhandled into Vladislav Tretiak's goal crease popping in the insurance goal, before hanging himself on the crossbar. Had it not been for the net he would have deked his way out of the Gardens onto Wood Street.

It was not only a stunning, memorable goal, it was a testament to what the

Canadian game was all about, and without question, *the* greatest goal I have ever seen. As a result, I have never forgotten Pete Mahovlich.

Over the years after the Team Canada series I occasionally ran across his path at golf tournaments, sometimes in press boxes, but it was a rare occurrence. He left the game in 1981, almost where he had begun, with the Wings following a two-season stopover in Pittsburgh, and finally with the AHL affiliate in Adirondack. It was 884 NHL regular season games later, 288 goals and 773 points after the Hamilton Red Wings, and three more Stanley Cups past Team Canada.

He stayed in hockey after his playing days were over, as a scout for his old Team Canada pal Phil Esposito when Phil was head honcho for the New York Rangers. Needless to say, when Espo went so did his selected people, and Mahovlich's next job was as a coach and GM of Denver in the Central League. He took the same position with the resurrected Dallas club in the same league before setting up house at the site of his final playing days in Glen Falls, New York, the home of the Adirondack Wings. There he opened a bar and restaurant called "Mahov's," and there he suffered the fate of many blue-collar-town ventures when the recession hit and so many of the customers he was banking on were not banking anything at all. The unemployment rate almost doubled in one year, from 9% to 17%, and the business was doomed.

He seemed to disappear for a while, then surfaced again as the colour man on Montreal Canadiens radio in 1993, which brought me up to date.

My next meeting with him was just before Christmas in the press box high atop the Buffalo Auditorium. It wasn't really a meeting, more of a finger-waving contest. Walking along the back of the broadcast booths on press row I spotted Mahovlich, and another old acquaintance, Dick Irvin, chattering away during a lull in the game below us. Scrunched into the tiny booth, Mahovlich sat sidesaddle style on his chair, knees on either side of the smaller Irvin hunched over the microphone. It looked like a heron was about to take a stab at a muskrat.

Mahovlich turned slightly as he caught me watching them work and raised a two-finger salute as he began to talk about the play just finished. Irvin, ducking down slightly under Mahovlich's arm slung across the back of his chair, squinted briefly at me and he, too, gave a quick wave. The thing that struck me as they continued their on-air conversation was the easy way Pete held his own, in direct contrast to the more schooled veteran, Irvin. What Irvin didn't know about broadcasting wasn't worth reporting, yet here was a first-year rookie holding up his end admirably. I attributed that to his enthusiasm and pleasant disposition, not to mention his knowledge of the game.

Three months later, mid-March, I caught up to him again, this time at the Montreal Forum. We had set up a meeting at a practice. The morning was cold and traces of dirty snow still stained the Montreal streets. As I approached the Forum, two young boys and their father stood in the downward blast of an air exhaust from the building, the only warmth on the street, Canadiens souvenir store shopping bags hanging off their wrists. Chattering in French, they studied a fistful of hockey cards each youngster held in gloved hands. I grinned at this family memory-in-the-making. The father simply watched and gave me an understanding smile as I passed. French and English understanding the other without a word being spoken.

Inside, safely through the pass gate with a tricolour pin snapped onto the collar of my trenchcoat, I entered the arena through the centre hall where doors on either side lead to the Directors' Lounge and the Canadiens' dressing room. The Canadiens had just finished their game-day skate to a sizeable bank of second-level spectators and a considerable group far enough up the social ladder to rate seats in the high-priced reds at rinkside.

Near the Canadiens' bench I ran into Dick Irvin again. He was heckling Canadiens coach Jacques Demers, who was signing autographs and posing for pictures with the railbirds. Only the last of the Montreal injured rehabs and lesser lights remained on the ice, watched over by assistant coaches Jacques Laperrier and Charles Thiffault.

"Geez, my dad must've been a genius," Irvin said in feigned surprise and loud enough for Demers to hear. He was referring to Dick Irvin Sr., the long-time Canadiens coach. "He won all those Cups and ran the team by himself." Those nearby grinned. Demers' only indication that he had heard was an almost imperceptible nod of his head in Irvin's direction and a slight smile.

For a minute or two we discussed publishing, having been put together at a book signing in Kingston in December, and we exchanged notes on speaking dates, another of our mutual interests. He also told me Pete Mahovlich would be late. Forewarned, I trailed the media scrum into the Directors' Lounge, a richly carpeted, warmly panelled room divided by a large curio shelf, stocked with decoys. Why? I have no idea, other than it has that "den" feel to it; I fully expected to find a smoking jacket, a pipe rack, and several cans of blended tobacco lying around somewhere among the comfortable furniture. Now Demers was holding forth from a sofa on one side of the divider, slipping in and out of French and English like the two languages were sets of floppy slippers. First it was a local French television show, then into English with the roundtable gathering of Philadelphia's Gary Dornhoefer, plus *Hockey Night in Canada*'s Chris Cuthbert, Scott Russell, Irvin, and producer Ed Millekin. The table was backed into a corner, against a mirrored wall on one side and another with two framed pictures. The first was an enlarged 34-cent Canadian stamp bearing the face of John Molson. The other was a colour reprint of a bearded Patrick Roy, Stanley Cup hoisted over his head.

Demers broke up the group by describing a scene where one of his young Habs is late for practice for the second time, guilty of having too many off-ice business activities. "You playing for the Canadiens, or starting up a doughnut-shop network," he said gruffly, describing how he took the kid down a peg. The laughter of appreciation was as much for the player's untenable dilemma as for the fact they were entrusted with the story. They all realized that it was a private yarn. The names and details would never be heard outside by the public.

Dornhoefer related a moment on the Flyers bus driving over to the Forum that morning. He talked about the radio DJ who was piped over the bus speakers commenting on the fact the Flyers were in town for the evening game, but for Montreal fans to curb their fears. "They used to be called the Broad Street Bullies. Nowadays they can't fight their way out of a brown bag." Dorny told of how he and Bill Barber, now an assistant coach and former teammate on the Flyers' two Stanley Cup teams, looked at each other and stifled their urge to laugh out loud. "The kids just sat there, stone silent, while Billy and I looked in different directions. I think they're beginning to get the message," he said, indicating the ex-Flyers had been trying to pass such a lesson along to the new players.

Wandering back out to the ice surface I watched the new "Bullies" circle the ice slowly, and picked out Rob Ramage, the former Leaf captain, presently in the last days of his career. We shook hands, he told me about working back from an injury, and then returned to the slow laps. Ramage didn't play that night.

Peter Mahovlich arrived dressed in a hip-length jacket, slacks, a denim shirt, suede topsiders, and a purple "Starter" baseball hat. At his height he might as well have been dressed in Day-Glo green. Six feet five inches is difficult to hide, at least around a hockey rink. Now that the Canadiens were long gone, we went up to red seats out of bounds to the mob of departing fans.

The Forum, to me, is a magic building. I'm just as star-struck as the kids outside with the hockey cards. It has that feeling of history, accomplishment, excellence, something almost tangible in the air of the arena. Sitting in the choicer-than-choice seats behind the visitors' bench I had a feeling of responsibility, of having to ask a question of suitable importance, yet Pete Mahovlich looked like one of those kids from the wrong side of the tracks who's never been awed by or who doesn't give a damn about the Forum's hallowed halls. I said he looked that way, full of (there's that word again) mischief.

I asked about how it was to play against his illustrious brother.

"It was — well, I'd say brief," he answered carefully, pointing out they had been teammates in Detroit before a season and a half of being on opposite sides. Straightening me out that way, he must have felt obliged to read my meaning into the unasked question. "To me, Frank was just another sweater when he was in Detroit and I was here," he said, thumbing toward the Flyers on the Forum ice. "And that was only a season and a bit. We were on the same team for the better part of four out of six years. Before that, he was with the Leafs, and I was in junior, so it wasn't as if we were a clan — like the Sutters."

This seemed to trigger something amusing. To my left I heard the un-mistakeable sound of a skater losing his feet and tumbling into the boards. Mahovlich signalled "safe" while the Flyers hooted and catcalled below. He laughed, but I didn't turn to look, doing my best to be professional. Instead, I asked the next most important question on my list. What about the short-handed goal against Tretiak?

"I only got the one against him in the whole series so I considered it a biggie," he answered brightly. The answer confirmed me in my conviction to hire a researcher for any further books. Again he seemed to sense my lack of defence. "I never really got to see it until the day after the game. They showed us the whole thing on TV and I have to admit I thought it was pretty good. You can only expect to use those moves once, you know." He grinned openly at his own assessment.

It went like that for ten minutes, me asking dumb questions, him playing cat and mouse, so I thought it was about time to turn and watch the practice. It was only then we slid into a casual conversation.

It started innocently, me remarking about Ramage, on the ice skating around with his eighth NHL team, and how difficult it must be to change his personal attitude toward opponents who become teammates.

"It was like that with Team Canada. A lot of owners and management people were worried about us getting together like we did. An All-Star game, OK, but for a month? They didn't like it. Look at me and Wayne Cashman. For three years in junior we were enemies, or so I thought. I was in Hamilton, he was with Oshawa. Central league? He was in Oklahoma City, I was in Fort Worth. When I was with Detroit and Montreal, he was with Boston. In '72? When we were going out to the airport in Moscow after we won it, a reporter said his paper's headlines read 'Canucks Tame Russian Bear.' So I get into the trainer's bag, get some tape and stuff, make a collar, a muzzle, and a leash, we put it on Cash, and go parading through the airport — me leading 'the bear.'

"The bear could do some tricks, too," he said, getting into the story, twisting around in his seat. "I had a water bottle, one of the squeeze kind, full of vodka. Every time the bear did a trick I'd have to give him a reward, right? Of course, his trainer had to have a reward, too. Man, we were beautiful. Those poor Russians could only stare at us. No sense of humour. I guess that happens when you lose. I know for goddamn sure there wouldn'ta been a bear if we'd lost."

Now we were getting somewhere. Were there any other sidebars to the Soviet series?

"The media was probably more uptight about the series than we were. At least we knew how we were gonna turn it around, all they could do was speculate and file stories.

"Red Fisher," he said, naming one of the premier sportswriters with the Canadians in Russia, "Red was primarily interested in keeping on top of anything concerning the Montreal players. Dryden, Savard, LaPointe, you know. So we had it rigged with the players, the doctors, the trainers, and at the end of a practice I took a header into the boards and just lay there, in a lump, then I started groaning. By the time I was carted off and came out of the dressing room, the word was I had hurt my shoulder, possibly a separation, or a hyper-extended elbow, take your pick. Rumours are like that, eh? Honest, I was taped up like a mummy, Red was running around trying to get every bit of info he could, demanding to see the team doctors, and pestering the hell out of trainer Joe Sgro. I did an interview saying I was doubtful for the next game.

"I go back to the Intourist Hotel and walk into the restaurant doing my mummy imitation. Then I run into the real Mommy. My mother, Cecelia, is there with Mickey Redmond's mom and she's really concerned, so I had to tell her it was a joke we were playing on Red. Boy, was she ticked off, told me no son of hers was going to do a terrible thing like that, made me peel off the tape and go up and tell Red, who had already invested two hours of typing to get the story out." Which to me meant he was more afraid of his own mother than he was of Red Fisher.

Later, as we drifted onto other matters concerning the game, he confessed to having a tough decision to make. Should he stick with broadcasting or not?

"The Canadiens have been fantastic to me, and being back in Montreal is great, too, but I've got a home and family in Glen Falls, and this winter has been pretty tough in that respect. It's not like when you're young and foolish."

"As in training bears, or drinking Bloody Caesars out of snifters holding a can of tomato juice and a half-bottle of Russian vodka," I suggested, recalling the story about the players being presented with expensive, giant crystal glasses after the game in Prague, and how the team finally got to toast their series win on the way home to Montreal's Dorval airport. Some say not one of the snifters made it back to Canada.

"Who told you about that one?" he grinned.

"Everybody," I answered, smiling as well, knowing he had been a teetotaller for the past few years and could afford to grin at the recollections.

"I meant more along the lines of you can't just pick up your family, and their home life, when they get older. I'll have to decide if I want to be a good analyst, and if I do, I'll have to put in more time. It's a tough decision that'll have to be made this summer by me — and the radio station."

As for today's NHL, he was pointed in his answer. "They have to get rid of this mentality that says better teams can be slowed down to a crawl with the hooking and holding, the stuff that seems to be acceptable in the game, which wasn't a few years back. I don't think they should penalize a good player. They should penalize bad general managers. Make them go out and get the right people, playing the game the right way."

The very next day I watched Pete Mahovlich play in an oldtimer game at the very same Forum. They wore the red travelling uniforms, in stark contrast to the other team in white and teal. Peter wore the familiar number 20 and the moulded skates with the black plastic-mounted blade he preferred toward the end of his career. They looked dated and somehow odd among the more sophisticated blades of those who retired behind him, because old pros tend to wear the last pair of skates they got for free. They also look dated and out of style because the opposition, like all oldtimer teams these days, invest heavily in the latest gear and footwear.

As the old pros' starting line-up got ready for the opening face-off, Mahovlich pulled himself off the bench to his full 6'9" in skates, and roared in mock seriousness as if it was Russia and Canada all over again: "Don't take any shit out there, *run somebody.*" The boys on the oldtimer bench giggled.

A short while later, during his second shift, to be exact, he used the old black blades to create a bit of that old black magic that embarrassed Vladislav Tretiak 22 years earlier. He scored the first goal of the game on two quick goalmouth feints. One-handed. He laughed about it all the way back to the bench.

From a player's standpoint he has every reason to laugh. As I said at the outset, Peter trailed Frank in every category, years in the NHL, games, goals, even penalty minutes. But they're tied in one of the most interesting stats in the NHL's history. The Brothers Mahovlich won ten Stanley Cups between them, enough to make the family unique. But they won two of those championships while on the same team.

Mom has got to be proud of that.

90-SECOND ALL-STARS

G — **Ken Dryden** *". . . always came up with a big save."*

D — **Bobby Orr** *". . . without question the best defenceman ever, in fact, maybe the best player ever."*

D — **Doug Harvey** *". . . if Orr was the best defenceman, Harvey was second."*

C — **Jean Beliveau** *". . . he knew how to play in the toughest situations."*

RW — **Guy LaFleur** *". . . he could generate his own offence."*

LW — **Bob Gainey** *". . . best man to have around, just in case the other team ever got the puck!"*

Brian Glennie

Moments of Impact

OVER THE YEARS I'VE WATCHED Brian Glennie go through three distinct stages.

When I moved to Toronto from Fort William in 1966, he was the captain of the Toronto Marlboro juniors, destined to win the Memorial Cup back in my hometown the following April. He already had a reputation as a banger, a latter-day Leo Boivin, a 1970s version of Boomer Baun. He was a muscular 200 pounds and spent time working on those muscles, because he knew his road to the NHL wasn't built on his offensive numbers or his double axels and triple toe-loops.

He played nine hard-time years with the Leafs, and scored a total of 12 goals. Ironically, his most fulfilling season in the blue and white, 77–78, would see him play a career-high 77 games and appear in 13 playoff contests. A tribute to conditioning, and modern medicine. For his efforts he was traded to Los Angeles in the off-season. His gold and purple jersey would only see 18 games for the Kings. He ended his career on the advice of team doctors, whose considered opinion said the pounding he had inflicted on others had now come home to roost. Their collective diagnosis was based on damage to the L4 and L5 vertebrae, where one more mega-hit might impair his ability to walk.

For most of two L.A. winters he languished on the Pacific seashore,

Hard hitter Brian Glennie: ". . . I caught him in front of the benches, and it sounded like somebody had dropped a car off a third-storey roof."

attending rehab, piling up a sun tan, and in his own words, "getting paid more money than Marc Dionne on a per-game basis." He was known to his fellow Kings as the "Mayor of Manhattan Beach," a pal who could be relied on to have the R & R prepared when they returned from those extended road trips the Kings were famous for.

When the race was over, when he left Los Angeles with a medical discharge, he couldn't adjust with gracious resignation to his exclusion from the game and subsequent retirement. Despite the injury, he never slowed down. The body that had been fine-tuned for all those years succumbed to a life of overeating and fun for the moment. It wasn't helped by the opening of his bar, a converted gas station a half-block south of Maple Leaf Gardens called "Wheels."

He admitted to me one evening that having been in hockey's grip so long, he didn't realize that "after lunch you don't lie down and have a nap." His mistake was living as if he was still playing. The occasional fits of exercise never lasted long. He philosophized, "If a guy puts on four inches around the waist, he can cover it up by putting eight inches on his chest." It was like whistling past the graveyard.

Being a bar owner and a party animal left little time for calorie counting. He ballooned to a size that came near to classing him as being his own tag team. He didn't bulk up gracefully, either.

In those days he drank rum and Coke when he wasn't drinking beer, ate chicken wings and french fries like peanuts, and was sometimes his own worst customer.

On a sunny afternoon, sitting across from him at an outdoor patio table, I noticed the shirt buttons straining perilously over his girth. Never one to miss an opportunity to heckle, I threw an arm across my face, startling both Glennie and my tablemates. Squinting out from behind an elbow I said, "Jeezzus, watch it, will ya?" Brian only looked perplexed. "What?" he questioned.

"That goddamn button lets go, it could take out an eye," I wailed, feigning fear. My pals exploded with laughter, but it wasn't worth it to me, because I didn't realize how much I had hurt his pride.

"Fuck you," was the muttered response, and he sulked off to the indoor bar where he obviously felt more welcome.

Eventually, I realized he wasn't so much angry at me, or us, but at Brian Glennie. He was a proud man, having trouble accepting himself and his position out of hockey, out of the group strength that goes with playing status.

Sadly, it wasn't enough to deter his running downhill. Eventually he lost the bar, and I lost track of him for a while, yet I always remembered his full beard, wild hair, balloon face, paunch, and a pair of the largest hands ever to wrap around a drink.

Although we talked a few times over the ensuing years, and randomly crossed paths, I was still shocked to learn he had suffered a heart attack. According to my source, Brian was a victim of excessive living, a pronounced disregard for personal well-being, and a bathroom scale that must have groaned out unheeded numbers of warning. Occasionally his name would pop up when players gathered and news was exchanged. The story was he had weathered the storm, was returning to work on a part-time basis, had seen the light, and was on his way back to near normalcy.

Even armed with this advance scouting report, I wasn't prepared for our first face-to-face meeting in over eight years.

The beard was trimmed short, and his hair had been cropped to almost military length. The face had receded and thinned out to a more youthful look. It was sort of like seeing a vintage car restored. But the missing 80 pounds was the most startling. I guessed him to be 220. When we shook hands, I remember thinking that if he could trim down those meathooks he'd be even lighter. The hands said he was still a big man, the grip said he was back in business.

So we sat, talked, and laughed, within the background babble of Shakey Walton's restaurant on Bloor Street. No one in the place recognized him, no one else wanted to chat, which was just as well. The recollections, plus his memory, brought out some anecdotes that were both new and insightful. We didn't need an audience.

He took me back to the days immediately following the hoisting of the Memorial Cup at the Fort William Gardens.

Glennie had been asked to join the Canadian national team by Father Bauer. The idea of playing hockey while working on his education held a lot of appeal, and the fact it was an Olympic year inspired other considerations. Waiting on the other side were the Maple Leafs and a dream, to play in the NHL.

Punch Imlach, short of defencemen, asked Glennie to play a game for the Leafs in Chicago. It was a strong temptation, so much so that he willingly went to the Gardens, tried on equipment, and left his skates to be packed for the train trip to the Windy City the next day. But by that evening he was having second thoughts. After talking to his father, he decided there was no guarantee that this single game wouldn't compromise his amateur status and more than certainly would preclude his chances of playing in the Olympics. The next morning he went to Union Station to relate his decision to Imlach. He was one worried and concerned young defenceman. Imlach, as expected, ranted, "What the hell do you mean you ain't goddamn goin'?" and proceeded to browbeat Glennie in front of some of the Leafs already on the train, looking out the windows, amused to see a raw rookie take the Big I down a peg.

But the worst wasn't over. Imlach implied that Glennie belonged to Toronto and would be well advised to be on the train later that night or on a plane the next day. He had better arrive in Chicago or else!

But his mind was made up. The Olympics won out. He went down to the baggage car, rummaged through the numbered bags — numbers familiar to any Leaf fan — until he came across his own, retrieved his skates, and barely made it to the platform before the train rumbled away.

"Punch ignored me for the rest of the year, anytime we met at the Gardens," Glennie recalled. "They had offered me a contract, once, and I turned it down for Team Canada. I suppose rejecting the offer to play a game with the big club was more than Imlach could fathom, and it was his way of letting me know about it."

Glennie had an outstanding year with the Nats under Jackie McLeod, and with Gary Dineen, Fran Huck, Danny O'Shea, Wayne Stephenson, and Ken Broderick almost pulled off a Canadian version of "The Miracle on Ice." It was a moment that Glennie still recalls with pride and some regret.

"All we had to do was tie the Russians and it would give us the gold. In the second we had played them to a standoff, and were getting good scoring chances. Then I broke my stick in our end. The play moved away and continued almost long enough for me to get to our bench, but not quite, and I was caught in a two-on-one. While I was scrambling back, I ran over my own stick, fell, and they walked in and scored. The whole flow of the game changed and they went on to whack us 5–0. We came home with nothing. I never forgot that broken stick."

The sting of defeat was tempered by the sweet feeling of vindication when, upon walking into the Leaf offices on his return, he met chief scout Bob Davidson, who again offered the defenceman the same contract.

"I thought, what the hell, I had a pretty good Olympics, go for more." Without hesitating he asked for a five thousand bump.

"Davidson said, 'Wait here,' went down the hall to Punch's office. When he returned he said, 'Punch says OK, we've got a deal. Welcome to the Maple Leafs.'"

For nine seasons he would patrol the Toronto blue line like a truck in a demolition derby, looking for the occasional dropping of the guard that would spell doom to forwards venturing into Leaf territory.

I recalled one night, with Pittsburgh at the Gardens, when speedster Jean Pronovost made a critical error and paid the price. The Penguins gained control in their own end and were making the transition to offence. Pronovost, near the hash marks at the right circle, took a quick look up ice to locate Glennie and spotted him turning to race back into position to defend the Pittsburgh rush. It may have been the last thing he remembers that evening, for as he accelerated and looked for the expected relay, Glennie, glancing over his shoulder, correctly sensed the quick release to Pronovost and slammed on the brakes just in time to catch the right winger about to accept the pass. I recall Pronovost being caught dead centre, right on the logo, taking a couple of steps backward from the impact, then sinking to the ice in a yoga-like position, before slumping over on his side, obviously unaware of the game, or anything else. It was a classic example of an old ruse. Pronovost did not reappear on the wing that night.

There was a later spring night in Buffalo, when another ex-Marlie captain, Gerry Meehan, was on the receiving end of a thundering body check. A big centre, at 6'2" and 200 pounds, Meehan made the mistake of hanging onto the puck while cutting along the Leaf blue line. Glennie, performing the same east-west move in the opposite direction, slammed into Meehan, sending the Sabre's stick spinning in circles and dropping him to the ice like a half-full equipment bag.

As the play continued, Meehan rolled to his knees, groping for his stick, resembling a guy looking for a contact lens. He struggled to his feet and shakily aimed himself toward the Buffalo bench, when the puck skittered errantly from somewhere onto his stick. Instinct took over and he wafted a backhand toward the Leaf cage. It looked more like a field goal attempt, floating end over end toward a tangle of players in front of the net. It found its way through the melee across the goal line. Seconds later Glennie watched disgustedly from the Leaf bench as Sabre trainer Frankie Christie tried to bring the still-groggy Meehan around with an ammonia cap. Meehan could be seen mouthing the question, "I scored?" and staring blankly at the centre-ice clock.

When asked for his own rating of the hardest hits of a career filled with monumental thumps, he selected two, and at the same time told me which player he considered the toughest he ever faced.

"Rejean Houle was the scariest check. It was in Montreal. He was on the ice out cold for a long time. Never moved after he landed. No dirt in the check either, just a clean shoulder hit."

Then he began to chuckle. "But tough? Brian Trottier. No question in my mind. We were on the Island. I think he was playing with a broken jaw. I caught him in front of the benches, and it sounded like somebody had dropped a car off a third-storey roof. It was one of those hits where you don't begin to feel it until a few seconds after the crunch. The puck went over the boards, or something, and the play was whistled down. We got up. I knew I needed a rest. I guess he felt the same. Just as we were about to step off the ice, I looked down the boards toward him. He was looking at me, too. We both nodded about the same time. He never said a word — probably couldn't because of his jaw — and neither did I.

"We both knew it was a career best," Glennie said, wistfully, like a man remembering nothing more than a good bottle of wine. It's the same tone of voice he used when talking about being asked to play for his country again. It was 1972.

"Harry Sinden called and asked me to report to the training camp at the Gardens. I remember saying a silent thanks to guys like Dallas Smith, who for one reason or another weren't going. I knew there wasn't much chance of me playing, but it sure was a thrill to be asked."

He was right as rain. He never suited up for any of the eight-game series, but he has nothing but fond memories of Team Canada and, in particular, one incident that carried over into the regular season.

By this time the people sitting nearby and around us had found our conversation more interesting than their own and the tennis on TV. Whether we wanted an audience or not, we were getting one.

"Stan Mikita and I got to be friends for some strange reason. We were miles apart as players. I was a workman, he was a superstar. I was a defenceman, he was a centre. On the Thursday night in Montreal we were told who was playing the first Saturday game at the Forum. I didn't think for a moment I'd be playing, but Stan — well, he had every right to expect to be in the line-up, and when he wasn't named, he was really down. So we went out and had a few. Maybe more than a few. Make that definitely more than a few."

A couple of the guys in the background broke into grins, like they'd been there before.

"Friday-morning practice, we were going through one-on-ones and right off the bat, I drew Stash. He comes weaving down the ice and just when he gets real close he pukes. Yeah, almost yarped on my skates. Man, I jumped out of the road, and he waltzed in without missing a step and popped one behind Eddie Johnston. He was so goddamn casual about it. Dennis Hull said it was a *hell* of a move to use on me, said there was no need to use tricky shit."

He paused to let the two patrons catch up from laughing.

"When we get back to the regular NHL, our home opener is against the Hawks. Wouldn't you know it, I get the first two-on-one of the game . . . Stan, and Cliff Koroll, I think . . . anyway I'm trying to stay between them until help comes . . . and you know Stan, he's not afraid to move close to you, hoping you'd make a play on him, then he'd just stick it between your feet to the other man. So every time he gave me that little move, I'd back off, still trying to keep them separated. It all happens in split seconds, but it seems like forever. Finally, figuring he's running out of room, he steps to the side and zips one into the top corner. I'm really burning about the goal, and as we turn to leave the ice, Stan's getting the high fives and says to me, 'Whatta you think I was gonna do — barf on yah again?'"

The people sitting behind us are openly laughing by now, making no pretence about not eavesdropping, suddenly clued in to who the speaker is, and ready for more.

He touched on Red Kelly and the famous "pyramid power" days when the Toronto coach had a hunch that charged ions held the key to success. The Leafs were in the playoffs against Philadelphia. On April 26, 1976, Darryl Sittler dared to place his game sticks under the pyramid. Brian, taking matters into his own hands, ventured his entire large frame under the contraption for a spell. The Leafs won the game 8–5, Darryl tied an NHL record with five goals, and Glennie took a Bill Barber slapshot in the face and broke his jaw. "So much for pyramids," he scoffed.

As many times as a high point will remain in the memory of a player, life's little underhanded shots stick out just as well.

Again it was the Blackhawks, only this time in Chicago. The teams had battled to a 0–0 tie midway through the second when the roof began to fall in on Toronto.

"I caught Chico Maki with a solid hip check and he got cut when he fell but gets up bleedin' and scores. They scored again the next time I was out, and it went like that shift after shift. With three minutes to go, they got us 8–0 and I've been on for all eight. I'm totally pissed off, frustrated, and when I charged through the gate after their eighth, I slammed onto the bench and fired my stick on the floor, just steamin'. Johnny McLellan comes over and before he could say anything I told him straight, 'Look, John, I don't wanna go out there. I'm snakebitten. Christ, I ain't playin' bad and I'm stung for eight goals. I'm just not playin' that bad, goddammit.' John just patted me on the back. Next shift, I wave him off, and he sends Claire Alexander out in my place and son of a bitch — they get their ninth.

"I just turned to Johnny, smiled, and said, 'See!'"

Like the others around us, he thoroughly enjoyed his own incriminating story, as so many of the players do. As we took our leave that afternoon, I shook the big hand with the red-stoned Team Canada '72 ring displayed so proudly, marvelled again at how good he looked at 225 pounds, and in my mind wished him luck on his way to a self-set target of 215.

He's a good guy, and a gamer. He'll make it.

90-SECOND ALL-STARS

G — **Bernie Parent** *". . . cool under pressure."*

D — **Borje Salming** *". . . he could start things going, quick."*

D — **Bobby Orr** *". . . who else? The greatest . . ."*

C — **Brian Trottier** *". . . toughest son of a bitch and a big play man."*

RW — **Wayne Cashman** *". . . check, then get the puck out to Trottier."*

LW — **Terry O'Reilly** *". . . the same thing."*

Jim Pappin

A Show of Hands

AS I MADE MY WAY UP THE escalators to the uppermost reaches of the Buffalo Auditorium where the press box, a vertigo sufferer's worst nightmare, hangs like a large flowerbox, I knew Jim Pappin was going to be there. Before crossing the mesh bridge from firm concrete to the totally unreasonable reliance on engineering, I was willing to bet he was either wearing a grey suit or a navy blazer, which as far as I've been able to determine are his "scouting" clothes. As the guard at the press box end of the bridge scrutinized my pass, I made my choice and bet grey suit. I lost. Sure enough, there he was, blue jacket and grey slacks, looking like an escapee from a Legion Zone meeting. I surmised it must be International Caravan night because he was sitting with two Pittsburgh scratches, Ulf Samuelson, the tall Swedish defenceman, number 5 on your program, number 64 on your shitlist, and another blue-liner, Jim Paek, hometown Seoul, South Korea. Paek turned out to be inscrutable, but Samuelson surprised me as a pleasant conversationalist. It only goes to prove you can't judge a hockey player by his fouls.

Pappin goes by two nicknames that I know of. The first being "Papoo," simply a derivative of Pappin, and "The Bird," which completely puzzles me.

After the introductions to the Penguins, The Bird went to work before the opening face-off, marking off the players not in the line-up according to the PA

Jim Pappin was traded from Toronto to Chicago on May 13, 1988: ". . . the best day of my life in hockey."

announcements and after reading through the Sabres' thick PR package of notes and stats. As the puck was dropped, he began the scout's stock-in-trade, marking down the line and defence combinations on each shift. By the second time around, after a few penalties to jot the numbers of the power-players and penalty killers, it became an easy routine to note the occasional changes to the original.

That night, it looked like an American Hockey League game. No LaFontaine, Mogilny, or Fuhr for Buffalo, and as for the Pens, no Lemieux to watch, no Samuelson to raise bile for the fans. Worse, Pittsburgh scored first, on a tentative Dominik Hasek, to a loud cheer. Why? Had Buffalo regressed to the point where the fans think it's an expansion team again, and aren't quite sure who to cheer for?

At the end of the period we sat and stared out at the rafters of the old Auditorium, and I noted the proliferation of balloons trapped in the sound baffles not 20 feet in front of us, curly ribbons and limp strings straggling down, coated in dust. One in particular I found intriguing. I pointed it out. It was a silver heart, trimmed in green, one of those birthday cake or gift tie-ons, filled with helium, that are usually a source of acute embarrassment to anyone who receives one.

It said, "I LOVE MAR . . . ," which was all I could make out. No matter how we collectively peered, grimaced, leaned, or shuffled to the extreme end of the press box, we couldn't make out the last part of the name. Being veteran pressboxers, we bet. Winning the toss, the Pens took MARY, and settled on MARLENE as their second pick. Cagey Papoo astutely pointed out, "It could be a guy," and went with MARK. Torn between male or female, knowing we're in Buffalo where names are sometimes spelled differently for dramatic effect or theatrical reasons, I wisely picked MAR-KNEE. A quick phone call by the now-involved guard to a group in a private box across the way, with binoculars and a perfect angle to see the remaining letters, settled the issue. It was MAR-CH 17TH.

I only point out this press-box lore to show you the depths to which people up there will stoop for diversion. This boredom, the routine of viewing a bunch of helmets move around like pinballs, which is the scene from that angle, needs skill-testing opportunities such as this to maintain a sense of balance.

It's the daily routine of a scout, at any level, and The Bird is a scout at any level. In arranging this meeting he was kind enough to forward his one-month schedule by fax, and more than anything else I can say, it spells out the job. The month is November, and the first day is open. From there, it's:

2 — Boston @ Detroit	17 — Atlanta @ Salt Lake City
3 — Florida @ Toronto	18 — Travel
4 — Islanders @ Chicago	19 — Phoenix @ Las Vegas
5 — open	20 — Las Vegas @ Phoenix
6 — Wedding ???	21 — Return to Chicago
7 — Edmonton @ Chicago	22 — open
8 — open	23 — Atlanta @ Milwaukee
9 — Team Picture	24 — Montreal @ Philadelphia
10 — Cleveland @ Kalamazoo	25 — L.A. @ Quebec
11 — Pittsburgh @ Chicago	26 — Ottawa @ Buffalo
12 — Cincinnatti @ Milwaukee	27 — Boston @ Toronto
13 — Las Vegas @ Milwaukee	28 — Moncton @ Cornwall
14 — Dallas @ Chicago	29 — Buffalo @ Toronto
15 — Travel ???	30 — open
16 — Kansas City @ Phoenix	

Sound romantic? Sounds like a guy with a sheaf of airline tickets in his hand wandering around airports with a bag of frequent flyer points. Yes, I agree the time between the 15th and 22nd could be a camouflaged golf trip, but you can also see why a bet on the next letters after "MAR" would be irresistible.

It wasn't always like this for Pappin, a full-time involvement with the game after a 14-year career. There were gaps where the only thing left to do was to enrol in a real-estate course and play with the Old Stars. But it helps to have friends in the game and an old teammate, Bob Pulford, eventually steered The Bird into coming back to Chicago as a scout, and it was a role Pappin was well suited to. According to the people he played with, he was the most clinical observer of the game, someone well versed and schooled, a logical choice to pick future prospects.

As a teenager back in Sudbury he was tall and rangy, an athlete with talent, both in hockey and as a shortstop in baseball. He left Sudbury to pursue the

NHL with the Toronto Marlboros and by the 60–61 season he was back in Sudbury, starting with the Eastern Pro League team there before moving onward and upward to finish the year with the Rochester Americans, Toronto's top farm club in the AHL. While the parent Leafs were winning Stanley Cups in the springs of 1962 and 1963 under Ol' Ironpants himself, Punch Imlach, Pappin was dutifully attending training camp in Peterborough each fall, then shipping out to Rochester. It was the way of life in the NHL of the six-team era and the days of big farm systems. You waited, patiently, learning your trade and earning your keep. Pappin once told me he would scrimmage with the Stanley Cup champions and be in awe of the names and the faces. He admitted to being satisfied, even resigned, to wait until George Armstrong or Ron Stewart was done or moved, such was his regard for the Leafs of the day.

But Imlach, always the hard driver, knew the young ones pushed the old ones and while captain George Armstrong was as much a fixture as it was possible to be, Pappin was brought up from the Americans in time to play 50 games with the Leafs and be a part of their third Stanley Cup, his first, in April 1964. Yes folks, there was a time when the Stanley Cup playoffs were out of your face before Mother's Day.

With a Stanley Cup ring, Pappin realized he had arrived, but a precedent had been set and the next season, after 44 games, he was odd man out when it came to sending people down to Rochester. He arrived in time to take part in the Calder Cup playoffs, lead all goal scorers with 11, and have a season-ending celebration anyway. The Leafs, meanwhile, had finished fourth and were out in the semifinal. The next season he broke camp with the Leafs and seven games into the season he was back in Rochester, again leading all goal scorers in the AHL playoffs, again sipping champagne. The Leafs? They moved up to third but were bounced in the semi's anyway.

In 66–67, a pivotal year for Pappin, he started with the Leafs, but by February he had only nine goals, and Imlach, at the suburban Tam O'Shanter arena where the Leafs worked out when the Gardens was busy, told him he was going back to Rochester.

"I went down, same old shit, pissed off, but in six games I had popped four goals and three assists, and they called me back with 20 games left in the season. When I got there we were at Tam O'Shanter again, but Punch was in the hospital, stomach or somethin', and King Clancy was running the team. He puts Pete Stemkowski, Bob Pulford, and me as a line for practice. Next game for us is at home to Montreal. We were down 2–0 in the second, and King sends us out for the first time. I score. 2–1. Our next shift, Stemmer scores. 2–2. We played the whole third period like regulars, and the next game, he starts us. First shift, I score. We went on a tear, won 15 of 20 games. In fact King's record in ten games was eight wins, two losses. We went from fifth place to third. I got seven game-winners and ended up with 21 goals. When Punch came back he left us together. We went on to beat Chicago in six games, and Montreal in six. You know, I led the goal scoring and total points in the playoffs and got the winner in the sixth game. George Armstrong scored an empty-netter to nail it down."

Left unsaid was that it was a banner year, one in which he showed some grit in being sent away, only to return and play outstanding hockey. He scored seven goals and eight assists in the 12-game playoffs, yet he never mentioned to me that Dave Keon won the Conn Smythe trophy as the Stanley Cup MVP with only three goals and five assists. But back then, if you weren't a goalie you had to be the leader, and Keon was a leader, a fact acknowledged many times by Papoo in our many conversations in restaurants, airports, and dressing rooms on our Old Stars jaunts.

With two Stanley Cup wins under his belt, having proven that he could perform during the regular season and under the intense pressure of the playoffs, he couldn't be blamed for feeling he had seen the last of Rochester. He was 28 years old and had waited his turn. The NHL had expanded and he was a valuable commodity, in a marketplace short on players of his calibre. But when he went to the pay car, he felt short-changed. It triggered a series of events that changed his career, and his life.

"The way I read my contract, I was supposed to get a bonus for 25 goals. I finished the regular season with 21 in Toronto, plus four in six games at Rochester. I was on a one-way contract, too," he said, referring to an agreement paying him the same salary whether he was in the NHL or the AHL. "To me that was 25. Never mind the goals and points in the playoffs! As far as I was concerned they owed me the extra, and that's exactly what I asked Imlach. 'What happened to the bonus?'

"Punch, of course, said, 'What bonus?' Couldn't understand what I was pissed off about. He asked me if I'd ever read my contract. 'It says 25 goals during the schedule . . . the NHL schedule,' he said. 'I can't give you a bonus, it'll open a whole goddamn can of worms.'

"He's madder than I am," Jimmy said, waving his arms around doing a creditable impression of Imlach. "So I said, 'This is bullshit,' and walked out. Then Clancy comes up from behind me and says, 'I'll sign yuh so's yuh won't have t'deal with Punch.' I kept on walking.

"Come training camp, I still hadn't signed, said I wanted the bonus first, and they simply said, 'We can't,' but offered to show me ways I could make up the difference. They made me an offer, and I asked for the bonus again. King says, 'It's already included in the offer.' Son of a bitch, I walk again. But, they wear you down. I eventually signed, knowing I'd never be happy, played 58 games, 13 goals, and then in February Imlach decides to send me to Rochester again. That was it! I told him no. He said, whether I liked it or not, I was going, so I did. Straight home to Sudbury for three weeks. I'd had it with this crap.

"Joe Crozier, who was always OK in my books, had Darryl Sly call me from Rochester to break the ice, and after a while I showed up, played two or three games in Rochester while Punch went and traded for Floyd Smith, Norm Ullman, and Paul Henderson. Big trade, very big. They sent Frank Mahovlich, Pete Stemkowski, and Gary Unger to Detroit. By the way, I got my money, and since I was eligible for the AHL playoffs, I stayed in Rochester, we won the Calder Cup, and I got a full playoff share, too."

Pappin raised his eyebrows and turned his palms upward, asking a question without saying a word. He does that move better than anyone I know.

On May 13, 1968, he was traded to Chicago. "I was playing golf in Richmond Hill with Wally Crouter and Dale Tallon. Dale was only 17 then, just a kid with the Marlies but already a hell of a golfer. Somebody from Wally's station, CFRB, got to us on the course. I couldn't believe it had happened — the best day of my life in hockey. It was a major item, at least for George Gross of the *Telegram*. He had a story running sayin' somethin' like 'Flash in the Pan, Jim Pappin.' He and Punch were always tight anyway. When I was told they had traded me for Pierre Pilote, I said you gotta be kidding. Pilote's 36, I'm 28. I found out later I was a throw-in from Punch, a way to get rid of me. Later they told me the Hawks' Tommy Ivan just wanted to get *something, anything,* for Pilote."

He laughed, and well he could, looking back on the change of scenery. All because of that measly bonus.

A lot of things happened quickly. Billy Reay, the Blackhawk coach, announced Pappin would start with Pit Martin and Bobby Hull. But the Golden Jet was holding out that September, and a succession of left wingers tried to fill the spot without success. Instead of lamenting the fact that Hull was AWOL, Reay turned to Pappin, saying, "I thought you'd be better, but you're not doing anything out there, and I don't like what I'm seeing. You can do better, I know you can, so let's see some production from now on."

Pappin had included the right to renegotiate his three-year contract if he reached the 30-goal plateau. He had everything to gain, and now he was about to be helped indirectly by the Golden Jet's late start. Reay moved brother Dennis to fill the vacant spot left by the elder Hull.

"We went 5–0 to open the season without Bobby. I had six goals. It was like magic the way we fit together, from the start to the finish. Dennis and I got 30 on the nose, the Hawks led the league in goals-for, but we missed the playoffs. All that did was tell Reay and Ivan that we needed goaltending, and they went out and drafted Tony Esposito from Montreal. Next year we started out 0–5, the exact reverse, with Dennis Dejordy in goal. Tony gets a start in Montreal and we tie 2–2. Now we know we have a goaltender. Hell, that was the year he got 15 shutouts. But as far as I'm concerned, the key for Chicago was the trade for Bill White from Los Angeles. He came with 22 games left. We had 17 wins, finished in first. But Boston won the Cup."

The MPH Line (Martin–Pappin–Hull) was a fixture in Chicago for seven seasons, although there was a personality wall between Pappin and Martin.

"We stuck together, on and off the ice, along with Dougie Jarrett. But it's amazing, to me at least, that Dennis and Pit still talk to me today, I gave them so much shit. I believe Pit realized our clashes were all from tension." He started to laugh as a mental picture came into view. "We'd go to dinner. We always split the bill. Goddamn Pit never had a salad, always a martini, and smoked a fuckin' cigar. Used to drive me nuts. Billy Reay had to have Dennis sit between us on the bench, in the dressing room. I think he always thought we were gonna start punching it out. Dennis was beautiful, didn't matter what Pit or I decided, he'd say, 'OK.' You know, 'Hey, Dennis, we're going for Italian tonight.' 'OK,'" he singsonged, mimicking the agreeable younger Hull.

It was a moment in hockey history when Pappin hung a little bit of philosophy and practical logic on Dennis and Billy Reay that made the rounds of NHL locker rooms for years.

The Hawks had tied the brawling Philadelphia Flyers in their own building the night before, then travelled to Montreal for a game against the Canadiens. The problem was, some of the Blackhawks had been caught redhanded in a hotel bar after curfew while others, not specifically nabbed in the incident, had missed the bed check in their haste to evade the raid. Billy Reay decided to change their posh Montreal hotel for one several notches lower, just to make a point, to teach the team a lesson. When they arrived at their new digs, the entire team sheepishly crammed into a meeting room and awaited their whipping.

"How do you like the hotel, Jarrett?" Reay asked, singling out one of the red-faced culprits.

"It's fine, Coach, just great," Jarrett replied, not wanting to sound like a griper. Reay's colour rose.

"No, it isn't great, or super, Dougie. It's second-class, just like you." Reay commenced to go through the entire room tearing off strips of hide, pride, and faded innocence. Finally, he came to Dennis, always one of his favourites, but one of the players he had bagged himself in Philadelphia.

". . . and *you*," he barked at the penitent Dennis Hull. "Of all the players in this room, I should have expected better from *you*." He left him to squirm for an extra moment. "Hell, you're exactly like your brother Bobby after midnight," Reay groused, referring to the Golden Jet's penchant for after-hours entertainment and hoping to inflict punishment on two Hulls at once.

Pappin couldn't resist speaking up. "Uh, well if it's all the same to you, Billy, can we reschedule our games a little later when we come to Montreal?" The full room of players fell apart laughing, and the lesson was lost.

Three months after the Buffalo meeting, The Bird and I got together again, at the airport Marriott in Toronto. It was Friday, Pappin was in for the weekend, arriving from a Thursday-night New York game in lots of time for a Saturday Hawks and Leafs game, then to Chicago for the second half of the home-and-home series. When I caught up to him he was awaiting the arrival of his long-time Sudbury pal, Darcy, who would often travel with us on any ground trips the Old Stars made in Ontario. Darcy didn't fly. Still doesn't. The boys on the Old Stars called him "American Express" because it seemed Pappy wouldn't leave home without him. Back in those dark days Pappin was looking for a job. Now he sat across the lunch table from me a respected member of the hockey intellingentsia, talking about the difference between winning and losing.

"Winning teams are more fun, simple as that," he said, turning the palms upward in the silent, rhetorical question. "We were winning. We had a lot of fun."

"Ebenezer Scrooge would have had a lot more fun if he was a hockey player," I chided. "How the hell can you avoid having fun with guys like Dennis, and Doug Jarrett, Dale Tallon?"

"Don't forget Maggie," he interrupted. The only place Keith Magnuson was fun was on his own team, I recalled.

"He was a university grad," Papoo said, determined to show me Magnuson's humorous side. "Denver U. But he couldn't remember what day it was, couldn't remember shit. Always carried a pad and pen in his pocket, always writing in a notebook. He'd write down stuff like what time practice was — the next day. Some of the boys stayed away from him. They thought he was writing a goddamn book. One day we're in the airport lounge. He's got the book out, frowning at it, rubbing his forehead, and one of the guys asked him what's wrong. He points at this line — 'phone Bill' — and says, 'I called every Bill I know, and I still can't figure out what the hell I wrote this down for.' Came back from the road trip, they'd disconnected his telephone." He cocked his head to one side as if to say "what," hands down, palms forward, then raised them to the "question" position. "You don't think that's funny?"

"Happens on a losing team, too," I answered, keeping a straight face.

"Yeah, but listen, I'll explain the difference. Just after Pulford hired me for scouting, the Hawks fire Orville Tessier and Pully has to take over behind the bench. Then he decides to bring Cliff Koroll back from the farm club as an assistant to see if he's ready to coach in the NHL.

"So, they ask me if I wanna go to Milwaukee and coach the Admirals. Sure, no problem, you know, they're not doing so good, but what the hell, I wanna take a crack and see if I can coach. They got some OK players, Stan Weir, Darren Pang in goal, Randy Boyd's a real good kid, Louie Begin, he could shoot a puck through a wall. We're gonna play Kalamazoo at home and then the next night in Michigan. I patiently explain what I want them to concentrate on. Plain, simple, nothing fancy. First fuckin' shift we're down 2–0 with two penalties to kill. We get waxed 7–2. After the game, they're sitting in the room waiting to hear what I have to say, but I keep my cool and pass on the chance. I mean, what's the big deal? Game tomorrow boys, get ready, we'll get our shit together." Pappin leaned back in the chair with arms spread wide.

"Next night, I go over what I want again. We stink the joint out, lose 6–3, and after the game I don't have enough time or breath to scream what I wanna say, I'm so goddamn mad. On the bus back they pull that old shit, 'Stop the bus in here, coach, we wanna get some pizzas.' Bullshit, right — they wanna pick up a few more bags of beer. I mean, do they think I'm stupid, never played or somethin'? Now we get to Chicago, rolling down the bypass on the Kennedy Expressway, and I tell the driver to pull into this plaza I know, stop the bus, and turn on the interior lights. By now some of these assholes are sleeping, but I get 'em all up. There's beer cans rollin' around, a bottle of vodka under a seat. I said to them, 'See over there?' pointing at the downtown skyline. 'That's Chicago. Do me a favour and take a good look at it, *because it's closest any of you bastards will ever get to it!*'"

I said I didn't think he was coaching material, the kind to bring young men along in the organization. He gave me the hand signals again.

Then we talked about being too young to play the game, referring to the youngsters who are put into the maelstrom of the NHL at 18, expected to do on-the-job-training in a dangerous and sometimes cruel environment.

"Some guys can handle it fine, others won't learn until they're too old. Look at me. I came out of Sudbury to Toronto, didn't even know where Hamilton was — 35 minutes away — Hamilton?" Again the hands expressed a question. Rather than interrupt, and ask *why* would anyone *want* to know where Hamilton was, I gave him my best rhetorical hand signal back. To the other patrons in the Toucan Bar, we must have looked like a couple of fair-skinned Italians talking about our last extra-end game of bocci ball.

"I was 23 before I knew what a mortgage was," he said, plowing ahead. "Davey Keon was mature at 21. Now there's a guy who knew how to play for Toronto. I didn't, I was one of the guys who had to be motivated to get me to take it seriously. Then I hit 40 and find out I've been taking the game too goddamn seriously, eatin' the ass out'a my linemates and screaming at minor-league hockey players." He shrugged it off as one of life's hard lessons. "Scouting is perfect for me."

There are very few triumphs in scouting. It's a business of watching and waiting, a job that demands a good memory and a keen eye for the little things. It takes a constructive mind to project today's performance into the future. It takes knowledge of the game, a feel for ability, to see how one player in another organization can fit into your team's system. I've always likened scouts to consultants, people paid to provide their advice or considered opinion. If a coach or GM doesn't choose to take the advice, a scout has to realize it's the other guy's call. In Jim Pappin's case he came up with two beauties.

"Chicago said they needed a goalie, gotta find a goalie. My son, Arnie, at school in Dakota, says there's a goaltender there, a crazy Blackhawk fan who's pretty good. So I go to North Dakota, and subsequently saw him play six times. Nobody had drafted him, and that's how we got Ed Belfour. Then they said we gotta get a centre, need a good young centre. A guy I know, Steve Lyons, calls me from Boston, says there's a kid out here playing college hockey you should take a look at real quick, so I did. Jeremy Roenick. I needed a bird-dog so I signed Lyons to scout the Boston area for us. Simple, eh?"

Yeah, right. Except you have to go out there to those arenas and actually take a look, and recommend the kid. And you have to know a Steve Lyons. Not simple at all.

After, we talked about baseball, another favourite of ours, and how, at age 21, he had a chance to play in the World Fastball Championship.

"Sudbury Park Hotel," he said, enthused again. "They were off to play in Florida. I was a shortstop and first baseman, led the league in batting," he said to my skeptical look. "I had a .249 average. Yeah, I could beat out bunts. Pitching is everything in fastball, and we had Booker Thomas from Detroit as our big man. I had to report to Rochester that fall, and Punch wouldn't let me go. That pissed me off, still does."

But the best is always for last and, since American Express hadn't arrived and we had finished our lunch, I ordered one more beer and he told me about his living accommodations in Chicago.

"The family didn't like Chicago and so I'm there alone during training camp and luck out in a place called Jay's, on Rush Street. I was staying at the Bismarck Hotel, owned by the Wirtz family, I think, but I wanted an apartment. Who do I run into at Jays? Paul Hornung, the Green Bay Packer running back. Very famous guy, eh? He says, 'I'm staying with a buddy from CBS TV, but I gotta move to New York. He'll be looking for somebody to take up the slack, so why don't you move in now?' Hornung moves out, the buddy is away, and I move in.

"The buddy comes home a few days later, I say, 'Hi there,' and he says, 'Who the fuck are you?' I tell him the story. He says, 'Well, isn't this goddamn lovely?' Now he tells me he's also out of the place in a month, so I'm back to Jay's, back to square one. Next thing I know I'm rooming with Ray Floyd. Yeah, the golfer. He's got a place that'd knock you out — winding staircase, pool table, fireplace. Did I mention we were in a high-rise condo?" I gave him the palms-up, with a head-cock and eyebrows, sort of a physical "who cares?" Pappoo understands immediately.

"After a few weeks, Floyd said, 'If you need any clothes, take 'em.' He had a closet — it'd go across this room. Full of nothin' but goddamn golf slacks. Drawers and shelves piled with golf shirts — not even opened. Sweaters, hats, shoes, golf gloves, the whole shitteroo. About two months later the Hawks are goin' to Oakland, and I don't have any summer slacks, none that I like anyway, and I go into the closet — 800 pairs of slacks — and pick out one pair of off-whites. Get out to California, take them to a tailor, and get him to let down the cuffs 2½ inches, figuring I'll get them rehemmed when I get back. About a month later I get a call from Ray. He's at the Colonial, or the Phoenix Open, leadin' the pack and it's Sunday, the final day. He really sounds steamed. 'Did you take a pair of my white slacks? I'm in the hotel gettin' ready to go, but my pants are piled so high around my ankles I can't see my goddamn feet.'

"Meanwhile I'm babblin' about how I was gonna get them shortened, but all the time I'm thinking, hundreds of slacks to choose from and I had to pick his favourites. Can you believe that shit?" He waves off my answer and slumps in the chair, resigned to being one of those people who never gets a break.

But I think he knows, deep down, he's been fortunate. One of the ones walking around with a couple of rings most hockey players would kill for. Besides, he's got a job he enjoys. There are a lot of people who can't lay claim to one of those.

Darcy fails to show before I leave, and as we part in the Marriott lobby I get Pappin to agree to send me next month's scouting schedule. "Why?" he asks, the hands, the eyebrows, the shrug in perfect unison.

"I got a buddy comes over once in a while. Hates to fly," I say over my shoulder, heading for the revolving door. "I'd like to give him your schedule and watch him cringe."

90-SECOND ALL-STARS

G — **Tony Esposito**

D — **Bobby Orr**

D — **Tim Horton**

C — **Jean Beliveau**

RW — **Gordie Howe**

LW — **Bobby Hull**

". . . don't have to say anything . . . see you later!"

Fred Stanfield

All in the Family

IF THERE WAS EVER A GOOD example of the importance of a general manager in the span of a hockey player's career, it has to be Fred Stanfield.

A skilled centre, with speed and good hands, he could pass both ways and was capable of directing power-play traffic from a spot on the blue line. He was not one to be cowed by unwritten laws or to follow blindly when the crowd moved off to greener pastures. He had implicit faith in his abilities, knew his limitations, and wouldn't look and see what other people were doing before doing what he thought was right. He also believed in fair treatment, which may have caused him some problems in his career and sometimes left a bad taste in his mouth.

The first time I ran across Fred Stanfield he was 36 years old, and had been the coach of the Niagara Falls Flyers Major Junior A team the year before. The season before that he had ended his 14-year NHL hockey career on the Buffalo Sabres' farm club at Hershey. In other words, he was two years out of hockey but not past the withdrawal symptoms.

My introduction came from our mutual friend, Dennis Hull, who had played with the NHL Old Stars and felt Stanfield would fit in. Hull was right. Although I was warned Stanfield could be a clubhouse lawyer — by players known to be clubhouse lawyers themselves — I asked him to join us. As far

Fred Stanfield: "... Freddie, Dennis, and whoever wants to straggle!"

as the NHL Old Stars was concerned, Fred Stanfield was a team player. From the first day he agreed to come along, I never had to worry about Freddie.

He signed on in the second year of operation. Driving from Buffalo to Toronto, he would sometimes pick up the errant and mercurial Turk Sanderson in Niagara Falls, and sometimes the late Larry Mickey, a neighbour in Williamsville, New York.

Besides his chauffeuring skills, what he brought to the team was a player who could start at centre, move to the wing later in the game, and double up on defence from time to time when injuries, the hectic schedule, and 24-hour "flu" from the post-gamer the night before got the better of our line-up. His two Stanley Cup wins didn't hurt our reputation, either. Although we had possibly the fastest and most talented oldtimer team in the business, able to take on all comers from Allan Cup champs to major junior A and university teams, we could always use the savvy and smarts, not to mention the marquee value, of a guy like Stanfield.

Depending on the personnel on a given trip, I would put Stanfield and Pit Martin on the same line, usually with Tom Williams, and it was something to see. Pit and Fred had crossed in midair in the blockbuster trade between the Hawks and the Bruins back in 1967. The trade helped make the Bruins so respectable they won two Stanley Cups. With the exception of Martin, it only made Chicago fans wonder. Now we had them on the ice together, as teammates on the same line, something they had never done through junior or pro.

All three had breakaway speed, could handle the puck in high gear, give and take rifled passes, and hit the top shelf without slowing down a notch. Williams, the best straight-ahead skater of the trio, was perfectly suited for either Martin or Stanfield. I remember the three as the prettiest line to watch. They turned the game of hockey into a musical. The only time the trio would change was when Dennis would make the trips. Then I'd say, "Freddie, Dennis, and whoever wants to straggle!"

Over four years Stanfield didn't miss many trips either, not when you consider he was starting up and running his own office equipment business at the time. He came to play, to relish the challenge of whatever and whoever we were playing. Hockey for the excellence of hockey. Sort of like a vacation. He rarely returned to the bench after a shift with anything but a smile, and he enjoyed the post-game get-togethers with the fans and the team.

Hull and Stanfield had begun their friendship as teammates back in St. Catharines with the junior Blackhawks, played in the Garden City Arena, where the golden tones of legendary Rex Steimer coughed up the play-by-play as he had done for Fred's brother Jack and Dennis's brother Bobby before. They roomed together, went to high school together, and made the jump to the NHL together back in 1964. They were also sent to the minors in 1966, and both returned to the Hawks in the 1966–67 season, but that would be the end of the parallel careers. The next time Fred would see Dennis as a teammate would be with the Old Stars.

It seemed that Stanfield was fated to wear the red, white, and black, graduating from the Dixie Beehives, whose home ice was not far from the Dixie–Dundas intersection of what is now the booming city of Mississauga. Both Dixie and St. Catharines wore the Blackhawk colours, and after four years it was expected that Stanfield would wear a real Chicago uniform. One of the ones who believed in the dream was Dennis Hull. Driving to a golf tournament a few years back, Hull confided to me how naive young hockey players can be.

"Freddie and I thought we'd go to the NHL, play with the Blackhawks, and retire. Just as simple as that," Hull said, tapping the steering wheel with a ringed finger. "Never occurred to us that it wouldn't be that way, that we wouldn't go on until the end as a pair."

Freddie and I reminisced about those early days in hockey one late afternoon at a neighbourhood rendezvous in the 'burbs of Buffalo called the "Libation Station." Judging by the crowd gathered around both corners of the squared-off bar, it was a halfway house for people on the way to their real houses. We sat at the only table available, in front of the jukebox, which was a mistake. We talked at a level akin to a couple of line workers in a bottling plant.

Over the golden oldies and bathed in the swirling, multicoloured glow from the jukebox lights, I heard about the expectations and anticipation all young players with the right skills bank on to reach the dream.

"Yeah, I'd say we always thought the NHL was in the future. Dennis and I used to talk about it all the time, and let's face it, we were a couple of the better players in the OHA then. I'm not popping off, you know. The last year we were together Dennis got 52 goals. I had 115 points, 39 goals, and finished third behind Andre Boudrias and Yvan Cournoyer. There were a lot of good players that year. Montreal also had Serge Savard and Jacques Lemaire, Hamilton had Pit Martin, Ron Harris, Pete Mahovlich, Nick Libett, and Paul Henderson, Peterborough had Andre Lacroix and Mickey Redmond, Niagara Falls had Gil Marotte, Ron Schock, and Bernie Parent. On the Marlies, Pete Stemkowski, Ron Ellis, Jim McKenny," His voice was getting lost in reflection, and the reggae strains of UB40.

"What about your other winger?" I yelled.

"Kenny Laidlaw. 'Stay-at-home Kenny,'" he roared back, smiling. It brought back Dennis Hull's description of Laidlaw, stuck on a line of offensive chargers. "Oh no," he replied to my question about Laidlaw possibly being a scorer, too. "Somebody had to mind the store. Kenny wasn't allowed to go over the other team's blue line." He shook his head, hiding a grin.

Like a prophecy come true, Stanfield and Hull went to Chicago in 1964, Dennis playing 55 games with ten goals, Fred playing 58 scoring seven. The following season they split time between Chicago and St. Louis, but under different circumstances.

In his rookie year Stanfield did what all rookies did back then, accepted the demotion as a checking centre, considering it an introduction to the rigours of the league. Soon he found the Hawks entrusting his line with shadowing the Beliveau line in Montreal, and the Alex Delvecchio–Gordie Howe line in Detroit. Tough work to lay in the lap of a rookie centre, but with grizzled Eric Nesterenko on the right side and grizzly Bill "Red" Hay on the other, he was in good company. So much so he experienced one of those "road hockey" dreams all kids enact.

Chicago had won the Stanley Cup back in '61, made the final in '62 and were surprised two-time semi-final losers in '63 and '64. In the spring of '65 they had once again clawed and climbed from third place to the final against the Montreal Canadiens, extending the series to the limit at the Forum.

"Here I was, a 20-year-old kid skating out to take the opening face-off of the seventh game in the Stanley Cup final. Against Jean Beliveau. Whatta picture!" he said, savouring the memory once more, over the voice of Phil Collins directly behind him.

The euphoria of the golden moment didn't last long. Probably less than 60 minutes as the Hawks exited the game and the series with a 4–0 loss. The problems between Stanfield and the Blackhawks were just beginning, and the end of the dream was getting closer.

Contract time is a fact of life in the professional ranks, an unpleasant task for the most part, especially the way it used to be, back when players were signed based on what they had done. Now it's different. Players air out their contract squabbles and renegotiation demands in the media, and gawky kids with changing voices are signed to million-dollar contracts without ever having played a game in the NHL. Back in the days of the six-team league the only weapon a player had was his last year's stats. In the case of Stanfield, the numbers seemed to lose a lot of their lustre without the daily exhilaration of the games. On paper the numbers looked bland.

He had scored seven goals and ten assists through 58 games, much of it on spot duty. In the playoffs he had gone through two gruelling seven-game series scoring two goals and an assist. In his mind he had done well, very well, for a rookie.

It wouldn't be the first time that a player had a different evaluation than management, and Chicago GM Tommy Ivan had a reputation for being a man with a converse sense of evaluation once contract time rolled around.

"I asked for a raise, and they refused. I went in again to see Little Hitler, as the boys referred to him, and again no dice. They held it in my face, like I was to blame. I was a defensive player, Ivan said. That was it. So I held out through training camp, and ten games of the regular season, sitting in the press box. Finally we met again, and he called in the arbitrator. Clarence Campbell. Seems as crazy now as it did then," he scoffed, referring to the practice of the day, in which the president of the NHL was called in to adjudicate a dispute between players and the owners Campbell worked for.

"I was getting conflicting advice, too," he added, putting the problem into perspective. "There were no agents in the six-team league, only fathers and the other players. Bobby Hull wanted me to play. He leaned toward signing. Red Hay told me not to. He said, 'They'll own you from now on if you do,' meaning I'd always be one of the last at the pay car if they were able to typecast me."

Like any young player, Stanfield succumbed to the basic fear of inactivity, plus the natural desire to play, so he signed and was sent to the Central League to get "conditioning." But the problems had only started. He borrowed defenceman Doug Jarrett's station wagon to move wife Anita and their worldly possessions to Missouri. At a motel on Route 66 the car was broken into, and everything — stereo, TV set, all the suitcases — was stolen, leaving them with only the clothes on their backs. It was an omen of things to come, going through "conditioning" for 24 games in St. Louis.

He made it back to the Hawks for half the season, but went through the same routine the following year. It's called being taught a lesson, something else that was an affordable luxury to GMs in the six-team NHL. He was spot-played for his last months in Chicago, dressing for only one playoff game in the spring of 1967. It was a bitter experience, a nightmare of packing and unpacking for the family, and a time of nagging uncertainty for a guy who was beginning to think the pinnacle of his career had come three years before at a face-off circle in Montreal.

A Rolling Stones ditty thundered out, and a pair of beers appeared as if by magic, gifts of the proprietors, Bob and Cathy, with Cathy endearing herself to both of us by mercifully toning down the jukebox.

"So what happened when the trade came down?" I bellowed, still not used to the lower decibels, startling the group at the far end.

"It was May. We were back home in St. Catharines and my mother-in-law Bertha called me, said she had just heard on the radio that I was going to Boston. The next call I got was from Milt Schmidt, the Bruins general manager." Stanfield grinned through the multicoloured glow. "Uncle Miltie we all called him. He told me straight, he said if I wasn't in the trade, it was no deal, and he said he liked the way I handled the puck."

Stanfield had worked the previous summer at a hockey school in Fenelon Falls, Ontario, where the other NHL names were defencemen Pierre Pilote of Chicago, Allan Stanley of the Leafs, and goaltender Ed Chadwick. Oddly enough, the head man was Milt Schmidt. Fred and Anita got out the boxes once more.

"I was goddamn happy about it, let me tell you. Boston had finished in last place, but I didn't care. What I liked was the way Milt called right away, the space I would have there, and the fact that they had no place to go but up." The sly grin returned. "And Bobby Orr was there, too."

It was a year of rebirth for the Bruins, and they made the most of it. Stanfield distinctly remembered a meeting at training camp in the fall of 1967.

"You had to be there, no excuses, no goofing off. It was held at the London Hotel after practice and a few beers," he said, taking the handoff of two such beverages from a patron between us and the bar. A raised finger from one of them indicated who the round was from. We waved our thanks.

"Let's see," he said, settling back into the captain's chair. "There was Eddie Johnston, Cheevers, Westfall, Bucyk, Ted Green, and the rest, plus us new guys, Esposito, Hodge, myself, Eddie Shack, and Derek Sanderson. He was a rookie. We knew that every position with the exception of Orr's was up for grabs, and we talked about getting some pride, proving something to the rest of the league, giving that extra push, sacrifice, all that stuff. But it was serious and it stayed that way. We finished third, in the playoffs for the first time in eight years. I mean to say, we *knew* we were getting there.

"The next year was a downer. We moved up to finish second and never made it through the semifinal. We had the Rangers down 5–2 going into the third period of the last game, took a bunch of penalties, and lost 7–5. It was a hard lesson, but a good one, and we *made* ourselves win the next year." For punctuation he took a long pull on the beer.

In 1967 they had talked about making it in three years, if they all stuck together. The Bruins may have been a year early on the prediction had they cashed in the year before, but they finally won it right on schedule in 1970. Though they moved up to first in 1971, the Montreal Canadiens forced their way back to win the Cup. Boston's second Stanley Cup came in 1972.

"The players in Boston wanted to win. Yeah, I know, everybody wants to win, but those guys *burned* with the will to win, and we got better and better. Harry Sinden was the best coach I ever had, bar none. Uncle Miltie got the talent and Harry moulded them into a winning collection, because Harry was perfect for our team makeup — or maybe it was the other way around. Like when he threw 'Chief' Bucyk, 'Pie' McKenzie, and me together. It worked from day one. Johnny McKenzie made me work harder just being around him. He was a hustler, a shit-disturber, a guy who kept everybody awake, all the time. He was perfect for me, and we were the speed. John Bucyk is in the Hall of Fame; I don't have to explain him. He was a scorer, and we had an instinct for where the other ones were on the ice. The two Johnnies made me better, and vice versa. Take a look at our Stanley Cup stats."

I did. Over 19 playoff games in those two Stanley Cup years Bucyk had 20 goals, McKenzie 9, and Stanfield 11. That's 40 goals, good for any line in any two years. But that's the past and so is sentiment. There was one more second-place finish with the Bruins, and although he had a no-trade contract he agreed to go to Minnesota for his next stop.

"Sinden decided he wanted to make changes and approached me. It was upsetting, but I apparently wasn't in the Bruins' plans. So, if I bought it, I was going to a good team at the time, under my terms, that is, a longer contract. The fact Wren Blair wanted me in Minny was another consideration." He stopped for a moment and shrugged. "Anita and I packed it up again.

"Jack Gordon was the coach, and for a year and a half I carried my end, did what I was told, putting players in the clear, but we never made the playoffs, and by the midpoint of the second season, I knew there was something going on." He leaned forward on his elbows. "Three times Punch Imlach came to Minnesota to scout me out himself, so I knew there was a trade coming up. In many ways Punch reminded me of Uncle Miltie Schmidt, a players' manager." Stanfield sat there making rings with the frosty bottle.

"Anita and the kids packed it up all over again?" I asked. He nodded.

"That's the hardest thing, you know. When I was a rookie in Chicago, we only had an apartment, just the two of us, getting established, but all I ever thought about was playing as long as I could with the Hawks and retiring in style, you know. People don't think about the other part. When we went to Boston, and again in Minnesota, we bought houses, settled in, figuring each time was the last move. The fans see a life of being in the spotlight, being on a team, travelling around to the best hotels. The spotlight is there, that's for sure — sometimes it's as bad as it is good, especially for the kids. But the moving, and packing, getting the kids out and into school, the pulling up stakes part is hard, really hard on the wives. But Buffalo was close to home, close to the families." The last part was drowned out by Phil Collins again.

"When I joined Buffalo, Imlach told me up front and honest, he needed a centre because Gil Perreault was hurt, plus he needed someone on the power play. He always gave me the impression he was grooming me for a coaching job, just the way he'd talk to me, take me aside, and ask me things. And he was good on his word.

"My last year, at training camp, Punch asked me to go down to Hershey and help out with the kids on the way up. Frank Mathers was the GM and Chuck Hamilton was the coach, but in the end I was coaching and it was another indication I was being groomed for something. We had some good ones down there. Tony McKegney, Larry Playfair, and Mike Boland all made it to the Sabres. Suddenly it was over. They fired Punch, and when I went in to see Scotty Bowman about something within the organization, nothing was offered, nothing."

He looked directly at me as if to say the easiest thing in the world is to get out of hockey. It isn't.

He tried other teams. "I called Slats Sather in Edmonton, and Ted Lindsay in Detroit, but nothing ever came of it."

He took a job as coach and GM of Niagara Falls at the major junior level, a team with Steve Ludzik, Mark Osbourne, Darryl Evans, Kevin McLelland, and Steve Larmer, but by the end of the year he learned the team was moving to North Bay. Without him.

"Reg Quinn, the owner, offered me the job, but I was happy in Buffalo. We weren't about to pick up and move again. And that was it," he said matter-of-factly, spreading his hands in resignation. For the first time the jukebox was silent.

"Let's slide over to my place and have some dinner," he insisted, so we said goodbye to the die-hards and the jukebox and drove the few short blocks to Williamsville.

Fred and I took a pre-dinner mini-tour of the house, and I noticed the Stanley Cup replica on the fireplace mantle. I'd also noted the large ring he was wearing and commented that a lot of winners I know don't wear theirs.

"Hey, Roscoe. I wear it every day. I'm proud of it."

Later as we finished off over a parting coffee, I asked him about the Old Stars.

"It was great," he replied. "It helped me satisfy my system for hockey at a time when I needed it, and still have fun. The best thing was playing with old enemies and finding out they're OK. You think I'd know better, eh, being traded three times. We sure as hell had a lot of laughs."

I wouldn't see Freddie again until he made a trip to Toronto to visit his ailing father in the Credit Valley hospital. Then I had the long-awaited opportunity to see the family "museum" I'd heard so much about, and got a whole new look at life in hockey.

The Stanfield family home in Mississauga is a long bungalow spread across an acre of lawn and garden, fronted by a very, very wide driveway that had to be a road hockey player's dream.

Down in the rec room were the collectibles of seven brothers, 20-foot two-tiered shelves covered in the hardware of sport, a bronzed golfer here, a pair of silvered skates topping a hardwood base there, MVPs and all-star trophies numbering in the dozens. There's a five-foot-wide rack of jumbled, standing sticks, all lengths and sizes, straight blades and twisting curves, the taped knobs as varied as the taped and untaped blades below, and the names are a trip through hockey's rosters, stamped into the handle, or scrawled with marker pen, some with numbers and others that didn't need numbers.

There's a Watson, Bugsy I presumed, and an Orr, which definitely nailed down two ends of the hockey spectrum. Mikita, and Howe, together at last! There's Esposito, Bucyk, Cashman, and Perreault. A Worsley stands alone simply because of the size and the gigantic three-inch knob crowning the handle. Heavy though it may be, it has an equal in the stick of Kent Douglas, a piece of fencing that might be mistaken for a wall stud. There's McKenzie, a Richard 16, G. Unger, and Coffey. A short stick, one I thought might be from a pee-wee or bantam Stanfield, turns out to be an early Bobby Hull. Although it is curved, it's without the intimidating hook that looked like a shepherd's crook.

Two handles catch my eye like parrots in a herd of sparrows. A hardly disguised "Espee 7" is one, and Kannegiesser is the other.

"Almost ran out of shaft on this one," I remark, and Freddie only grins. I can't help but think this must be the best company Sheldon Kannegiesser was ever in.

Next there's the four-walled side show of plaques, crests, certificates, badges, and photos by the score, no pun intended. An underwear-clad Fred with father Gord and the Stanley Cup, and another one, this time the multiple long johns of Freddie, John "Chief" Bucyk, and Johnny "Pie" McKenzie, cigar in hand, mugging over the Stanley Cup once more. Two certificates hold a special place on one panel: 1974 and '75 All-American selections for brother Vic while with Boston University. Across the way there are photos of the eldest, Jack, in Houston Aero skivvies, with the Avco Cup, champions of the World Hockey Association.

Then there's the fireplace. A grey stone floor-to-ceiling beehive, a tribute to the "Beehives" of Dixie where the Stanfield family spent all of their winters over two decades of scheduled practices, games, playoffs, and tournaments. On the mantle running around the midpoint are replicas of the Stanley Cup and Avco Cup, the top silverware in North American pro hockey. It's all the trimmings from the seven Stanfield brothers, and their father, Gord, a retired deputy chief of police.

One might say a police chief would be the least you'd need to corral a group only two outfielders away from its own baseball team, but sports, as so often is the result, becomes the outlet and direction for young boys and channels their energy and determination to succeed in the right direction.

Jack, the eldest, played in the American, Western, and Central leagues before joining Gordie Howe and the Howe boys in Houston for two Avco Cups. Fred was next, then came Jim, who played in the AHL, the Central League, and logged six games with the Los Angeles Kings. Joe was another of the Dixie Beehives, but took up the fireman's trade in Mississauga. Vic played his junior year in Dixie and went on to captain Boston University, twice the MVP of the prestigious Beanpot Tournament, two NCAA All-America selections, and 12 years playing in Germany. Then came Paul, another Dixie junior grad, and the youngest, Gordie Jr., who split his all too short hockey time between Dixie and the Streetsville Derbies before becoming the victim of a fatal auto accident.

Taking the tour with Fred as a guide has its moments. He goes out of his way to underline the achievements of the brothers and of his dad. He tells me about his mother, saying she was the best fan in the world, and how she bestowed the same amount of attention on each of her sons, the Stanley Cup winner, the All-American, the fireman. Clearly, pride shines through in this room of achievement, even without the pictures and doodads, and the glitter from what most people refer to as "dust collectors." The appreciation is both parental and fraternal, the points of interest carefully highlighted by the guide so the tourist doesn't have any misconceptions about this sweater, that trophy, or the photo on that wall, and their significance.

My closing glance around the rec room told me it's not just the all-encompassing sense of accomplishments that gives the room a special personality.

It's about hockey. Without GMs, coaches, or moving vans.

More importantly, it's about family.

90-SECOND ALL-STARS

G — **Glen Hall** *". . . an absolute competitor."*

D — **Bobby Orr** *". . . guts and brains, he made you play the limit."*

D — **Serge Savard** *". . . the backbone of Montreal's defence."*

C — **Stan Mikita** *". . . patient and smart, never gave up the puck."*

RW — **Gordie Howe** *". . . finesse, respect, and mean."*

LW — **Bobby Hull** *". . . one shot and you win."*

Walt McKechnie

A Jersey with Air Miles

THE SIGN SAYS "McKeck's Place." The storefront facade is about 20 feet across, one large window facing the street, a doorway on one side, two steps up to get in.

It's a rinkwide pass from the main intersection in the town of Haliburton, Ontario. Highways 121 and 519 to be exact. Through the front door the hockey motif begins. There are pictures. Everywhere. Teams, action shots, personal photos, hockey sticks, and pucks abound. A sign over the bar saying "Welcome to McKeck's" is underlined with two autographed sticks.

It's as small as the storefront dictates, but only in width. A walkway divides the bar stools from a wall-length row of empty tables in the midafternoon lull, but the bar chairs support a few of the regular patrons. Like a pigeon I home in on the seat next to the designated town booster. Lou Hodgson's family roots go back forever in the region. He is, I find out later, referred to as the "Mayor of Haliburton," but the title doesn't tell it all. His father was a Member of Parliament for the area, and Lou was the Conservative member of the provincial legislature, as well as a municipal politico of note. It happens, doesn't it? Everytime you think you're being put-on, one of these characters turns out to be the real thing.

Both Mike the manager and Gail the bartendress relayed the same message.

Walt McKechnie as a Maple Leaf: ". . . Conn Smythe came around one day and said to me, 'Son, wear the Maple leaf the way it should be worn — proudly.'"

"Walt says to wait. He'll be back when he picks up Kate and Shannon from school." With our little meeting on hold I cruised the picture gallery. There's Phil Esposito in a Team Canada uniform, obviously not '72, but which Team Canada? Another colour shot is of McKechnie in Detroit being checked by Pete Mahovlich and Guy Lafleur. Walt and Buffalo netminder Roger Crozier. Walt and J.P. Parise of the Islanders. Walt as a Colorado Rockie leaning into a slapshot on Ranger goalie Doug Soetaert. The puck is frozen in mid-flight, forever, and I wonder if it was a goal or just an interesting photo. Up the angled staircase to the second floor, the warm wood colours continue into an open loft. More tables, more pictures, and a lot of sweaters.

The framed photos are black and white, from an earlier era. Walt and Derek Sanderson, shaking hands back in their junior days, and another with Walt Tkaczuk. There's one of the London Nationals, partially dressed in their equipment and uniforms playing cards and obviously waiting for a game to begin. My favourite was an 8 × 10 taken of Walt with four of his Phoenix Roadrunner teammates, Gordie Readall, Del Topoll, Harry Shaw, and Rick Charron. They all have their bridgework out, and five pairs of eyeteeth surround nothing but air. A regular Dracula look-alike convention.

The nine sweaters lining the east wall are another thing. Detroit, Toronto, and Team Canada are numbered 11, Cleveland, California, and Colorado are numbered 8, plus there's a Boston 18, a Minnesota 22, and a 93 — it's a Leaf jersey with "Gilmour" on the back. Even with this named and numbered checklist staring me in the face, it doesn't tell the story of Walt McKechnie's hockey career, which spanned 16 NHL seasons, because all the sweaters aren't there. I'll be damned if I could remember which ones were missing.

But "McKeck's" wasn't finished either. I stepped up a slight rise at the back of the second floor and walked into "The Dome," a replica of the SkyDome with nothing but Blue Jay logos, posters, and pictures. What appears to be little more than a small-town diner from the outside is a hell of a lot bigger on the inside.

It's a long way from the rah-rah of hockey to the Haliburton Highlands. Life's a lot more sedate up there, unless you count the summers, when the yahoos from the city come in droves and make the locals rich. Or so they say. McKeck's Place has become a favourite year-round spot, and the McKechnies — Walter and daughters Kate and Shannon — have settled into the quiet life of rural Ontario, living on a lake, surrounded by trees, with a 4×4 parked at the end of a long driveway leading into a home all us city dwellers tend to be envious of when we consider cottage life.

Maybe this idyllic lifestyle makes up for the rough ride he had in hockey.

His hockey roots go back to six years of junior, four in Junior B where he was a teammate of Phil Esposito in Sarnia. How good a prospect was he? Good enough to be Toronto's first pick, sixth overall, in the 1963 amateur draft. He then played two seasons with his hometown London Nationals, the Leafs' major junior affiliate in the OHA. He didn't stay with the Leafs when he turned pro, which turned out to be an omen of things to come. Instead he began in Phoenix of the Western Hockey League, where he scored 24 goals and 30 assists. It earned him the Rookie of the Year award. After a mid-season trade, he found himself with the Minnesota North Stars for nine games in the Stanley Cup playoffs, scoring three goals, adding two assists. An auspicious beginning to a pro career, to be sure, but it guaranteed nothing. He wouldn't see another Stanley Cup game until 11 more years had passed.

While looking over the list of trades and reserve list additions and deletions in a 16-line rap sheet below his NHL statistics, I recalled him telling me that he had once been on five team rosters, one only on paper, in the space of 12 months. The fact he weathered 11 years between Stanley Cup games was tempered by the point that he had 12 points in only 15 games, seven of them goals, in only two Cup series over his entire 16 years. Not bad, but the only thing a record like that is good for is improving your golf game. Was he a bad player or were they bad teams?

Any player who scores 214 goals and 392 assists for 606 total points over 955 NHL games while balancing a moving van and airline schedule has truly performed a remarkable feat, in my opinion. To give you an idea of how tough that schedule was, consider this: he changed NHL teams 12 times with stops in the minors four times.

Were they bad teams? The best was a second-place Boston Bruins, where he saw limited duty in 53 games before moving on to the first of his Detroit stopovers. Early in his career he had a brief stint with a third-place Minnesota club, but it wasn't until 78-79, for his first of two long-awaited seasons with Toronto, that he contributed to a worthy cause. The Leafs placed third that season, McKechnie chipped in with 25 goals, and seven more in his last six games of Stanley Cup play. He was 32.

There were other years, better years, when the goals came, the total points were there, but the team finish wasn't. His last year with California he scored 23 times in 63 games. The Seals were 16th in a 16-team NHL for the second time in a row. In his first two full seasons in Detroit, he logged 80 games both times. In 75-76 he had a career year: 26 goals and 56 assists. The Wings finished fourth in their division. The following year he had 25 goals and they slipped to last place in the Norris.

He played on nine teams that finished last or were destined to be tail-enders before he was traded. With only part-time exceptions, the best full year he put in was with the third-place Leafs. His career ended with the last-place Red Wings.

McKechnie walked in with no sign of surprise to find me on his doorstep. Walt isn't given to histrionics or backslapping. It was June, he was already tanned a reddish brown most people would fight for, accented by the blond-haired, blue-eyed good looks that seemed to fit perfectly on a relaxed 6'2" frame. The hands are large, a characteristic I remembered from a long-ago first handshake when he played ball with the ProStars.

As we sat in "The Dome," away from chance visitors, I expected to find some bitterness, and who could blame him? But out of two hours of conversation I listened to very little, with the notable exception of three little incidents. The first came up as we talked about the great beginning in Phoenix.

"Phoenix was a good place to break in. They had great guys there. Sandy Hucul, Bob Kabel, Dick Lamoureaux, Dougie Dunville, Tommy McVie . . ." There was a reflective pause, as if to indicate enough was said, but then he continued. "I learned how to drink with Tommy. He split more beer than most of us drank." There was an edge to his voice.

"Yeah, I loved the Western League. When they announced I'd won the rookie award, we were playing against Seattle in the playoffs. You ever hear about Guyle Fielder?" he asked, probing my knowledge of one of the great minor-league players of all time. I only nodded. "You know what he said to me? He said, 'Kid, you ain't gonna be around here long, get yourself a straight blade.' He was trying to help me out. There were a lot of guys like that back then.

"I remember sitting on the Minnesota bench with Ray Cullen beside me when Larry Hillman ran Gordie Howe. Next thing I know they're calling for a doctor out on the ice. For Hillman. Ray leaned over and said, 'Don't be running at Howe.' I said, 'It would never enter my mind.'" Walt laughed. "Good guys," he said, almost lost in reminiscing. But then another thought pushed him out of a slouch and into a smile.

"In Oakland, the team was bad, almost out'a control. Whatta group: Bobby Sheehan, Ivan Boldirev, Ernie Hicke, Hilly Graves, big Pete Laframboise. We were in New York playing the Rangers, Gilles Meloche is standing on his head in goal for us, we're down 1–0 and it should have been 10–0. At the end of the period they announce the shots on goal were Rangers 23, Seals 2. In the dressing room Stan Gilbertson gets up and asks, 'Who are the two wise guys?'"

Warming up to the California Seals situation, McKeck moved some glasses around again and told a story about the Philadelphia Flyers coming to town for the last game of the season between the two clubs.

"Hell, they were the tough guys, we were just the punching bags. At practice one of the boys said let's just play the game, don't start any shit, and get it over with. Next day Hilliard Graves was quoted in the paper saying something like, 'If they wanna get tough, they know where they can find me.'

"That night, before the game, in comes Laframboise . . . big afro hair cut, big moustache, big trenchcoat, he really looked like a tough guy should, you know, 6'2", rangy, walked like a goddamn farmer. At the time he was on a line with Graves and Stan Weir. You could see he was pissed off, never even took off his coat, just sat down, took out the paper, already turned to the offending article, smacked it with a backhand, and said, "Can you fuckin' believe this shit? They got the Hound, the Bird, and the Hammer' — referring to Bob 'Mad Dog' Kelly, Don Saleski, and Dave Schultz. Glancing up he pointed at himself and his linemates. 'And whatta we got? We got Big Mouth and the Two Chickens.'"

"What about 1974?" I asked when we'd settled down. "In Boston."

McKechnie leaned back into the chair once more, and chose his words carefully. "You don't realize until you're actually there what it's like to play with great team players. Everything is done at a higher level. Even practices." He pushed the chair away from the table, putting his elbows on his knees and sitting forward, a position you'll see most hockey players assume often. It's the way you conduct business in a dressing room. There are no tables there to lean on, or hide behind.

"Bobby Clarke used to piss me off big time, but you can't let a guy get to you, or at least not let it show. I used to beat him on a face-off and he'd start chirping about how many losing teams I'd been on. He was always yapping." The bitterness showed through for the second time. "Once, I stepped away from the face-off and asked how he'd like to wear my sweater for a trip around the league for a change. I said, 'It's easy to play on a good team, Clarkie. *Anybody* can play on a good team — even you.' And it's true. When you play with a better club, your own level of play rises. In Toronto — and you can ask anybody who was there at the time because that was a goddamn good team — playing with guys like BJ Salming and Darryl Sittler forces you to come up a couple of notches."

"First time in Detroit?" I asked.

"Yeah, the first time around was OK, had two good seasons personally but never got into the playoffs. It's hard to tell sometimes, when you come into a team from the outside, because they looked good on paper, but there were some strange ways of doin' things around the old Olympia. They had a strength coach, an old football player from the Lions, who was always telling us hockey was for sissies, and hockey players were stupid, football players were smart. You know, 'You'se guys couldn't remember da snap count.' We'd say, 'Gol-lee . . . what's a snap count?' just to grind him.

"He was a big asshole, six feet, weighed about 230, could bench press a thousand pounds or some ridiculous number. He was in great shape, but a crusty old bastard. And egotistical, too. One day we set him up. Had him do his toughest bench presses. He'd just barely make his last push when we'd get a new guy in the room and say he'd like to see him do it. Goddamn dope would do it all over again. Finally, we had him almost helpless, whacked-out, inoperable. We jumped him, taped him up on the bench and shaved the dummy bald. Chest, head, arms and legs, crotch, everywhere." Laughing uncontrollably, McKechnie made Cyrano de Bergerac gestures like he was slashing with a sword.

"There was Nick Libett, Dan Maloney, Denny Hextall, Bugsy Watson, and me. The poor son of a bitch was gurgling and growling like the Tasmanian

Devil. Couldn't even talk he was so fuckin' mad. Chased us around the Olympia like a maniac for about an hour." He shook his head and glanced up at the oversize Blue Jay logo for a moment.

"In 1977 I was picked up by Team Canada for the World Championships. Pretty good team, too," he said, and I recalled one of the colour photos on the main floor wall, a multi-rowed picture of helmetless NHLers in blazers and striped ties. Sittler, Dallas Smith, Tony and Phil Esposito, Rod Gilbert, Paul Henderson, Ron Ellis, Pierre Larouche, and others who had been knocked out of the NHL playoffs. I also recalled they were named "Team Ugly" for their on-ice behaviour, finishing out of the running when the Russians suddenly contracted amnesia, forgot how to play hockey, and went into the tank, losing to Sweden and thereby eliminating the Canadians. That was in the spring. The fall would be just that, a fall from grace.

The next team on the list, the sweater I had missed on the wall, was Washington. McKechnie had come off playing all 80 games for Detroit in both years, with 26 and 25 goals respectively, but the Wings finished fourth, and last. Still, a new year always brings new players, new hope, and in this case a new coach in Bobby Kromm. Walt never got to add Kromm to his list of mentors.

"Ted Lindsay, the Detroit GM, told me they had signed goalie Ron Low from Washington, and the Caps had compensation coming. Originally they had asked for Dan Maloney or a first-round draft pick. The Wings backed off, but counteroffered me and 100 grand. We haggled back and forth, they sat me out, but now Washington wanted me. The Wings said I had disgraced the team by turning back the offer and didn't want me around."

"Did you turn down the deal?" I asked.

"Damn right, I did. It was the only time in my career I balked, and believe me I had lots of reasons and lots of opportunities to balk." The bitterness began to show in a new way.

The deal was ultimately made, involving second- or third-round draft choices down the road on both sides, and McKechnie shipped out once more and ran into his old buddy from the Western League, Tommy McVie, now the head coach of the Capitals.

"We were at training camp in Hershey, and I find out McVie is a fitness bug now that he isn't a player. We had guys like Gerry Meehan, 'Ace' (Garnet)

Bailey and Gary 'Axe' Smith in goal. McVie calls us the 'Fat Squad.' He's got us doing laps around the building, using weighted sticks, ankle weights, all kinds of stupid shit. This from a guy who used to drink his weight in beer," he said, and I had the distinct feeling we had reached the main source of McKechnie's rancour.

"By the time we've played 16 games we're no wins, two ties, and 14 losses, and the media is saying it's time for McVie to go, stuff like that. So what does he do? Calls a team meeting, in a bar. What the hell can I say? We had a guy who coached in the I (the International League) and we had a bunch of kids he'd brought with him from the I. We had a lot of vets, too, so you can't blame the kids, but he's looking for a reason why we're horseshit, except where it belonged. McVie starts talking about 'the problem' and Axe Smith considers it for a moment and says he knows what the problem is. He says, 'The problem is, we're in the wrong fuckin' league.' Bill Riley, one of the regulars, went apeshit. He was really hurt. He grabbed Smitty by the shirt, started yanking him around. Smitty was cool, kept saying, 'Let go of the shirt, Billy. You're gonna rip the shirt, Billy.'

"It was a circus, believe me. At practice McVie kept harping about hard work — hard work gets the job done. Hard work doesn't work if you don't have talent. You can work till you drop and if you don't belong in the league you're gonna get your ass kicked. It came to a head right then and there. He called me in and told me I was 'a cancer on the team.' Guy Charron and I had four goals each to lead the team at the time, but he sat me out for a month, even though other teams were interested in me. It was the worst management treatment I had experienced up until then. They traded me midway through December to Cleveland. From last place to last place, but I had a pretty good four months — 12 goals and 22 assists. At the end of the season, Minnesota put me on their reserve list, because Cleveland and Minnesota merged, and bingo! I was traded to Toronto. Man, was I happy."

It was 1978 and the Leafs were on a roll, finishing third in their division, settling into a better line-up, starting to come back from the doldrums with some young stars who could score goals: Lanny McDonald (43), Darryl Sittler (36), McKechnie (25) — even the combative Tiger Williams scored 19 in that peek-a-boo year for the Toronto fans. But it wasn't to be. The mix was about to change.

"Jim Gregory was the GM, Roger Neilson the coach, and they treated me first class. They had the makings of a 'team.' You know what I mean by 'team.'" I nodded in the right place. "Then Punch Imlach came into the picture the next year and it all went to ratshit." I knew he was referring to the conflict between Punch and the captain and team leader, Darryl Sittler. For Punch it was a power struggle, and I remembered back to the time when he told me, "No goddamn player is gonna run *my* team." That's what he perceived as Darryl's assumption of duties, aside from playing, that had been accorded him in the Gregory years.

There are those who say Imlach resorted to trading away any and all who were tight with the captain because he was contractually unable to get at Sittler. He sent hard-nosed Pat Boutette, Sittler's buddy from way back to their junior days in London, to Hartford on Christmas Eve 1979. Lanny McDonald, a budding superstar, was next, traded to the Colorado Rockies on January 10, 1980, and Dave "Tiger" Williams, even though a personal favourite of owner Harold Ballard, followed — sent to Vancouver on February 18.

On March 3, 1980, McKechnie was traded to Colorado. Sittler remained.

"I still have a hard time accepting what happened to that team," McKechnie said quietly. "You were around Imlach for a while. Can you?"

Behind the question was another story about the new coaching regime of Floyd Smith, Dick Duff, and Punch.

"Sometime after New Year's we played three games, Wednesday, Saturday, and Sunday — 21 goals against, just absolutely horseshit. Monday, we go to practice, 45 minutes of 3-on-0's. Then they tell us 'now we're gonna skate.' So I said to Smitty that in 11 NHL years I've never seen a 3-on-0. Dan Maloney pipes up and says 'Walt's right,' and we were kicked off the ice, and off the next road trip. No instructions, no nothing. I called my agent, Bill Watters, and he advised me to get some ice time with the Marlies. When the team came back I went to practice, put on a black sweater — as a joke, you know, the Black Aces crap. The boys are laughing, asking who's the new player — and that's when management asked Sittler to tell me to leave. He said 'Tell him yourself,' but they got rid of me anyway. I think Gunner (trainer Guy Kinnear) was the one to tell me, and he was the guy who called to tell me I was back a few days later.

"We played Detroit on a Saturday, tied them, I was picked third star, and then it happened. Monday after practice I'm at Bobby Rubino's Ribs in Mississauga, and Dan Maloney calls me there. 'You've been traded — to Colorado.' Billy Watters got to me with the news that there was a one-way ticket at the airport waiting for me, and I had to hustle down to the Gardens to get some gear and sticks. To this day, Roscoe, to this very day," he said, tapping a stiff finger on the table, "not one of those people has ever told me I was traded. Not Smith, not Duff, or Punch."

It would be another eight months before I saw Walt, stopping at McKeck's Place after a speaking engagement in Lindsay. Mike was managing, Gail was bartending, Lou Hodgson held down a middle bar seat. I stood beside him and soaked up some local politics and lore all over again. The sticks were still there, the sweaters and pictures remained in place, country and western still played to the half-dozen customers lingering after lunch. This time the visit was just for atmosphere, since we were actually meeting at his home on a lake north of the town.

We had dinner with his daughters, talked over a couple of beers in front of a huge stone fireplace, and watched the Leafs play Chicago in a playoff game, then packed it in for the night. Next morning, after the girls went to school, we had a chance to walk down the front of the property to the lake. The docks were yet to be put in the water, the pontoon boat sat safely up on blocks, and a weathered case of empties from last year's staff get-together still hid along the wall of the bonfire pit.

Back in the cottage, over coffee, we talked about the laughs and the good times in hockey. It seemed to centre on that one special year in Toronto.

"They were the best of times," he said, fingering some notes he had written earlier, things he had recalled and items to jog his mind for this last conversation. "Jim Gregory and Roger Neilson were first class, number one. They treated you like men. We'd be chartering out of Toronto after a Saturday night game and he'd have the bus stop at Grapes — remember Turnbull's place on Church Street?" I nodded. "They'd always let us load on a pile of sandwiches, a couple of boxes of beer." Ian's bar was around the corner from Maple Leaf Gardens — just south of the bank on the west corner of Church and Carlton. It was nothing more than an old house, repaired to appear like an eating establishment. The kitchen was in the basement, orders were hustled up the stairs, and beer was served over the bar out of Coleman coolers. Winston's it wasn't, but it was frequented by the hockey crowd, and that's all that mattered.

"Ballard was a funny old guy back then. He'd come in the dressing room and start ragging on Tiger Williams, saying, 'If we could get ourselves *one* tough left winger, boys, we'd be OK,' and they'd start wrestling, sparring around the room. Goofy old bugger, he could have been hurt horsing around with the Tiger. I also remember Conn Smythe came around one day and said to me, 'Son, wear the Maple leaf the way it should be worn — proudly.' I'll always remember that. Just like I'll always remember that team."

I asked if he and Jim McKenny had ever run into one another. It immediately brought a smile, as it always does with most players.

"Never got a chance to play with him, but we were at the Minnesota-Cleveland training camp when the NHL merged the two teams. It was brutal, all those guys fighting for jobs. I mean, one bad shift and you were gone. They had fights every day, real punch-outs. One time a guy bit off the tip of another player's finger. They were goddamn serious. Looked like the set of *Slapshot*. Jimmy and I made a pact in the dressing room. Whenever there was a fight and we were on the ice, we promised to grab one another and waltz around until the shit settled."

I asked him about the coaches — he had had so many, could he run down them and comment?

"Turk Broda was my junior coach. He said, 'Kid I'll make you an all-star.' Of course he said it over a bottle of scotch, sort'a like storytime." I smiled and said I was thinking along the lines of NHL coaches.

"How much time do you have?" he groaned, clasping his hands together and leaning forward. "In Minnesota I had John Muckler for a cup of coffee, Wren Blair, Parker McDonald. Blair was a piece of work. One time we were playing L.A. He came in the dressing room chirpin' and fumin' about big Bob McCord not kicking the crap out of Real Lemieux when he had the opportunity. He screeched it about three times, 'Why didn't you punch that Frenchie in the head?' McCord was sitting there, head down. Finally he looked up at Blair, who was red in the face, and said, 'How'd *you* like a punch in the head?' Wren took off." McKechnie leaned back and laughed out loud.

"In California it was Vic Stasiuk — he said our team set hockey back 20 years — and Freddy Glover. In Boston I had Don Cherry. He was another coach who went by the theory that if you played good, didn't duck behind excuses, you could have a couple of beers. Just as long as you performed, that's all. In Detroit, the first time, I had Doug Barclay, Fats Delvecchio, and Larry Wilson. They were all geniuses compared to what went on later. Then there was Washington and Tom McVie. In Cleveland it was Tex Evans, a good guy, but — he had to send us off the practice ice once. The smell of booze was so bad, he said, somebody was gonna get hurt. Toronto, Roger Neilson, then Floyd and Company. Colorado, Don Cherry again. Geez, he had that town humming, the place was rockin' every night we played. If they had left him in there and didn't get in his way, the NHL would still be in Denver today. Then came Billy McMillan. Enough said." I reminded him he had played two seasons in Detroit.

"Don't worry, I remember. Wayne Maxner the first year, then Nick Polano. I had left Colorado as a free agent and signed with Detroit, without question the best sports town in North America, bar none. But this guy Polano was a minor leaguer, never got close to the NHL, and couldn't coach. You have to wonder how in the hell . . . well, anyway, after October and November the second year we're lower than whale shit and he decides to call each guy in to his office for a lecture. We've been playing one forechecker in their end from the start and we have diddly to show for it. So the guys in the dressing room — Reed Larsen, John Ogrodnick, Nick Libbett — start harping on me to tell Polano about changing the checking. I told them, 'Tell him yourself.' I'm coming to the end of my career, tryin' to get 1,000 games in and I ain't sayin' shit. That's it. So it comes my turn, and Polano starts on me, saying I'm not doing this, I'm not doing that, I'm one of the veterans they were counting on and I should be leading, and all that B.S. So I asked him if he minded if I said something. I said, 'How long did you play in this league? Exactly. If you play in one end of the ice all night, even *you* could play in the NHL.' I said, 'You have to have *two* forecheckers in this league, start playing in the other team's end for a change.

Send two guys in with reckless abandon — but have a plan! One guy stays high in the zone.' He says, 'Show me what you mean.' So I did, on the blackboard in his office. When I finished I said, 'That's the way you play in the NHL, and I'm only telling you what the guys in the other room wanted me to say.' Then he had me do it again in the dressing room." He nodded his head as if asking a question. I nodded back, because sometimes you have to wonder.

But at the end of that season Detroit cut him free at the age of 36, with 955 NHL games to his credit.

"I tried to sweeten a deal to get me those 45 games. I offered to take a one-third pay cut, help out with coaching, be a spot player, but Jim Devellano said they were going with younger players. Next thing I know they signed Darryl Sittler and Tiger Williams, both in their mid-30s, too."

But it was over. Even a minor-league playing role in Salt Lake City where J.P. Parise was coaching ended when it became apparent there was no chance of returning to the NHL. The new kids were taking runs at him. An old gunslinger on the way down.

A tinge of bitterness showed, but disappeared quickly.

When I left McKechnie that morning, we stood for a while talking beside the car. I asked him what advice he gives to young players these days. "Stay away from Tommy McVie?" I suggested.

He grinned. "I know I'm the kind to say it straight, and I know I burned a lot of bridges back then. I know I'm opinionated, especially when it comes to hockey. But I tell kids to love and respect the game, play as long as you can, and save your money. There aren't very many jobs like it out there, and there sure isn't the money."

Driving away, I thought to myself, at least he doesn't have to worry about getting a phone call telling him he's traded. That was in the past. Today the concerns are about two little girls, about putting in the dock, and about a 20-foot-wide restaurant and bar called McKeck's.

I had to smile. There was a time when he didn't worry about anything, and my mind went back to a picture on the restaurant wall of five smiling young players in faraway, exotic Phoenix.

Back then, they didn't even worry about teeth.

90-SECOND ALL-STARS

G — **Ken Dryden** *". . . covered so much of the net. Unorthodox, but he got the job done."*

D — **Bobby Orr** *". . . the ultimate competitor. He'd find a way to create a goal."*

D — **Denis Potvin** *". . . best passer I ever saw. Big money player."*

C — **Phil Esposito** *". . . he'd thrive on the situation . . . tremendous desire to win."*

RW — **Guy LaFleur** *". . . had the speed, and the shot."*

LW — **Clark Gillies** *". . . intimidating — if the puck goes in the corner, he's gonna get it."*

Doug Favell

Like Picking Cherries

THE RESTAURANT WAS SEMI-CROWDED. Diners were scattered haphazardly through the tables, while a bunch of "no-friends" sat or stood appropriately distanced around a rectangular bar. Our little group of hockey instructors took over four stools plus my prerequisite stand-up spot, and ordered the usual from a bartender we were getting to know all too well. The place was called Chatterly's, or Chudley's, or Chuckie's, but it's the closest to Ridley Hockey School, a summer spinoff of the prestigious, preppy Ridley College in St. Catharines, Ontario. As per usual, we'd been on the ice three times that day. The first session was at 6:30 a.m., another one in the afternoon, and once more that evening. Combined with the usual meals, supervisors' duties, and final reports, it had taken another 16-hour day out of us, but the next day was a late-morning start. Time to relax a little.

I had an interesting story to tell my fellow instructors. It concerned a question from "The Judge." The man was a bona-fide jurist from Shaker Heights, Ohio. His son was a 14-year-old in my class of 32 Canadian and American kids who had just closed out their fifth day of workouts. The next day was to be the showcase intra-squad game, which the camp counsellors appropriately called "Sissies versus Pissies." The kids themselves preferred "the Nerds and Turds Tilt."

Doug Favell in Philadelphia with the "sunburst" mask: ". . . I didn't think about style. Well, all I concerned myself with was stopping the puck . . ."

I had been forewarned about the "blowhard judge from Cleveland." Armed with that knowledge, I was prepared when confronted by Big Daddy, here to pick up his offspring and solicit an evaluation of his son's merits.

After an initial toast and quaff, I started out.

"I'm coming off the ice, nose dripping, hoarfrost on my ass, and he steps right in front of me and demands a word — in private. I lied, said I didn't like to do that because some of our senior instructors had been viciously assaulted in the weeks gone by, by irate fathers, and I put on my best concerned face. 'Jesus, I'm a judge,' he says, offended that I don't know who he is — a loud voice of reason and calm, a dispenser of justice. We step to the side, but he wants to go even farther along the boards. I told him I wasn't allowed to step off the rubber mats."

Steve Davies, the co-director of the school, and an ex-WHA goaltender, managed to choke down a gulp of beer before it passed through his nose.

"He's gettin' real pissed off, and asks me if I've ever heard of Notre Dame. I put a finger to my lip, looked up at the ceiling, and said, 'Yeah, it's in Saskatchewan, isn't it? The place where Gary Leeman played?' He looked at me like I had opened my fly in a convent. 'No, no, the school,' he says waving both hands. I said 'Oh yeah, right, it's that school run by the Dogans, team's called the Hounds. Courtnall played there, too.'"

My buddies are all chortling by this time and savouring the story. They've all had to put up with His Bargeship and the man's quest for attention.

"'Naw, the Fighting Irish, fer Christ's sake,' he says, steamed that he's run into another dumb Canadian. I just stood there wiping my nose, looking puzzled. He asks, 'How's my boy doing? Scholarship material?' I don't know what got into me but I couldn't resist. I told him Pete's doing real good, a little more work on his catching hand, and once he gets the angles down . . ." Then I did my best Judge imitation: "'His name is *Pat* — *Pat,* not Pete — *Pat,* the goddamn defenceman, not a freakin' goalie.'"

This time Davies did the beer trick completely through the nose, coughing and hacking while the others laughed as much at him as the story.

At that point, across the bar, I noticed a smile buried in a ruddy tan, the eyes scrunched up in the usual happy face, shoulders jiggling a bit as the man listened to my little performance. I recognized the laugh and chastised myself for not noticing him earlier.

Douglas Favell. Free spirit and former NHL goaltender.

This chance meeting was a welcome change from the bitch sessions of hockey school, and certainly more than a quick relief from the daily routine. In an instant it brought back a lot of good memories.

The first time we met was at Maple Leaf Gardens. Favell had just arrived from Philadelphia, completing a deal giving the Flyers the rights to Bernie Parent. Again! Jim McKenny, a Leaf defenceman and a good pal of mine, introduced us, explaining that he always tried to ingratiate himself with goalies at training camp, since "it makes it much more difficult for them to criticize me later, when it counts with the coach."

Back then, my first reading was of Favell being a true maverick, a tad flaky, a guy whose list of priorities put hockey in fourth or fifth position. It simply proved I didn't know him very well.

Of course we'd all heard the stories. Here was a guy who wore a pumpkin mask, a hideous orange ball that covered his entire skull from front to back. Maverick. Not satisfied, he later changed it to orange and white, something resembling the flag of wartime Japan. He euphemistically referred to the design as "sunburst." Flaky.

Favell was the one who, during a fit of horseplay in the dressing room, sliced his Achilles tendon on a skate blade and missed half a season. Add irresponsible. Later he had his bell rung so hard he went around living in la-la land and wondering about dates and places, talking about teammates who were no longer there.

He played professional lacrosse during the summer months, a definite no-no for those wishing to remain within the good graces of the NHL pooh-bahs. One career-ending summer injury in a game that invited hospital bills, and his on-ice career was over, his hockey contract null and void. Flaky, bordering on nuts!

He was the kind of goaltender who perpetuated the stereotype. A fun lover. Yet he had the credentials, and the record, to indicate better things were possible in hockey.

His junior time was spent with the Flyers in Niagara Falls, a 15-minute drive from his home on Princess Street in St. Catharines. In those days the Flyers were part of the Boston system, much like the Marlies were for the Toronto Maple Leafs.

Niagara Falls would win the Memorial Cup in 1965 with a line-up of youngsters who went on to make their way in the NHL. Bernie Parent, a future Hall of Famer who would dodge in and out of Favell's NHL career, was the other goalie. Gil Marotte, Barry Wilkins, and John Arbour were a few of the defencemen. Up front the Flyers had Ted Snell, Rosaire Paiement, Jean Pronovost, Don Marcotte, Bill Goldsworthy, and a yappy, crew-cut centre named Derek Sanderson.

That summer Favell would win the Minto Cup in lacrosse with Oshawa's Green Gaels, qualifying him as possibly the only junior to have won two of Canada's national championships.

Then it was off to Oklahoma City for several of those Niagara Falls Flyers, including Parent. While Bernie would get the first tryout with the parent Bruins, both he and Favell were scooped by the expansion Philadelphia Flyers in the 1967 draft. The fact that two ready-to-wear goaltenders came from one organization to the same expansion team showed the depth of the Bruins at that position, with Eddy Johnston and Gerry Cheevers sitting pretty and Dan Bouchard coming along, and that someone in Philly was a very astute observer of the game. Why? Because "Favvie" would go on to 12 NHL seasons, six with the Flyers, three with Toronto, and another three with Colorado. Meanwhile Bernie, in 13 NHL campaigns, picked up back-to-back Vezina trophies, consecutive Conn Smythe awards as the MVP in the playoffs, and two Stanley Cup wins while on his way to the Hall of Fame. That's why.

Back when he was a kid growing up in St. Catharines, lacrosse was a summer replacement for hockey. In Favell's case there were some bloodlines to the sport. His father, Doug Sr., was a qualified star of the game, enough to put him into the Canadian Sports Hall of Fame. The heat of Southern Ontario days would find the younger Favell between houses on Princess Street with stick and ball, endlessly firing shots off the wall of the family home, doing the things kids have done for years to master the deft stickwork required to be successful.

Next door, in the spacious garden, Wayne Hillman and another junior Blackhawk teammate named Bobby Hull, no stranger to garden work himself, would tend the neighbours' burgeoning vegetable spread, chores the future NHLers enjoyed and performed as an unrequired part of the room-and-board deal many of the out-of-town teenagers did for their landlords. While

Hillman and Hull hoed and sweated, Favell was short-hopping his own bullet rebounds off the paved driveway between the two houses. Favell recalled his first meeting between the Flyers and Hawks, accompanying his story with the chuckling that surfaces in all Favell's conversations.

"Skating around in the warm-up, Bobby and I passed each other in opposite directions and I'm sneaking a peek at the Golden Jet just like any rookie, especially a goaltender. Geez, I almost fell over when he said 'Hi Doug.' Hell, I must'a been 12 back when he last saw me, before he moved up to the NHL. How the hell did he remember a snot-nosed kid from back then, never mind my name? I was impressed, believe me.

"Then during the first period, Bobby comes barrelling in over the blue line, one-on-one, with defenceman Eddie Van Impe all over him, stick between Bobby's legs, arms grabbing and pulling whatever he could, like an octopus. I come out to cover the angle, and about the time Van Impe is gonna bulldog him, Bobby lets a bullet go and I spear the damn thing with my catching hand. Roscoe, I'm not sure whether it was going in the net or out of the building, but I've got it anyway, you know, doin' the splits, the whole ball of wax, a photographer's dream. While I'm posing, Van Impe and Bobby hit the ice and slide into the goal crease submarining me, and we all pile into the netting. I'll never forget it, especially since there was no penalty."

By now Favell is snuffling into a napkin, shoulders shaking to the rhythm of the memory.

"Think I could leave it alone? Nope. What the hell, I'm a rookie, and cocky to boot. 'Just like pickin' cherries, eh?' I said as the three of us were untangling. Jesus, Van Impe went haywire. Got right in my face as Bobby skated away with that little smile he used to use, sort of saying 'I'll be back, sonny.'

"Van Impe had a round face and he looked like a red goal light gone nuts. 'You asshole,' he growled about two inches from my nose. 'Are you fuckin' crazy? Don't ever rile him up like that. I got enough goddamn problems out here without you stirrin' up shit.'" Favell rocked back and forth in his seat in a full-fledged laugh. "Somebody else must have got Bobby upset, too," he gasped. "He got 58 goals that year."

It was the beginning of a six-year rollercoaster ride with the Flyers. Management was assembling the cornerstones of the Broad Street Bullies, first under Keith Allen, then Vic Stasiuk for the first four seasons, to be followed by Favell's final two seasons with the Flyers under the enigmatic, yet philosophical, Fred Shero. Philadelphia was where two events in Favell's career would add to his reputation as a flake, and another twist of fate would see the coveted Stanley Cup be snatched from his grasp.

Goalies are on the same rung of the athletic ladder as left-handed relievers in baseball. For the men in the nets, idiosyncracies become folklore. Gump Worsley hated to fly, so the word was out he arrived at the gate tipsy. Glen Hall would throw up before every game. Mike Palmateer was considered the leading expert on arena food around the league. It wasn't unusual, so "they" said, to see him enter the dressing room before a game munching on a bag of popcorn.

On a bus taking the Molson ProStars to Oshawa, unable to figure out any other way to approach the subject, I asked Favell head on what the real story was behind the near-career-ending Achilles tendon injury he had suffered in the dressing room back in 1969.

"Nothing to it, really," he replied, quiet and reflective. "Just standing around in a towel, talking to Bobby Clarke and Reg Fleming after practice, when I stepped back to return to my chair. Reggie's skates were on the floor, and sliced me pretty good." The mere mention of the incident made me wince.

"So, it wasn't a towel snapping bit of horseplay, or a rassling match gone sour?"

"Nope. Turned around is all, and that was it." He fixed me with the pale blue eyes that were normally crinkled in a big smile. Then, as if on cue, the big grin dropped down like a theatre curtain. Now, I thought, I'm going to get the real story.

"Funny," he chuckled, "Reggie and I fought a couple of times." Somehow, it was difficult for me to picture the slim Favell trading punches with the barrel-necked, muscular Fleming. The first word that came to mind was mismatch.

"Reggie was with the Bruins, and I was just turning pro with Oklahoma City in the Central League. We had an exhibition game in Boston, and he speared me. So I speared him back with the big stick next time he came around the net. You should have heard him squeal." His shoulders shook with laughter. "He had that high-pitched voice. Reggie, built like a brick shithouse, and then he'd talk with that pipsqueak voice." The others around us on the bus at the time were now joining in the cackling.

"Yeah, and a couple of years later — he was with the Rangers by this time — he speared me from the side. I whacked him with the stick — cut him, too, but you couldn't hurt him. Crazy bastard," he smiled at the recollection, and added with a grin, "I hated him."

"Next year Reggie came to Philly. Nicest guy you could ever meet. Honest, he was a great guy, and after all the stuff we'd dished out to each other on the ice, I bump into his skates and miss the rest of the season. Ridiculous, eh?"

What about the stories that hinted at living in the future?

"That must be from the amnesia," he answered routinely. "I was out for a skate on game day. Since I was playing that night, I had my gear on, but no gloves, and was stickhandling a puck — you know, pulling it into my skates, kicking it forward. I stepped on the puck and fell backward into the boards and cracked my head a good one. The boys said I got right up saying I was OK, but Vic Stasiuk started asking me questions, then he called Frankie Lewis, the trainer, over and he asked me more questions. I told them, 'Hell if I can't play, Bernie can.' Problem was Parent had been traded to Toronto a month or more before, and Brucie Gamble was at the other end of the rink doing the practice. By the time they finished with me I had lost two years. Couldn't remember my telephone number, or that I had been married for six months. Didn't even know what kind of car I was driving. Yeah, I was rung up pretty good. You know, in all the time in Philadelphia, we only practised twice in the afternoon at the Spectrum. When I cut my heel, and the time I got conked onto Dream Street. Both those practices were at 4:00 p.m."

So much for the rumour mill. But the most ironic thing about Favell's Flyer career wasn't the injuries, regardless of how celebrated but mundane they may have been. The fickle finger of fate, so common among professional athletes, denied the ultimate goal.

By 1972 Keith Allen and Fred Shero were nearing the end of the search for the ingredients to produce a Stanley Cup. Their Flyers were big, rowdy, truculent, and intimidating. They were guided by their coach, Shero, who subscribed to a forechecking theory that said, "Go to the man with the puck, and arrive in a bad mood." They were led by an angelic, curly-haired centre who resembled Goldilocks posing as Dracula. Bobby Clarke's eyeteeth showed through the grimace of effort on every shift. He was the heart and soul of the Flyers.

One critical piece of the puzzle was missing.

"I really respected Shero," Favell said one day over lunch at a place called Prudhommes, just outside St. Catharines on the Queen Elizabeth Way. "His system said it was OK to allow a shot from the angle, but no chance at a rebound, no second shot, no loose pucks. If you made the first stop and somebody wanted to barge in and take another crack at it, Freddie wanted them to pay for it. As a result, not many teams we played wanted to go to the net, which was great for a guy like me, a reflex goalie. When you gamble like I sometimes had to, you're gonna get some crazy rebounds." He grinned out the window at the parking lot and the whizzing traffic on the highway. "Occasionally, when I made one of my more spectacular saves, I'd also be out to lunch. Everybody had to be covered." The grin got wider.

"Vic Stasiuk once said I looked like an acrobat having a seizure." The thought brought a chuckle. "I didn't think about style. Hell, all I concerned myself with was stopping the puck — a throwback to road hockey. Any way you stopped a goal was the right way. The media got on my case sometimes and I told them straight one day. I said 'When I'm playing bad, according to you guys, I'm guessing. When I'm playing well, I'm anticipating.'"

In the spring of 1973 he got into 44 games and Philly finished second. Favell went on to play in the first series the Flyers ever won in post-season play, racking up 11 games and a 2.60 goals-against average. It was a sign of better days to come, and Favell knew good things were going on and that the Flyers had a shot. He was right, but the "goings on" didn't include him.

By the end of the 1973 season, Bernie Parent had turned his back on the WHA and had no intention of ever returning to his former team, the Toronto Maple Leafs. Several deals were tendered, but the one the Flyers accepted for the right to deal with Parent included Doug Favell coming to Toronto.

What was good for the goose was good for the gander, and Favell, who until then had signed one-year contracts, used his drafting by Ottawa of the WHA as a bargaining tool. With the threat of the Leafs losing yet another goaltender to the WHA, Favell and agent Bob Abbey were able to negotiate a three-year deal. At that stage, looking more for security than money, Favell took it a step further, agreeing to a little less money but a five-year deal with an option.

"I talked it over with my dad, and while it was a real blow to be traded away just when things were coming together for Philadelphia, the disappointment was tempered by the fact I was going to the Leafs, which made us both happy. I think it's every kid's dream." The serious statement was again broken by a grin. "Didn't hurt to be one of the secret top-paid players in the game at the time either. And, we never, ever, negotiated with Ottawa."

If Philadelphia was on its way to three straight appearances in the finals, coming away with two Stanley Cups, the Leafs were destined to wallow in the doldrums. By September of 1976, Favell was sold to Colorado. The end of the line. Yet he was able to cut a new three-year deal with the Rockies and still remain one of the highest-paid goalies in the NHL.

"The only risk was if Colorado folded. The Leafs were making up the difference and I was happy, but busy. In the first game there, I got a 4–2 win. Stopped 45 shots, though. That was the pattern for the rest of my time as a Rockie."

"What about the big picture?" I asked. "What other memories come to mind?"

He raised his eyebrows and looked at me briefly before turning to gaze out the window again. "You mean all this other stuff isn't off-beat enough?" and he began to jiggle and laugh all over again.

"Well . . . I think I was the first goalie to use white tape, figuring they wouldn't see a poke check coming. I was the first goaltender to use a painted mask. Frankie Lewis, the trainer in Philly, painted the mask orange, like a pumpkin. What the hell, it was Halloween. Then next year we did the sunburst thing. I always maintained a guy coming in on a breakaway looks up and what's the first thing he sees? A wild and crazy mask. Maybe it might put him off just enough."

I asked if Gerry Cheevers may have had the first painted mask, with those marker pen stitches he plastered on it.

Favvie shook his head, determinedly. "Doesn't count," he said, just as firmly. Then he captured a thought.

"When I was in Philadelphia I played the first game in five NHL arenas.

Yeah, four in one year. In 1967–68 I played in the Long Beach Arena against the Kings. We lost 4–2. I got a second star." Who says he had amnesia, I wondered? "Naturally I played the first game in the Spectrum, a 1–0 shutout, then the new Madison Square Garden, we lost there, 3–1. I was second star. Next one was back to L.A. for the opening of the Forum." He looked pleased with himself, and looking up from my notes I asked, "How'd you do at the Forum?"

"We won 2–0. I was the first star," he snickered self-consciously.

And the fifth arena?

"Oh that was in '76, the McNicholl in Denver. We beat the Leafs 4–2. The team that traded me." He grinned from ear to ear. I had to ask.

"Get a star?"

"Yep. First." He slouched back in the chair in a fit of laughter, shoulders shaking. "I even got the Visiting Player of the Year in New York for the first expansion year. We only played there twice, but I think it was because I smoked Reggie Fleming. Hey," he sat up quickly, "that might make it the first hockey fight in the new Garden!"

"Any players you had a rough time with, excluding Reggie?" I asked. Between the spearing, fighting and severed Achilles tendon, Fleming had to be his nemesis as an opponent, *and* a teammate.

"You know, I never had a problem with Bobby Hull, or Dennis, Phil Esposito, Lemaire, those kind of guys — but Bob Berry! How many goals did he score over his career? Whatever it was, he got half against me. Same with Kenny Houston. I bet if you check his stats he got all but ten goals against me. Nightmare players."

"I suppose the lowest point in your career came when you were traded?" I asked, scribbling quickly.

"Nope. The lowest point in my life came when Buffalo beat us out of the playoffs in '72. All we had to do is get a tie and we were in, Pittsburgh was out. We had the puck in the Sabre end with 13 seconds to go — 13 seconds — and Gerry Meehan fired a knuckler from inside the blue line and it goes in. There was only four seconds left on the clock. They win 3–2, and we're out. The story kept growing. First it was a shot from the blue line, then outside the blue line, then the red line . . . ahhh."

"How far out were you?" I asked, a regular question to ask a goalie since a good way out of a tough situation is to be "too deep."

"Not far enough," Favell chuckled, unperturbed.

"Was it a good goal?" Another escape question.

"To me it was," he answered, breaking up into snuffles and jiggles.

"Were you ever thrown out of a game?" I asked, changing the subject, since he was having so much fun and I was trying to get serious.

"Once. John Ashley, probably one of the most even-tempered, nicest refs you could ever meet, called a goal on me in Buffalo, with Jim Lorentz standing *behind* me, he was so far in the crease. Man, I went coo-coo. I was in his face all the way to the timekeeper's bench, eatin' his ass out because he wouldn't listen to me. When he'd had enough of my bullshit, and I was tossed, I told him — no, I screamed at him — the only guy more behind me than Lorentz was the goddamn goal judge."

We both had a good laugh over that one.

And that's Favvie. The injuries he suffered over the years all came out in the interview as laughs, things to poke fun at, typically a hockey player's view. His style was exciting, his career was a theme park ride, and through it all, he maintained the smile, the chuckle, and the shoulder jiggling. He closed off the reminiscences with a quote I highlighted in my notes.

"Bernie Parent was better — but I was more fun to watch."

When the end came, as it does for all players, there were no regrets, no cursing the injuries, no handwringing over fate. There was a radio colour job for the Colorado Flames in the Central League, and coaching spots at Denver University, Thorold, Ontario Junior B (where he doubled as GM, then tripled taking on coaching at Brock University, all at the same time). There were the two years with the Buffalo Sabres as a goaltending coach, and there was life after hockey.

Now, every Tuesday he leaves home to pursue his auto sales business, driving to the Milton auto auction, looking for and finding those deals on Porsches and Mercedes, exchanging car talk with the other buyers.

But hockey is only an instant away, triggered by a casual reference to a name, or a year, or a familiar face.

90-SECOND ALL-STARS

G — **Bernie Parent** *". . . his record speaks for itself — he delivered."*

D — **Barry Ashbee** *". . . a great player, tough, and respected."*

D — **Bobby Orr** *". . . nobody compares."*

C — **Bobby Clarke** *". . . tenacity. He'd win the draws."*

RW — **Gord Howe** *". . . very hard not to go with him on that side."*

LW — **Bobby Hull** *". . . that shot, and his skating. He was explosive."*

Dale Tallon

First Pick,
Second Pick

A S I WALKED UP TO THE LOBBY of the downtown Buffalo Hyatt, a couple of the young Blackhawks stood outside, surveying the bleak site in front of the hotel. They looked out of place in their oversize trenchcoats barely hiding shirts and ties, amid a swirling swarm of team jackets and baseball caps. Both six-footers, they stared over the scene of unaware youngsters beside a tinted-glass bus that was idling, growling out pollution over two jammed parking lots and a one-way street leading to the Buffalo Auditorium. Boring. We used to call them the game-day blues.

Once inside the Aud, I found the lobby awash with more excited young athletes in straggly, supervised line-ups, checking in for the regional Special Olympics. Definitely not the place to be for a lunch meeting, but then I spot my appointment, striding along the back wall, another six-footer in a large black winter coat, a sort of off-ice Darth Vader. Darth is smiling.

It had been a couple of seasons since I last saw Dale Tallon. It was at a practice, Maple Leaf Gardens, and he was a member of the visiting media doing the colour for ESPN's Chicago telecasts then, as he does now. On that occasion Pat Foley, the long-time Blackhawk play-by-play announcer, was expressing interest in our conversation about Dale's time with the Old Stars, his reporter's curiosity stimulated by the laughs it provoked between the two

Dale Tallon, on being a Chicago TV broadcaster: "I used to take notes, interview guys, but I do it my own way now. Just listen to the players and watch the game."

of us. When Tallon left to pick up some information from the skaters on the ice, I mentioned to Foley I had a once-in-a-lifetime picture of our mutual pal. It showed Tallon caught in nothing but cowboy boots and jockey shorts, posing in a dressing room somewhere in the wilds of Nova Scotia. He had his back turned to the camera, prominent hockey player's butt barely covered by the shorts, which had been pulled up to appear like the bottom half of a string bikini, and he was smiling provocatively over his shoulder at the camera. "Pure cheesecake," I said, "a wedgie to remember, and well worth the asking price of season's tickets to the Stadium."

Although he balked at the price, and I settled for a more modest fee, he agreed the photo was exactly the kind of pop art needed for the opening of the next season, a spot devoted to offbeat snaps of the broadcast crew. This one, he agreed, was a "gotta have."

On this day the photo subject looked much the same, even though fully dressed, and except for a tinge of grey, he still had the expectant grin, and mischievous eyes of "Mikey," the kid in the TV ads who'd eat anything. As we threaded our way to the restaurant, a sports bar filled with TV sets all playing the Canada–Russia Olympic game, we exchanged our latest Dennis Hull lines, which turned out to be the same ones.

"It was Dennis who got me to Chicago as a player," he said, pulling up a chair facing the set, while I did the same in another direction. "And it was Dennis who called me about this broadcasting job, too." His eyes were riveted to the screen overhead. The bartender swooped in and gave me a choice of bottle or draft, the draft coming in a frosted glass that looked suspiciously like a flashlight. I took the draft, Dale opted for diet cola. Broadcasting does that to you.

I had heard the story before. How Tommy Ivan and Billy Reay, both skeptics about the value of Team Canada and apprehensive about what it would do to water down player animosity within the league, had asked Dennis if there were any people on the Canadian team who would look good in a Blackhawk jersey. One of those he named was Tallon, who was traded for defenceman Gerry Korab and goaltender Gary "The Axe" Smith following the 72–73 season. Following his injury-forced retirement in 1980, he returned to Toronto, working at various projects but not really settling into a groove.

"You guys (the Old Stars) had just come back from playing at Charlie Brown's place," Dale recalled. "Santa Rosie's . . ."

"Santa Rosa," I corrected, watching Canada fall behind by another goal.

"Yeah. What the hell's that cartoon guy's name? Dave Shultz?" he asked, watching the replay.

"Charles Schultz," I explained, thinking Dave "The Hammer" Schultz was as far away from a cartoon as you could get, while signalling the bartender for another flashlight of draft. From behind the bar he held up two glasses, one longer than the other. "What do you think Dale, should I go for the three cell, or the five cell?" He never hesitated, holding up one hand, fingers splayed. I overruled, ordering three fingers.

"Dennis called from Chicago and said there's an opening coming up on the Blackhawk radio network, why don't you get in here and audition? So I did. Flew in, and Pat and I have been together ten years now.

"I got a couple of more to go on this contract, then I'll sit back and make up my mind," he said, just as Canada got back into the game with a quick goal. "Why the hell didn't they do that at the start?" he muttered.

"Don't worry," I answered, "they start slow and come from behind. Done it a couple of times already." He shook his head, as if to say it wasn't a good practice. It was then I remembered the first time I had really come into contact with Tallon was here in Buffalo, back in 1970 when he and Gilbert Perreault went one-two in the draft.

June of 1970 came and Punch Imlach selected Perreault first overall, then Vancouver, who had been beaten out of the first choice by the tacky over-and-under wheel used by the NHL to decide the order, took Tallon. For most of that spring it had been a topic of sports media speculation: who would be the first pick, Perreault, the flashy offensive star of Quebec, or Tallon, the hard-nosed defenceman, sometimes centre, from the Toronto Marlies? I was to learn firsthand, and early, that for Imlach there was no grey area. Imlach also touted Rick McLeish and Reggie Leach. But Imlach chose Perreault first, and Tallon went second, becoming a starting Canuck, and one of the most watched, almost overnight. Between the periods on TV Tallon ran over his thoughts about Vancouver.

"It was a big surprise to me, getting picked second, I mean. I never thought I would go that high. It seemed every time we played against Perreault, I

played well. I figured for sure the Canucks will take a Western guy, but . . .
I remember Hal Laycoe, he was the coach in Vancouver, asking me where I
wanted to play. This was the first time I met the guy, and *he*'s asking *me*? So
I said the four words I'll always regret, 'Anywhere I can help.' I had a great
training camp, playing defence with Dennis Kearns, then they started playing
me at centre, then back on defence, and we'd go through it all over again.
After I came back from Russia, Vic Stasiuk, the new coach, put me at centre
again and I told him I should be playing right D. We never hit it off and I
never got back on track. It always seemed to be a secret, where they were
going to play me. Maybe if I'd understood . . ." He shrugged off the "what
if."

But it wasn't all doom and gloom in Vancouver.

"We had a great group, especially for a kid like me. Andre Boudrias, Bobby
Scmautz, Gary Doak, Orland Kurtenbach, and Pat Quinn, veterans, and good
guys, too. I had a membership at the Point Grey Country Club, and on St.
Patrick's Day we got a foursome together and went out to play. Quinnie
showed up in a green sweater, bow tie and a bowler hat, and we celebrated
St. Paddy's on the greens, so to speak. Next day a letter showed up in my
locker telling me my membership was suspended for one month." He laughed
out loud at the very idea.

Not bad for a kid from Noranda, Quebec, being a talented hockey player
who took up golf and found he was more than good at that as well. Bilingual,
he was sought after by the Francophone broadcast crews from his junior days
in Toronto and throughout his professional hockey and golf career. In
addition, as a young pro golfer, he added a double shot of publicity to his time
on the Canadian Tour.

Like most bilingual players, he could joke and heckle in both accents, and
I reminded him of the time he told me the story of driving back to Toronto
from his dad's place in Quebec, tuning into the local FM station, which
switched DJs from French to English and back again regardless of the quality
of enunciation. We both said "Under My Thumb" at the same time, startling
the bartender into another diet cola and a third frosty flashlight.

"The station had times for French and English, but sometimes the announcer would be an English guy on the French time, and vice versa. I'm
heading back to Toronto and tune the station in because up there you go a

long way between channel selection. Most of the time it's static. So I get it tuned in right, and this guy comes on saying, 'And now, we 'ave da new 'it single from da new h'album, dose guy called da Rolling Stone — H'under My T'umb.' I almost drove off the goddamn road laughing."

Believe me, nobody does a francophone speaking H'english better than Dale Tallon.

In Vancouver, he took time to set a record for rookie defencemen with 42 assists to go along with 14 goals the first season and followed up with 17 and 13 goals in the next two years, although the Canucks failed to make the playoffs. Then came the trade and five seasons in Chicago.

"Whatta difference! More fun, with class. On defence we had me, Dougie Jarrett, Keith Magnuson, and Phil Russell. Hustle, Bustle, Muscle, and Russell. Whatta group! Maggie, Phil, and I were single and we hung out together, went on vacations, everything. You haven't lived until you've seen Maggie in a Speedo on the beach in Hawaii," he assured me with big eyes.

"Keith was such a fierce competitor. Christ, he cut *me* three times . . . after the whistle. He and I had to have an agreement. I told him, "I won't let you touch the puck, and you don't let anybody touch me!""

The recollections came as fast as the Canadian comeback on the screens, and the answers were offered freely now rather than pried out. Such as my mention of his playing with Bobby Orr when the superstar left Boston to become a playing assistant coach with the Hawks.

"Oh, it was tough on him. Certainly as much as it was tough on us. I mean hell, he'd watch the drills standing to the side on those gimpy legs, and you could see the way it was affecting him, you know, having more skill than anyone out there, and being tied to the boards. Shit, he could play the game hurt better than all of us combined. One day he stared at me for a long time, and I was uncomfortable. Finally I said to him, 'I can't play like you. Nobody can.' Yeah, it must'a been hard for him to adjust."

As it was for Tallon. In his second Chicago year he suffered a dislocated hip, courtesy of a sandwich from Vancouver's Tracy Pratt and Mike Robitaille. Three months off. That was followed by a broken wrist, a souvenir from Philadelphia's Eddie Van Impe. He bounced back from the injuries to score 15 goals and 47 assists, breaking a Blackhawk record for defencemen held by the legendary Pierre Pilote. But by the time the 1978 season began, he found himself banished to Pittsburgh with a cast of characters resembling the *Dirty Dozen* of Hollywood. Pete Mahovlich, Greg Shepherd, Randy Carlyle, George Ferguson, Ross Lonsberry, Dave Schultz, Orest Kindrachuk, and Dennis Herron in goal were some of the others who had fallen afoul of management.

"Johnny Wilson was the coach, and we were 0–11–1. One crummy tie in our first 12 games. He laughed aloud as the waiter dropped a five cell. "What was next? The American Hockey League? But, we got it together, finished the season in second behind Montreal with 85 points. Denny Herron, the human coat hanger, backstopped us." He laughed again, remembering Herron's squared-off shoulders, even in equipment.

The next season, though he was riding a full crest of promise and hope, was to be Tallon's exit. An early-season injury would signal the end of a career.

"Compound fracture of the tibia," he said, watching the TV screen and the winning Canadians. "They set it in Vancouver, didn't put a plate in. It was never right after that. I had to take some legal action, but it was settled and I was gone."

Then came the Molson ProStars ball team, to be followed by the NHL Old Stars, where his special brand of humour made us all the better for it.

He was the one I called "Do-it-all," because as he said himself after a game, "I think a pass is something you give your wife to get in the game for free." He was the one who hung the nickname "Logo" on Turk Sanderson for hanging around the centre ice face-off circle while the rest of his teammates battled it out in the defensive zone. Dale was the one who egged Eddie Shack into getting the Air Canada flight attendant to give us our "meal vultures," a word she more commonly knew as "vouchers."

He was the one who advised Dennis Hull to buy a dozen of those Day-Glo orange golf balls, claiming Dennis would never lose one.

"What do you mean you never lose them?" Hull asked, skeptical but interested. "Have you ever found one?" Dale deadpanned.

And "Do-it-all" hadn't changed, as I was to discover on this lunch break in Buffalo. As we shuffled into our coats, he remarked how easy his job had become after I suggested he might be better off preparing for the game between the Sabres and Hawks than sitting with me in the restaurant.

"Naw, I used to take notes, interview guys, but I do it my own way now. Just listen to the players and watch the game — it's simple. When Foley once said maybe he was taking up too much of our air time, I told him, 'Go for it, Bud, I ain't gettin' paid by the word.'"

He sure as hell doesn't get paid for cheesecake photos, either. I'm glad I never gave up the snapshot to Pat Foley, and I probably never will. I'll just keep it handy, in the frame mounted on my office wall, and show it to anybody and everybody that comes by. Sort of a word-of-eye campaign. It's slower than television, but a lot more fun, and I believe Dale would approve.

As I said before, not bad for a guy from Noranda, and this summer I have an invite to show up at Tamarack Golf Club in Naperville, Illinois, just outside of Chicago. There he'll be doing whatever the club pro does, 'cause that's his job.

And he doesn't get paid by the stroke, either.

90-SECOND ALL-STARS

G — **Tony Esposito** *". . . he was a big-game player."*

D — **Bobby Orr** *". . . the best I ever saw."*

D — **Larry Robinson** *". . . you can count on him, both ways."*

C — **Phil Esposito** *". . . because of the Team Canada performance."*

RW — **Jim Pappin** *". . . a clutch player. He scored when it counted."*

LW — **Bobby Hull** *". . . the best."*

Gil Perreault

Never Know
'til You Get There

AN UNWRITTEN LAW SAYS THAT what happens in the dressing room stays in the dressing room. For some, especially the superstars, it is the last refuge of shelter from the all-seeing eye of the public. It's a place where you can be yourself, mix and mingle with your peers, experience the protection from that common thread of uncertainty, fear and apprehension, without having to second guess or provide excuses. It's a home where the inhabitants are no worse off, or better off, than the least-skilled member. Wearing the same sweater has its advantages.

For Gil Perreault, the dressing room was a haven, a place where he could be one of the boys, able to heckle and be heckled with impunity in that rarefied air that the people in the seats seldom experience. This was a player who used the cloak of the dressing room, the sanctity of the team, to the fullest.

I never really appreciated his position when he first arrived in Buffalo in 1970, but I do now. Back then no one knew he would play 17 seasons with the same team, score over 500 goals, over 1,300 points. Nobody knew he was going to be the rookie of the year, centre a line that was to be remembered far past the short season and a bit it was together. No one knew. We were told he had a truckload of talent, we were assured by the sages inside hockey this guy was the real goods. The problem with reassurances was that the same sages were so often wrong. Somewhere there's a long list of players touted

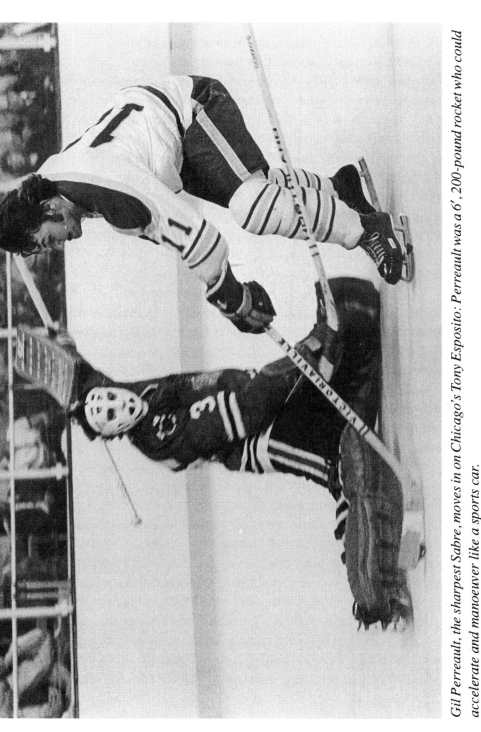

Gil Perreault, the sharpest Sabre, moves in on Chicago's Tony Esposito: Perreault was a 6', 200-pound rocket who could accelerate and manoeuver like a sports car.

by the sages who never made it to Christmas. Although the pull to show up the pundits is strong, charity forbids naming names.

On the other hand, from the moment Gil Perreault played his first exhibition game, and every game thereafter, he seemed to grow in stature. To me he was distant, aloof, and withdrawn outside the dressing room. At the time I would guess his French/English was 80/20. However, despite the difficulty with English, he understood the language of hockey. His teammates could have been Turkish for all the difference it made. Excellence is excellence. Even the bad players could read the way he played. But off the ice, outside the dressing room, he was reticent, stilted, given to hurrying through crowds with one thing on his mind. To get where he was going. As a result, he appeared to be difficult, some even said a prima donna. But it wasn't like that at all.

The first year in Buffalo, 1970, he ran neck-and-neck in public awareness with his general manager and coach, the rambunctious Punch Imlach. In the collection of minor leaguers, retread NHLers, and hope-so's that made up the Sabre roster, the two of them posed the only marquee value for the team. Neither disappointed. Imlach was outrageous, opinionated, spoke from the hip at all times, battled and clawed for every advantage he could get for his patchwork team. Nothing had changed in the season he had been out of the game and he remained the sweetheart of the media, the Teflon Kid, who had nothing negative stick to him. He was popular on both sides of the border. With adoring fans in New York State, and the still-disgruntled fans in Toronto, unhappy with the fact Punch was fired in the first place, and disillusioned at what had transpired since he left.

For his part, Perreault was everything he was billed to be, a five-star player who could lift the spirit simply by taking a rush up the ice. The Buffalo fans were treated to a show many other teams could not find in a single performer. But realistically, hockey is a team game, and with all due respect, Perreault didn't have the supporting cast other teams took to higher places in the standings. Nevertheless, he did what was expected of him. He put pucks in the net, asses in seats, and smiles on the accountants' faces. The magnanimous Buffalo owners, Seymour Knox III, brother Norty, and a directors' list that rivalled the length of the team roster, could point to Imlach and Perreault with pride, knowing the magnificent duo had put them on the NHL map.

When the first season ended, Perreault had set a goal-scoring record for first-year players (38), won the Calder Cup as the NHL's Rookie of the Year, and established himself not only as an offensive threat, but also as somebody you didn't fool with. He was tougher than his junior clippings gave him credit for.

He had started out in his hometown of Victoriaville, Quebec, which was also the home of his idol, Jean "Le Gros Bill" Beliveau, before moving into junior ranks in Thetford Mines, Quebec.

It was only a stopping-off place on his way to the Montreal Canadiens juniors, the only Quebec team in the topflight Ontario major junior league. There he would become the captain, a player who rivalled the NHL Canadiens in celebrity and recognition. His nickname was simply "le Gros," the Big, and he needed to be, playing with a line-up that included coming NHLers Rejean Houle, Marc Tardif, Bobby Lalonde, Richard Martin, Josh Guevremont, Guy Lapointe, Andre "Moose" Dupont, and Pierre Bouchard. The scouts saw very early that he wasn't out of place lining up on the blue line for the national anthem. Aside from the nickname, Perreault *was* big, a 6' 200-pound rocket who could accelerate and manoeuvre like a sports car.

That Buffalo was lucky come selection time back in 1970 has been documented by myself and others. Imlach, notorious for his superstitions, pulled off every trick in the book to nab the first pick in the June draft. He wore his lucky suit, stayed in a lucky-numbered room, and avoided anything, or anybody, he considered a jinx. But there was a factor coming into play that may have been the most fortuitous one of all. For many years the NHL had granted the Montreal Canadiens exemptions on two French Canadiens from selection, effectively sewing up the choice of the best La Belle Province had to offer the hockey world. The year 1970 was the first the exemption was null and void. Gil Perreault became a Buffalo Sabre.

The first training camp was held in Imlach's old Maple Leaf digs in Peterborough. Eager to get some firsthand information from the untried superstar-in-waiting, I remember meeting with Perreault, Charlie Barton, the long-time hockey writer for the Buffalo *Courier Express,* and Phil Goyette, the veteran centre picked up from the St. Louis Blues, who sat in as a part-time interpreter.

Perreault, I observed, had a disconcerting habit of looking at something

behind or above the questioner. He did his best, only occasionally asking for
a translation or clarification, although he seemed to be answering the world
at large rather than the interested trio around him, and continually shrugged
in the negative as a substitute for a reply. I wrote down "shrug/shrug/shrug"
as he bobbled a question, until he asked Goyette in rapid French for an
explanation, then gave up his only smile of the interview, bobbing his head
in approval. I jotted "nod" on my notepad. Things went along like that until
Charlie, ever the fan, asked what I thought was an unnecessary, even dumb
question, not the kind you'd expect from a veteran journalist.

"Do you practise your stickhandling moves?" Barton asked from behind
Elvis Costello black-rimmed spectacles.

"Pardon?" Perreault said, using the French pronunciation, puzzled in either
language, looking to Goyette for help yet again.

Barton plunged forward into the dark. "I'd like to know if you practise
stickhandling, you know, ten repetitions of this, ten of that," he said moving
his hands with nothing more than a ball-point pen for an imaginary stick.
Goyette and Perreault engaged in a minute-long discussion in their mother
tongue, complete with moves and gestures. Barton decided to speed up the
process.

"Gil . . . do you practise certain moves you'd use coming up on a defenceman, or a goalie?" Goyette translated again. Perreault frowned, put his arm
across the back of the booth, and stroked his chin with his finger, another
habit surfacing often in the interview.

"No," he said finally, "I don't practise dat. 'ow can I? 'ow do I know what
I'm going to do until I get dere?" I wrote the reply down, knowing I had heard
one of the all-time definitive replies to the question of stickhandling, and I've
never forgotten it.

Over the ensuing years we met, but only on sporadic occasions. Golf dates,
walking down the halls of the Aud, or at a Sabre function, always hockey-
related. It was only a nodding acquaintance. He knew me, and I certainly
knew him.

Strange, then, when he was inducted into the Hall of Fame in 1990, that I
felt a surge of pride, and relief. Proud that he would rightfully be the first
Sabre into the Hall, and relief that after all those seasons of trying, he at least
had this distinct honour to put beside his name. Until then he had been another

in a long list of great players who never experienced the thrill of winning a Stanley Cup. At least this was a crowning recognition of his talent, and his longevity.

Now, it was almost 20 years after I had last seen him face to face. We made telephone arrangements to meet in Montreal, where he was in to play a game with the Canadien Oldtimers.

Marc Verreault, the dapper head honcho of the Montreal team, graciously ushered me into the dressing room on the visitors side of the Forum, and I found myself in a scene that I'm sure would seem like a fantasy for many hockey fans. Stepping through the bags of equipment and past players in various stages of getting ready, I was greeted by some of the greats of the game. Pete Mahovlich, Don Awrey, Jean Guy Talbot, goalie Steve Penney, Rene Robert, Pierre Mondou, Jacques Laperriere, Steve Shutt, Pierre Bouchard. And in the far corner of the room, my destination, sat Mario Tremblay, Gil Perreault on one side, Yvan Lambert and the legendary Maurice "The Rocket" Richard on the other. Maurice, suited up as a referee for the game, was listening intently to Perreault, who had waved me over to the corner, and it was obvious from Richard's attention that Gil was in the middle of a joke. Just as I sat on the bench, both sides of the room exploded in laughter. I only grinned and hoped the joke wasn't about me.

The game is predictable, with the exception of the two goaltenders for the Desjardins team, decked out in spiffy white uniforms with teal stripes. They play over their heads, no disrespect to either of them, and having been with the Old Stars I knew this was to be expected. They were good goaltenders to start with, but there is something about lining up against shooters of this calibre that makes opposing players either turn to jelly or come up with a big game. Standing between the two benches, I can see and hear the loose talk on the pros' bench, and the earnest exhortations from the amateurs.

The Desjardins make the usual mistakes, falling over the boards on a line change, then two players break out on a two-on-one and wind up jostling each other, shoulder to shoulder, easy pickings for Laperriere. It's called nervousness.

The game is also unusual because Steve Shutt takes an accidental stick in the face and has to repair to the Canadiens' dressing room, followed by the heckling of his teammates.

"Don't worry, I got the bastard's number," says one.

"Too bad he got you on your good side," says another.

Shutt sails past, towel held to his nose, eyes glistening with pain. Don Awrey, on the end of the bench, turns to me in dead seriousness. "This could get ugly," he mutters earnestly then slaps a gloved hand over his face and peeps out at the other bench, laughing from between his fingers.

The game is tight, and Steve Penney is forced to come up with a couple of brilliant saves to keep the score even. Mahovlich makes it 1–0. Then it's 1–1. The two Sabres, Perreault and Robert, return to the bench with a bogus complaint for Verreault. They're not being passed to, but take it upon themselves to grab the lead on their next shift when Robert gracefully tips in a wicked point shot that never leaves the ice.

In the dressing room, the heckling continues.

"Looks like we gonna have to open it up, boys," says one.

"If we open it up, they're gonna have to open me up," says Pierre Bouchard, indicating a scalpel cut down his chest with a thick finger, then tearing open his soggy underwear. "Hey Bert," he yells at Perreault, "how come you don't wear da shoulder pad?"

"Same as you," Perreault fires back. "If I wear da shoulder pad, da sweater don't go over my stomach." Mondou, Tremblay, and the Rocket like that one, breaking up, laughing and pointing.

In the second period, Perreault bursts into one of his patented rushes, blowing past white and teal jerseys until the goaltender makes a phenomenal stop of a laser shot to the top corner. Perreault circles behind the net expressionless. In the third he undresses the Desjardins defencemen and walks in, but is turned away again by another great save. The crowd eats it up, and number 11 skates back to the bench, his work for the night completed. The Canadien oldtimers win 4–2.

Back in the dressing room as the slow stripping starts before the welcome showers, the mutual regard is obvious between the older Richard and Perreault, both Hall of Famers, but separated by two generations and the accumulation of legend. "Don't get any of that Grecian Formula shit on me," carps one player as the Rocket passes. Perreault grins at Richard while the Rocket rubs his fingers together, indicating money. The two laugh at an inside joke.

Later, Perreault and I met at Le Texan across the street from the Forum, a throwback to Arnold's in the TV series *Happy Days*. I almost expected to see the Fonz coming out of the can combing his hair. It had the old wooden booths, and the kind of licence that requires food before you can order a drink on Sunday. We placed an order and I let Gil do the talking. There's no way this Anglo is going to ask for french fries in Montreal.

Perreault slid into the corner of the booth, threw an arm across the backboard, and assumed much the same position he did over 20 years ago with Charlie Barton and Phil Goyette. He occasionally stroked his chin throughout our conversation. The English was excellent. Occasionally an "H" would be dropped, or added, a plural "s" would go missing, and from time to time a "d" found its way into his language in place of a "th" sound.

"You must have come in here a lot as a junior," I said.

"Pro, too," he answered quickly. "It was da place to go, everybody did." We talked about those heady days as a junior in a town supposedly in love with the major-league Habs.

"We used to beat the Canadiens in attendance on a regular basis. In fact, I think we still hold the record for a hockey game — twenty-one thousand something. We played the Russians that time. You know how it feels? The atmosphere in the Forum, the excitement in the building, the fans. We beat them 9–3. It's still my 'most anything' game," he said, grinning openly but self-consciously at the disclosure.

"How did you feel about leaving all this, going to Buffalo?" I asked, knowing how difficult it had been to step into what for him must have been a foreign environment.

"I was happy. Actually, I was looking forward to it, you know? I t'ought I had a better chance of making the team, playing as a regular. Here, it's a problem, eh? Punch just tell me to score goals, put da puck in da net, it's a tough job, eh? He says you have to be careful out dere. Dat guy Daigle in Ottawa reminds me of when I went to Buffalo, what I went t'rough. In a lot of ways we are da same. Language problem to overcome, new franchise, not a very good team, eh? But, you gotta give him time, he's only 18. I was 20 years old. He's just a kid. Dat's why I understan' da Russians, and the English guys going to Quebec, they stick together, and the wives, too. You see them sitting together, they have a problem, that's for sure. I was like that."

"Seventeen years, Gil. Did you think you'd be up there that long, or did it ever cross your mind?" He only shook his head and stroked his chin.

"Did I ever tell you I ask to be traded?" he said suddenly, catching me off guard.

"You *asked,*" I repeated. "When?"

"After the '78 playoffs. We had good teams, from 1975, but we couldn't get that extra, the push you need, eh? You know I t'ought we were the team for da next five year. Always a hundred points, but we were behind Boston and Montreal all da time. I t'ought, hey, maybe it's time for a change. I think it's not bad for a guy to move, you know, he's in one team for so long, it's better he moves, get a change, some new scenery, different attitude. So I said to Punch, if you want to trade it's OK, and I told him maybe it's better. But he ask me to stay, said we're going ahead. I should have gone."

"Why did you stay? Loyalty?"

"Yeah . . . I guess so. But then Imlach got fired, Scotty came in, 1979, and he traded to rebuild — so he said. And den again in 83–84 they trade some more, to rebuild. I'm thinking, how many rebuilds can a person go t'rough, eh?"

I thought back to his career, watching him absently rubbing his chin again. He had won the Calder Cup, fulfilling the promise of the press clippings. Won the Lady Byng trophy in his third season, always increasing his point total. He wasn't the first Sabre to crack the top ten in scoring, but he had a hand in it when Richard Martin came seventh by the end of 1974. The next year the "French Connection" all made the ten leading scorers, Rene Robert finishing seventh, Perreault and Martin ninth and tenth. Though they had gone their separate ways as a line, they were still the force on the power play, and the Sabres pulled off the unthinkable taking the Philadelphia Flyers to six games before losing in the 1975 Stanley Cup final. It was an incredible achievement in such a short time but, sadly, as close as any of them would get. Perreault continued his scoring ways, finishing third, fifth, and eighth in the following three seasons, missing the next in an injury-shortened year, then bouncing back to reach fourth place in 79–80. He was twice a second-team All-Star selection at centre during the 1970s. In a nutshell, he had done everything asked of him, and more.

"Don't get me wrong," he said, starting up again. "It was good, yes it was fun. I play with a lot of good guys, no regrets." I asked how he liked playing on a line with Eddie Shack. He laughed aloud, turning around in his seat for the first time.

"Eddie always wants the puck there," he said, holding his large hands stretched in front. "A little bit ahead so he can step into it. He used to call me 'Gros' . . . dat's it, 'Gros.'"

I didn't tell him Eddie had practised his French pronunciation on me when I told him I was going to do a story on Gil. "*La — Grow, la — Grow.*" Shackie growled the two syllables as only he can, no difference in emphasis, inflection, accent, or timing on either. *La — Grow.*

In that first year there was another thing people don't associate with Gil Perreault. Fighting. I asked him about the Dan Maloney fight in Chicago.

"Yes, I did that. It was time, it was going to happen so it did. I had t'ree fights dat year. Maloney, Gerry Hart in Detroit, and someone else. I can't remember anymore, eh?" Unwilling to discuss the scrapping, he switched channels on me again.

"You remember the big storm in Buffalo?" he asked, referring to the killer storm that struck Buffalo in January of 1977. It was the only clue necessary. Despite radio and television warnings, many people were caught in their cars during rush-hour traffic on the streets of the city. Several died within sight of the downtown buildings, stranded on the elevated roadways, or buried in the canyons of the freeways. It always puzzled me why the NHL never cancelled the Buffalo game in Montreal, and I assumed it was because it wasn't snowing in Montreal.

"Danny Gare picked me up. Because he had a bad back, I had to get out and push four times. The toughest part was getting off my street, and I don't know how the hell we made it to the airport. When we got there it was very bad, and the worst was yet to come. We got on this two-prop job, Air New England I think, and honest, we were staggering down the runway, bucking t'rough drifts. I don't think you could see 50 feet on either side of the pavement. Only 13 guys showed up, but we made it, played the game, and tied the Canadiens 3–3." It was January 29, 1977.

There was a time when he felt the weight of his looming retirement, a spell when he felt he should be stepping aside for the younger players, but the "last chance" was always just around the bend. As the last game neared, he rightfully expected some kind of job with the Sabres. Though he waited through May 1987, nothing was forthcoming from the team. He announced his retirement on June 5, even though five teams were interested in his services. He still felt there was a hope for some duties with the only team he had ever known, the only team he ever played for.

But it never came. Only a public appearance deal, which, if you know Perreault, is not his strong suit.

"Yes I was disappointed. I felt I could advance scout, help with coaching, work with the young players, stuff like that, but they came back and only offered a guarantee for so many appearances for this much money. We pulled up stakes and went back to Victoriaville. What the hell, I only visited kids in hospitals and stuff like that. I never went out to sell my name, and I'm no speaker. So, that was it. But I would go back to Buffalo," he said, staring at the far wall and finishing the remark with a shrug.

Home meant an involvement with the Victoriaville Tigers of the Quebec Junior A League, all the way up to GM and coaching duties as well, but now it's only "a piece of the action, playing with the oldtimers and watching the boys." For Gilbert and wife Carmen, the boys, Sean 8, and Marc-Andre 16, are the main interest now. Marc is 6'2" and 180, playing triple A midget. Is there another Perreault on the horizon?

"That's for him to decide, eh? For now, it's enough to try to keep up school. The elusive, cherubic smile crosses his face once more.

He made the Hall of Fame on his first year of eligibility, and rightly so. Though he professes to have no regrets, it's a wistful Gil Perreault who talks about memories and Buffalo, at least in the confines of "Le Texan," where the dreams of 25 years before were of different things.

"At my retirement, they gave me a highlight video, you know? It was funny sometimes, but there was one goal that caught my eye. It was against Los Angeles, the goalie I don't remember, but I was holding off a defenceman with one arm, and I deke the goalie with one hand on my stick and score. It was a good one, but unless dey show me, I don't remember that, eh?"

It took me back to the question from Charlie Barton, and the answer I never forgot. It seemed such a long, long time ago, many games past, a lot of ice melted, many things gone wrong, many gone right. Today, he's in the Hall of Fame.

And a kidding buddy of The Rocket.

90-SECOND ALL-STARS

G — **Rogie Vachon** *". . . he'd challenge any shooter."*

D — **Bobby Orr** *". . . the greatest."*

D — **Serge Savard** *". . . a perfect match with Orr. Always had a great view of the overall game."*

C — **Jean Beliveau** *". . . he's my idol."*

RW — **Guy LaFleur** *". . . quickness and a great scoring touch."*

LW — **Bobby Hull** *". . . a very powerful, dangerous player."*

Jean Beliveau

"Première Class, Merci"

THIS IS THE FIRST STORY about the boys of winter where I have no personal anecdote or experience to relate involving myself and the subject. Only observations.

I have never formally met Jean Beliveau face to face, or shook his hand, or played a game of golf with him, or closed a bar or sat with him in a press box, or even called him to book an appearance.

Like most of the hockey fan public, I'd seen him play, both live and on television. In 1970–71 I was around the Buffalo Auditorium to see him close out his NHL career. All told, I've heard, read about, and seen Beliveau for 40 years or more.

As I said, I don't really know him. However, we have locked eyes on occasion, nodded in each other's direction from time to time, and in three separate instances, for some unknown reason, he has smiled and specifically said "'allo" to me, and I, being magnanimous, have always smiled and said "hello" in return.

Twice I held a door open for him. The first time was during his playing days. He was entering the Montreal Forum, I was exiting. Backing off first, I stood smartly to attention and he breezed by pleasantly, saying, "Première class, merci." I replied in my best fractured French, "Pas de problème." He simply continued on his way, an imposing figure in a flowing, flapping

Jean Beliveau in the first NHL game ever played at the Buffalo Auditorium, October 15, 1970. Goaltender is Roger Crozier.

trenchcoat, with a momentary incline of his head, as if to indicate we had completed a tricky, intricate manoeuvre of some kind. In a word, he had style.

Once, speaking at a dinner, I was asked if I had ever done a piece on Beliveau, and I recall the regret of having to say, "No, the opportunity never presented itself." While working on this book, the memory of that question came to mind again and it got me to thinking back across the years, over the infrequent instances when I was in the vicinity of Beliveau. He always impressed me with his bearing and his dignified elegance, even in something as ordinary as a hockey uniform — albeit the red, white, and blue of the Canadiens. Some players, straight out of the dressing room for the warm-up, look like they've been dragged behind the Zamboni. Beliveau *always* looked like a page out of *Gentleman's Quarterly*. Even during the overtime!

Fashion statements aside, how good was he? Good enough to play 20 years in the NHL wearing the same livery. Good enough to play in 12 Stanley Cup finals and win ten times, five of those championships consecutive victories with what many agree was the greatest roster ever to lace up skates. For nine of those 20 years he was the captain of the Canadiens' dynasty. He scored 507 regular-season goals and 1,219 total points. In 162 Stanley Cup games, he totalled 178 points, better than a point a game. In 1956, his third year in the NHL, he won the scoring race, his first Stanley Cup, and had the temerity to tie the record of his teammate and national idol, Maurice "Rocket" Richard, for playoff goals, at 12. He was also named the league's Most Valuable Player and, just to show it wasn't a flash in the pan, achieved the honour again eight years later. That was in the six-team league, too.

At the advanced hockey age of 34 he won his sixth Stanley Cup along with the inaugural Conn Smythe Trophy as the MVP of the playoffs. The jury is out on how many Connie's he would have won had they been available. Over his 20-year career he had ten All-Star selections at centre, trailing only Wayne Gretzky — but then so does every other hockey player in every other category, with the possible exceptions of penalty minutes and skate size.

The most interesting thing about those 20 years listed in the *NHL Guide*, is that he played only two games in 1950–51, and three in 1951–52. The first year he scored a goal and an assist. In year two he had five goals in three games.

The next logical question would be, why? Why did this incredible 19-year-old prodigy wait until he was going on 22 to join the NHL on a full-time basis? Good question, and to get a good answer I had to turn to my buddy and former office neighbour at *Hockey Night in Canada,* Frank Selke Jr., a former host/interviewer on the HNIC telecasts out of Montreal who moved on to become the general manager of the ill-fated Oakland Seals, and then onward and upward to vice-president at HNIC. Selke's father, Frank Sr., was the Montreal GM for almost 20 years and certainly not one to turn his nose up at a good player. But Beliveau, a star junior with Quebec Citadels, had moved up to the Quebec Aces senior team, coached and managed by Punch Imlach, rather than turn pro.

"Jean was still an amateur," Selke stated. "The fact of the matter was Quebec City had a good thing going. There were major sponsors locally who kept Mr. Beliveau in a style that was certainly on a par, or better, than NHL standards. He had no reason to leave, despite the fact he was also becoming a national figure, well outside the Quebec provincial borders, and his nickname, le Gros Bill, the big one, a Paul Bunyanesque term in French, was familiar to hockey fans across the country. Sure, the Canadiens owned his professional rights, through his signing of a C form as a junior, but he was still playing amateur hockey."

Selke Sr. had by now whetted the appetite of Montreal fans by bringing Beliveau up twice in two years on the "loan" basis allowed at the time. Finally, when other enticements failed, he turned the entire Quebec Senior League professional and moved the 21-year-old Beliveau up to the big team. Frank Jr. explained this sudden turn of events. "Being the cash cow for the senior league, Montreal was able to convince the member teams to make the move, and Beliveau became an inevitable, and well-paid, Canadien."

He was a scarce commodity: 6'3", 200-pound centres were rare in those days. In fact, hockey players of that acreage were the exception at *any* position. His skating, stickhandling, passing, and scoring touches, plus his God-given feel for the game, made him something for any owner or general manager to slaver over. But there was one problem for the other five clubs of the day. Beliveau, like it or not, belonged to Montreal. And he was very, very good.

My second brush with le Gros Bill came in the late 1960s at a golf tournament held at the Board of Trade in Woodbridge, just outside Toronto.

It was, as I recall, an American Airlines event in cooperation with the fledgling NHL Players' Association. The hockey biggies of the day were there, and following their rounds of 18, Beliveau and Stan Mikita went up to the autograph tables under an awning set up adjacent to the pro shop.

It seemed the organizers had considered the hockey season when making the fairest pairings on this day. Mikita had 30 goals, Beliveau 33. Stan had 97 points, Jean 82. The reformed Mikita had 52 penalty minutes, Beliveau 55. But when it came to team results, there the similarity ended. The Blackhawks and Canadiens were at opposite poles in the East Division, the Habs in first, the Hawks in sixth. Beliveau had his ninth Stanley Cup, Mikita was reduced to being a spectator.

Mikita, a golf pro in the off-season, was coming off another of those seasons where he had demonstrated the restraint necessary to be considered for his third straight Lady Byng trophy, which was a remarkable thing. When he first arrived in Chicago he was a feisty, cantankerous, ornery 160-pounder, and his penalty minutes were often over 100 minutes, and hit 154 in the year (64–65) when he won his second straight NHL scoring trophy. For Stash Mikita, belligerence and production went hand in hand. However, bowing to the logic that being a small man in a violent game dictated staying away from the endless line of opposition bone-crushers, he changed. On this afternoon the restraint was being sorely tested as he appeared ready to wrap a three iron around the neck of anyone who dared speak to him. Conversely, Beliveau strode tall, languid, affably at ease with the blatant adulation of those lined up to await this special, once-in-a-lifetime audience. As Beliveau neared the tent, I was just ending a conversation with a couple of American Airlines people and turned away in time to see him approaching. Courtesy of Wayne Cooper, then the PR director for St. Louis, I was wearing a St. Louis Blues golf hat, the large blue and gold "music note" logo emblazoned on the front.

Beliveau smiled, giving me my second nod, and said "hello." Was he acknowledging the hat, a cut above the souvenir items sold in stores, or just being friendly?

A short time later, as I watched the autograph seekers from my vantage point behind the two stars, I couldn't help but notice the differences in the queues. Mikita's line was impatient, and from time to time the kids bickered, as if this were a line-up for popsicles at a company picnic. But Beliveau's line-up was well-mannered and contained more adults, all calm, cool, and collected.

Mikita was stiff, darkly silent except for the occasional gruff murmur of acknowledgement, churning out his signature automatically, while Beliveau was relaxed and patiently gracious, neither warmly open nor coolly disinterested. It was the first time I had seen the regal bearing that was becoming my considered opinion of this unfamiliar superstar. After a few minutes, he turned, looked at me with only the hint of a smile, and held his hands and shoulders in the universal gesture that meant "what can I say?"

On October 15, 1970, we crossed paths again. It was opening night for the Buffalo Sabres. The Auditorium was not completely refurbished, holding only 10,000 for the first season, but on this night it was decked out like a hooker on a Saturday night, scrubbed and painted, a new necklace of glass that had absorbed gallons of Windex sparkling under a battery of new television lights. Onto this dazzling glare of white ice would step the Montreal Canadiens in their red uniforms, and history would be made.

Trudging down the police-patrolled hall leading to the end boards and the players' gates, I noticed I was trailing some of the Habs, who were making their way up the incline from a temporary visitors' dressing room, straggling along over the black mats laid down for the occasion. Out of habit, I followed the rubber mats, too, although there was ten feet of space on one side, completely empty. As I was about to pass the Montreal dressing room, Beliveau stepped out of the doorway. He's tall, make no mistake, but with him in skates and me in shoes, he was absolutely gigantic. We managed to put on the brakes simultaneously, coming within inches of colliding, but I did a double toe-loop that would have made Toller Cranston green with envy, and admonished the lofty Jean-boy to "keep your head up out there." He nodded in agreement a few times, said "bon chance" (assuming I was a Buffalo supporter), and waved a gloved hand to acknowledge the free advice. I supposed he hadn't recognized me without my Blues hat.

At the All-Star game in Minneapolis, January 25, 1972, I did my second stint at opening doors. My wife and I had flown in from Phoenix the day before, leaving mid-80s sunshine behind for a mind-boggling wind-chill factor of 68 below in the Twin Cities. To give you an idea of how cold minus 68 is, the doorman who greeted us was wearing a red and black snowmobile suit and boots, a ski mask, *and* ski goggles. I was already in the lobby of the Radisson South, and I could see Beliveau alight from another airport van. He defensively covered his head with the collar of his coat and was wrestling a suit bag and briefcase through the outer glass doors, so I stepped forward and held open the inside door. He came through muttering "brrrrrrrr," blinked through watery eyes, and nodded his appreciation, too cold to speak.

The next morning, Beliveau displayed the same quieting grace and (dare I say it about a hockey player) charm he exudes when he walked into the morning dining room of the hotel. We were sitting across from our breakfast companions, Sabres Gil Perreault and rookie Rick Martin.

Beliveau stood waiting at the hostess station. This time it was a navy blazer, beige slacks, white shirt and Canadiens tie, the tiny C/H discernible only to the practised eye. Once more I watched as the talk grew quieter, heads turned, and muttered explanations flew from behind napkins. He walked majestically, towering through the tables as he followed the hostess, who had no idea who he was nor how most eyes in the room were following the two of them. Perreault and Martin were too busy eating to notice, but as he turned to sit with his back to us, he looked up, wearing that enigmatic smile, and nodded to me, mouthing a silent hello as if we were in a church.

Was it Martin and Perreault? Was it our sun tans? Was it surprise at seeing the doorman dining with the guests? Whatever the reason, my wife was impressed.

In the summer of 1972, at the Queen Elizabeth Hotel in Montreal, where the NHL held its annual draft meetings, I had the chance again to see Beliveau's dignified personality impose itself, this time on a much tougher audience. A crowd of his peers.

Having lost two of the greatest stars it had to offer the previous season in Beliveau and Gordie Howe, the NHL Hall of Fame had seen fit to relax the rules covering the waiting period for eligibility and offered the "foregone conclusion" of induction to Gordie Howe and Beliveau at the same time.

Howe had finished off his "first" career, retiring at the end of the 1971 campaign, as had Beliveau. At 43, Howe, in his 25th season, closed out with a respectable 23 goals and 52 total points. You had to look back 22 seasons to find a lower point total for the big guy, but back in 1949 he was a callow 21, and only three years into his "first" NHL career. For Howe the end must have been as much in the fact Detroit finished last in the East, and a lowly 13th, just ahead of the last-place California Seals, as it was the age factor so many said was the major reason. After all, how many team rebuilding programs can a man go through? Little did anyone know at the time he would return to a "second" career and retire all over again nine years later.

On the other side, Beliveau, at 40, had gone out on the highest note possible: 25 regular-season goals, 76 total points, tied with Toronto's Dave Keon and Fred Stanfield of the Bruins for a ninth-place finish in the scoring race. Better yet, he said farewell to hockey contributing what was then a playoff record ten assists, and his tenth Stanley Cup.

Now I was about to see them in an up-close study of contrasts.

The mezzanine floor ballroom was studded with member team tables, surrounded by little platoons of officers who held different ranks but were all in the same army. You can always tell the difference in rank. The real hockey people are dented, scarred, gimpy. Dentures and bridgework are the order of the day. Suits and sports jackets are off the rack.

Then there are the owners, club directors along for the ride, and the lawyers. It's always a cinch to pick out the team counsellors. For the most part they are the ones with capped teeth, year-round tans, tailor-made suits, and ties that match.

Standing in the large foyer off the main ballroom, I waited along with the Buffalo media for the grand entrance of Punch Imlach, the Wizard of the Aud. Imlach, resurrected from the hockey junkyard the year before, wasn't the poor cousin any longer. Not since he had plucked Gil Perreault off the top of the list in the previous year's fiasco draft. Just to rub it in, Imlach and his cherub superstar, together with a team resembling "the gang that used to be," finished fifth in the tough East, and overall were even-up with Los Angeles, but ahead of Vancouver, Pittsburgh, California, and the Red Wings. No wonder Gordie had decided to hang 'em high.

No, Imlach was once again a man of substance, a man to be reckoned with. However, his grand entrance would not be the big story today, at least not for me.

As the elevator bells dinged and disgorged their cargo, heads would turn, faces would be recognized and duly noted, then the rattle of conversation would continue.

When Gordie Howe emerged, the last man off a car from the upper floors, the conversation didn't stop, it picked up in tempo and resonance with hearty well-wishes and the occasional pockets of applause thrown in as he made his way down the gauntlet of wall-leaners and gladhanders.

The next Oscar-night event was good ol' Punch. Hatless, he had outgrown the lucky suit he had shoehorned into the year before when he copped Perreault, but no doubt he was wearing some other garment of equal super-stitious worth, because that's the way he operated. He nodded to all the right writers, assumed a humble pose now and again for those who passed along words of praise, and briefly stopped for a radio-type who stuck a small tape recorder in his face. He formulated a quick answer with the typical pained expression he always adopted when being asked the obvious, then swept into the ballroom with his little entourage in tow.

The mood in the hallway was almost carnival-like. First Gordie, then Punch. What's next? Eddie Shack?

Once more the ding, once more the doors opened, and the first man to step out was le Gros Bill, Jean Beliveau, and the room went through a whole transformation.

I'll never forget the abrupt stop in the general hubbub, or the way the hockey-hardened media toned down in a matter of seconds. It was followed by an air of quiet respect that filled the hall.

Beliveau was dressed in a grey suit, a pale blue shirt, and a red patterned tie. His jacket was done up with one button, fashionably pulled back to allow one hand to slip into a pant pocket. He walked through the mob of people who gave way to his presence, and while he received subdued well-wishes and congratulations, it seemed some were almost hesitant to speak, and not one person moved forward to slap him on the back or shake his hand. You don't tug on Superman's cape.

The difference between this, and the reaction to Gordie and Punch, was startling. True, Beliveau was in Quebec, where his stature was almost religious, and yes, there were a lot more Montreal types in the area than the rest of us Anglos. But the man couldn't have had a more dramatic effect had he been an envoy from the Vatican. In fact, the thought finally struck me that he was more akin to royalty in both carriage and demeanour than those "royals" in London. I believe a Prince Charles would have to do something very un-royal to gain more attention, or something very stately to gain more respect, than Jean Beliveau did on that sunny morning in Montreal 20 years ago.

Years later I was pleased to discover, listening to Dennis Hull expound on the charismatic Beliveau, that he agreed with me.

Howe and Beliveau were all-time favourites for Dennis, along with brother Bobby of course, and if nothing else, you can say the man has great taste in idols. He, too, found Beliveau regal and dignified, despite the added burden of having to play against him. So much so that he found himself in one of life's embarrassing moments during a playoff at the Chicago Stadium.

"It was game one in the 1971 cup final, and Beliveau was rushing up the ice, two on two on the far side. I was coming back on my wing, minding my own business, and suddenly our defenceman, Bill White, must'a tripped over the blue line, and big Jean cuts toward my side to go around on a breakaway. Geez, I hustled up a few strides just in time to give him a two-hander from behind. You know, to distract him, but it caught him across the gloves. Perfect. The stick comes out of his hands and the puck squirted right to Tony Esposito, who dives on the loose puck, the whistle goes, and there's no harm done. Honest, I expected a penalty, though I didn't get one, but the worst thing was Beliveau is hurt, holding one hand in the other. He skated by me givin' me that look and says, 'Dennee, I never h'expeck dat from you.' Shit, I was embarrassed, crushed, I mean I really felt terrible. One of my idols, a guy who wouldn't hurt a fly, I've tried to cut off one of his limbs. In fact, like a jerk, I skate all the way to the Montreal bench with him, saying, 'I'm real sorry, Jean, but I didn't have any other choice,' and stuff like that.

"I'm not kidding, I was really ashamed, and tryin' to apologize. Hell, I almost put my goddamn arm around his shoulder. All the while, 20,000 people are cheering their asses off, cause they think I'm gettin' tough, right in his face, in addition to the foul."

One thing came up in my research into Saint Jean of Montreal that might help Dennis Hull feel less contrite. Aside from the fact I've never heard Beliveau described as anything other than regal, stately, elegant, dignified, majestic, charming, noble and, to quote the late Danny Gallivan, "magnificent," this guy had a rap sheet.

His final stats show 1,125 games. It also shows he spent 1,029 minutes in the penalty box. You get time in the box, Mervin, for being a bad boy, and that's almost a minute a game. For comparison I took a look at that arch-criminal Dennis Hull. For 959 games, 261 minutes. Not even 15 seconds a game in the brig. Wait a minute, does this mean Sir Galahad has fallen off his horse? And by the way, what other long-service players fell short of Beliveau in the sin-bin department?

John Bucyk of the big bad Bruins, 20 seconds a game. Serge Savard and Allan Stanley, both defencemen, weren't even close at 40 seconds a game. Stan Mikita, the Sheriff of Nottingham to Beliveau's Robin Hood? "Stick 'em" Stanley played 22 years, 1,394 games, and with 1,270 penalty minutes came in at just under a minute a game.

Gordie Howe? Mr. Elbows, the guy who perfected behind-the-play muggings, the one player the media described over four decades as "a mean mother"? He played 1,767 games and served 1,685 minutes in penalties. It works out to the identical percentage as Monsieur Beliveau.

So much for the halo, Jean.

Someday I hope to be formally introduced, to be able to sit down and chat with le Gros Bill and see if there's a sense of humour, or a sense of his own importance. Until that happens, I'll have to wonder if those "'allo's," smiles, and nods, are due to my hats, my tan, my breakfast companions, maybe the company I keep.

Or the fact that I'm a first-class door opener.

90-SECOND ALL-STARS

G — **Jacques Plante**

D — **Bobby Orr**

D — **Doug Harvey**

C — **Stan Mikita**

RW — **Maurice Richard**

LW — **Bobby Hull**

Derek Sanderson

Lobbying in Montreal

THE MAIN ENTRANCE OF MONTREAL'S Chateau Champlain was buzzing with activity. My vantage point was one of two comfortable chairs separated by a low table, affording an all-encompassing view. Perfect for an experienced lobby-watcher.

A bank of five brass-doored elevators set into a marble facade returned Sunday churchgoers to their rooms after unloading the checkouts wearing a variety of Canadiens' clothing and hats. Sprinkled into the mix was the occasional bright orange of Philadelphia fans brave enough to show their allegiance. What the hell, it had been *Hockey Night in Canada* and the Flyers had tied the Canadiens the previous evening, even though the Phillies were up 4–2 at one point.

A new breed appeared on the scene as a beefy, bearded, biker type, in a black Boston road jersey, ragged jeans, and cowboy boots ambled over to the reception desk. His out-of-place Celtics hat had a ponytail sticking out the back. The Bruins were in for a rare Monday-night tilt, and this guy obviously was an early arrival, as were the Bruins, chartering into Montreal after a Saturday-night game in New Jersey, a rare day off on the road. At the counter, Carl Lindros, Eric's father, was going over a bill proffered by the attentive clerk, who had no idea who the person in front of him was. The Boston boy,

Derek Sanderson pushed the "bad-boy" image to a new high: latter-day Slip Mahoney of the Bowery Boys, with everyone else in the world playing Satch.

D. SWEENEY worn proudly across a broad back, heard the Lindros name, squinted as if assailed by a sharp pain, the recognition factoring in, and stepped back to size up the older hotel guest. Like son, like father. Carl Lindros looms at 6'5" and though sporting a bit of a paunch is a size to give pause. The Beantower turned, grinning with a smile that had boycotted dentists for years, scanned the lobby for any of his friends, and was disappointed to see none were present. A moment in reflected glory wasted.

My glance at the other lobby-patrollers revealed small pockets of out-of-town Montreal fans, plus a Hall of Famer, sitting in a corner in front of the large windows reading a hardcover novel. Tom Johnson won six Stanley Cups as a defenceman for Montreal and another as coach of the Bruins. Periodically, he glanced over the edge of the book, checking out the lobby activity, going unobserved and unpestered in this 40-storey hockey melting pot. Even D. SWEENEY missed the chance to meet a real star of the game, a man who has spent almost 30 years with the Bruin organization.

The diversion of the Boston-shirted fan missing Tom Johnson caused me to overlook my own quarry coming off the elevator. Derek "Turk" Sanderson for some strange reason seemed taller than I remember, or maybe it was just the difference in the gait. A six-footer at the best of times, he has gone through two hip replacements, and his walk has changed to a more practised stride from the strut I vividly remember from days gone by. To the uninitiated, the characteristic supreme confidence bordering on arrogance is still there. Only the walk has changed.

Now 48, the hair is grey and so is the moustache. The sports coat, shirt, tie, and slacks are impeccably coordinated, fashionably subdued. The shoes glow. I couldn't help but note that this man, who has run with the hounds of hell, simply didn't look the part, with the exception of silver in his hair.

We shook hands and he surveyed the notepad I had been jotting in, then my large briefcase. "Where to?" was all he said. He answered himself, hands stabbing left and right: "Here, there, or coffee shop. Coffee shop. All the pews here are filled," he added, in defence of this decision.

He casually beckoned to a bellman, ever alert for a known spender. "Hey, Mac. Take this suitcase and stash it for my pal," he said, dipping into his pocket and slipping the concierge a deuce, dismissing his "yes sir's" with a muttered "yeah, yeah, good."

"Whad'ja have in there, your fuckin' lunch?" he asked as we walked down the hall to the restaurant. I was glad to see the recent stories I'd heard about the Turk were correct. With the exception of no more drugs and drinking, the man hadn't changed. At the doorway we were greeted by a "host" in a double-breasted suit. Before the man could ask, Turk filled him in.

"Two. Smoking — and let's not go for a hike, bud," he stated flatly, surveying the 11:00 a.m. expanse of empty tables. Miffed, the host paraded us up two stairs and around the entire upper deck of the room to a booth in the back. Near the cash register. "Thanks for the walkathon," Sanderson mumbled as the host dropped a pair of menus and left, while an aproned waiter scurried up empty-handed. Turk gathered up the menus, handed them back, and pointed to me, then himself.

"Coffee. Café au lait. A round of Juan Valdez. OK?" he said without looking up, rummaging through a series of pockets and producing a deck of cigarettes and a scruffy pack of matches. The cigarette was fired and tapped on the edge of the ashtray after a practised shooting of the starched shirt cuffs, à la Ed Norton. I couldn't help but stifle a laugh as I looked away toward the empty tables. Still the big wheel, still in command, still the king of the walk, a latter-day Slip Mahoney of the Bowery Boys, with everyone else in the world playing Satch.

It seemed all his young years had been spent becoming a legend. Like all kids who play road hockey, and shinny, hanging around rinks for the free ice time, he was a rink rat in every sense of the word, and in every game he ever played. He was a pest, a skilled but irritating pest, the kind of player who could beat you two ways: with his defensive smarts and his street smarts. He was the type who, when facing impossible odds, would smirk at *your* predicament. More often than not, as the pendulum swung toward his side, the opposition was left to grind their teeth at what they thought was his mindless luck.

Derek Sanderson became a legend — but not the one he had in mind. Nobody starts out deliberately to be self-destructive. The more he created the image, the more he felt the pressure of living up to it. He was, in the words of my grandfather, "like a bear running downhill. Pretty soon your ass goes over your head, in a mad tumble to the bottom." The operative words here are "mad" and "tumble."

His career had the earmarks of a screenplay. He won the rookie award in 67–68, the second Boston player in consecutive years to do so. Some kid named Orr had won in 66–67. Sanderson was another new building block in the Bruins' resurgence. In that turnaround year the Bruins also welcomed the arrival of Fred Stanfield, Ken Hodge, and Phil Esposito from the Blackhawks. Eddie Shack was another who came to Boston that season and, playing the right wing on Sanderson's line, managed to bag 23 goals of his own.

In the playoffs his second season Sanderson led all goal scorers with eight. The following year, 69–70, he led the playoffs in penalty minutes. The notable difference in 1970 was that the Bruins won their first Stanley Cup in 29 years. The next season, though Boston finished in first place, they didn't make the finals and watched the Cup slip from their grasp, a bitter lesson. Sanderson had scored 29 goals — a figure he would never match again — while sitting out 130 minutes in penalties. They came back with a vengeance in 1971–72, winning their second, and last, Stanley Cup over the New York Rangers.

The role of luminary fit Turk Sanderson like a pair of compression shorts. He revelled in the life of notoriety that success and two Stanley Cups can bring, not to forget the associations with co-stars like Orr, Esposito, and a cast of tens. He was flamboyant, bordering on pompous, haughty, and imperious. Below it all he was still a kid from Niagara Falls. A crazy bastard, true, but fun to watch. Regardless of his own assumption of superior ways, he was a favourite of the fans. All that was about to change in 1972, the year of the World Hockey Association. Mr. Sanderson was about to become a millionaire.

He signed with the Philadelphia Blazers. Bernie Parent, the Toronto Maple Leaf who missed Philly so bad he went back, signed as well. Bernie played 63 games, earning his money. Turk played eight games before returning to Boston the same year, playing 25 games with the Bruins. His money was guaranteed.

The eight games made him a millionaire, but probably cost him a chance with Team Canada '72. Not that he ever indicated he cared, but it was a given that if he were eligible, he would have been coach Harry Sinden's choice to fill one of the centre spots.

He began a life of living the part, if in fact he ever left it, cruising with the upper echelon, owning his own bar. Daisy Buchanan's was on Newbury

Street, the Rodeo Drive of Boston. He was into good wine, hard liquor, and drugs. It began to show. The fall from grace was not pretty, and it only took five hazy years.

The first time I met him was at a ProStars fastball game at Stamford Park in his hometown of Niagara Falls. It was the Molson-sponsored team's first season, the summer of 1976. By this time Sanderson was an ex-Bruin, an ex-WHAer, an ex-Ranger, and was now about to be an ex-member of the St. Louis Blues. He was also well on his way to being an ex-millionaire. He would suit up with three teams in the upcoming season, even though he had posted career figures for the Blues the year before. In 65 games he had scored 24 goals and added 43 assists for 67 points, his best ever by four. After 32 games, St. Louis tired of dealing with his ego and sold him to Vancouver, and finally the Central League became home. He then played 13 games for the Pittsburgh Penguins, who took a chance and signed him as a free agent in what was to be his final season of pro hockey. It was 1978.

In 1968 he was the Rookie of the Year in the NHL. Ten years later, at the age of 31, he was relegated to watching the game on TV at his father's house.

I saw him again the next year. It was a ProStars game at Exhibition Stadium in Toronto, and he was suited up with the Buffalo Sabres. He didn't look good, even though he appeared in good spirits. No pun intended. Playing catch on the sidelines, a cigarette clamped between his teeth, he said something unintelligible to me as he dropped the ball for the third time in three throws. I have to admit, his bumbling ball-handling was done with a certain flair, but I still had twinges of concern for his well-being on the field. I should have known better. It seems God *does* look after the helpless. He played first base without a miscue, and in his only at-bat went down swinging at a vicious fastball thrown by the Leaf's George Ferguson. I thought it was a good at-bat because the cut he took on strike three was at least in the vicinity, and who knows what he was seeing through his eyes. I'm not sure whether he was replaced as a safety precaution or took himself out of the game, but I suspect either way there was a feeling of relief under the veneer of nonchalance.

The next time our paths crossed, he was a new recruit on the NHL Old Stars. Fred Stanfield suggested I contact Turk, now living back in the Falls, drying out, trying out his new run at life. It was 1980, and he played his first game in Timmins against the junior North Stars. Oddly enough we had opened the season in Welland and Niagara Falls. No Turk.

I recall our conversation on the phone. Sanderson has a way of running words together that makes him almost unintelligible. Easy if you're face to face, but on the telephone you get the feeling you have reached a foreign embassy, and in this case he did nothing to make me feel comfortable. At risk was our team's reputation with Labatt's and our spotless record, to this point anyway. I recall spelling out the rules clearly and I told him if there was one drink, one reason for me to suspect anything, he was on his way home. *No problem,* he said, and he was right.

That's not to say he wasn't a pain in the ass. He didn't have any equipment, for starters. Joe Sgro, our trainer, had to outfit him, down to his inner jock. He wasn't too happy with our Victoriaville sticks, which come through a deal secured with some difficulty. The fact that they were free didn't impress him either, but he used the "cues" just the same. Labatt's bought all the team members tailor-made blazers, and Ron Williams, a clothier and old pal for many years, came out to the airport when the need arose to measure up players such as Turk, whose only trips to Toronto were to make our flights for the next set of games. When Turk received his jacket he said something to the effect of, "I didn't know Canadian Tire sold clothes. Did your tailor work in garden supplies?" We had a private talk about the remark, and I reminded him, "While the jackets aren't up to millionaire standards, none of us are millionaires any more, are we? With the possible exception of Shackie." It's the only untoward moment I experienced in the 18 games he played with us that year. In between he was a source of humour for all of us, and as he rounded into some semblance of shape, he became a showpiece for the team.

Since Freddie Stanfield had rediscovered Derek, he also became his steady roomie, much to Freddie's dismay. The Turk isn't the easiest guy to share living quarters with, as I discovered on various visits to their room on the road.

Once, in Stephenville, Newfoundland, I dropped in to find Derek lying in bed surrounded by a jumble of empty pop cans and discarded chip bags, on the phone arranging room service as if we were at the Harbour Castle in Toronto. Stanfield was in the shower and his share of the room looked comparatively unscathed, as opposed to the mishmash on the other side. The telephone conversation went like this.

"That's right, two orders of eggs, one scrambled, one over easy. What? Yeah, one whole wheat. That's what I said, the brown stuff, got it? And one white. What the hell's so hard about that? How many colours of bread you got? True, I never thought of that, darlin'. Both with bacon — back bacon, none of that front stuff. Never mind. Two orders of bangers. What? Bangers. Sausages, Porky Pigs, Jimmy Dean's, it don't matter. Hey, you got those little potatoes? Home fries, whatever. Or french fries, it don't matter. Load 'em on both orders." He waved his hand in a circle overhead, indicating he wanted the poor girl to get moving. Just then Stanfield emerged from the bathroom, wrapped in a towel, looking for a shirt from his suit bag. The ordering continued.

"Yep, two. One orange and one grapefruit, and don't forget to put double jam and stuff, OK?"

"Nice," I said to Stanfield, admiringly. "You got your roomie trained to order for you."

"Me? You gotta be dreaming," Freddie snorted. "That's *his* breakfast."

Whatever incredulous surprise I must have registered was wiped off my face, because at that very moment Sanderson casually held out the handset to Stanfield. "Fritzie, you wanna order somethin' or you going downstairs to eat with the general public?"

Another time, on a bus rolling into Amherst, Nova Scotia, there was a lively discussion about habits and strange practices between long-time room-mates. Eddie Shack was explaining how he had to leave the bathroom light on for Bob Nevin. One of the others wanted to know if Nevin was afraid of the dark.

"Naw. Ever since Nevvie took a header over my suitcase," and the rest was buried under the guffaws of The Nose That Knows.

"Ever think of movin' your goddamn suitcase?" Nevvie asked, moustache twitching.

"Any more *rules*," Shackie bellowed, laughing at his fellow bridge part-ners. Freddie Stanfield shifted in his seat to face the aisle.

"Turk and I have only two rules. You have to have one foot in the bathroom to fart, and no spitting on the walls," he said disgustedly, looking over at the snoozing Sanderson.

If anything, the Turk was simply another source of laughs and good stories for the group. We all had to be. There wasn't any room for crab asses on the team. By the time we reached Charlottetown in November 1980, Sanderson had four games under his belt and was becoming oriented to the atmosphere. While his hotel habits left a little to be desired, he was fastidious in his preoccupation with statistics, keeping his own numbers because no one else kept track of anything. Imagine my surprise when he would report to me after every game: how many face-offs he had won, and what his percentage was in "critical puck control situations," meaning face-offs in the corners. It was noteworthy enough for me to pass along to the members of the team, and in Charlottetown he not only "controlled" the critical face-offs but scored a hat trick that evening against the Junior A Islanders. The team determined he had accomplished this feat by hanging around the centre ice paint all night, hence the nickname, "Logo."

The next day we were in Fredericton to play the University of New Brunswick, coached by Don MacAdam, who would go on to coach in the NHL and American Hockey League. The arena and facilities were first class, and so professionally handled that the PA announcer came into our dressing room looking for me, handing over an official game sheet for me to fill out. Even though I explained our usual drill, that he could look on our program for the numbers, and that we didn't give a big rat's ass about goals or assists, he stubbornly stood his ground, hand extended with the form until I took it and scratched in the line-up. As I remember, I added a few names. Orr, Howe, M. Richard, P. Trudeau, and John Candy, number 27, just to aggravate him.

As I handed the official PA guy back his official clipboard and official line-up pen, Jimmy Pappin, who had been watching the scene, collared him and steered him into the official shower room, arm around the man's shoulder. For a while I thought the boys were going to "hose" him down, but he left the dressing room officially dry. It wasn't until after we had first scored that I realized my trepidations about what kind of plot had been hatched in the shower room were unfounded.

"Labatt's Old Star goal scored by Dale Tallon." So far it was routine, and then the script changed. "His sixth of the year, assisted by . . ." This place was so damn official, I remember thinking to myself, they even keep track of the number of goals. Then the little light went on.

"Labatt's Old Stars goal scored by Dennis Hull, his 12th of the year . . ." It was followed in order by Eddie Shack's tenth, Tom Williams' seventh, and Bob Nevin's fifth. Sanderson by this time had been shut out. In fact, nobody even gave him a pass until after Nevin had scored. Suddenly the rink-wides were hitting his stick rather than being in his skates or behind him. Opportunities for Logo, patiently hovering around centre ice, waving his stick for attention, were now finding the mark. Finally he scored on a breakaway, circled the net with a look that said, "It's about time, boys," grudgingly accepted the high-fives and hair ruffling, then headed for the bench and a well-deserved rest.

"Labatt's Old Star goal scored by Derek Sanderson, his first of the year." As soon as the words were uttered, he turned to me.

"Who the fuck is keeping the goddamn stats around here?" he groused. "I got three last night . . . son of a bitch!" he yelled as the assists resounded over the speakers. I could only shrug and shake my head. The guys on the bench looked away as he skated over to the timekeeper's bench. Hunched over, speaking through the hole in the glass, we could see him holding up three fingers, and arguing. The official scorecard man held up his game sheet with the official up-to-date goals listed neatly beside each name. Figures don't lie. Suddenly Turk started to laugh and skated away, shaking his head, pointing his stick at our bench as if to say "gotcha." We never ever got the latest face-off stats again.

The last time I saw him in uniform was in our second-last game of the season, at Indianapolis, April 1981. He didn't show up for the final game in Orillia. Turk had disappeared, for all we knew. From time to time I caught hearsay and rumour until he came to Toronto to have hip surgery. A bedside television interview with Dick Beddoes was the only news of him, until I began hearing about his foray into the TV field as a colour commentator for the Bruins. When I finally caught a Boston broadcast I marvelled at the diction and elocution of this man who under normal conditions was a rapid-fire mumbler.

Here in the restaurant of the Queen Elizabeth Hotel in Montreal, he was a model of good health, with the noted exception of the hip replacements and the notable exception of an attraction to cigarettes. We sat across the table and he told me how it was to be an alcoholic and a drug user. He told me that he has spoken to over 400,000 young people about the abuse and the life. He told me how his employer, Tucker Anthony Investments of Boston, provided his speaking dates free of charge to anyone, anyplace. He related the story of being on an open-line show in St. John's, Newfoundland, with a 15-year-old boy with a serious drinking problem on the line, desperately looking for help.

"Where are you, pal?" Derek said, with his hand to his ear, listening to an imaginary headphone, re-enacting the moment. "The kid said the name and I jotted the phone number down, saying I'd call back after the show and we'd get to him. So I asked the producer how long a drive is it to Corner Back —"

I hold up my hand and correct him. "Corner Brook."

"You bin there? Place is a 12-hour drive. I said maybe, a few years ago . . . with a case of wine . . . but we got somebody to him anyway, and that's what I do now. That, and work at the investment business, got diplomas and everything, play some golf, look after my family, the wife and two little boys, Michael and Ryan. Speak to the gangs in the projects — like that." He shot the cuffs again and waved the waiter over for more coffee. We talked about hockey and a life that has changed so drastically it should be on the silver screen.

"Yeah. I can see that happening," he said matter-of-factly, like it was a mystery why a Hollywood type hasn't made contact as yet. The idea triggered a memorable scene in his mind, and he suppressed a laugh. "Can you picture this," he said, holding his hands up, thumbs touching, fingers tight in the time-honoured signal for a lens frame.

"I've just signed my contract. Two-point-six-five million," he said, holding up two fingers on one hand, all five on the other. I suppose I looked skeptical, possibly because the figure I remember started with a one. Sanderson shook his head and held up the fingers again.

"Not bad for an overrated penalty killer," he said, shaking his head at my faint objections to the handle, as if to signify he had come to terms with the meaning of life. "I'm in this cab going down the main street — Broad Street, right? — and I see this car dealership. Keenan's. Rolls-Royce and Bentley. I tell the cabbie to pull in and pay him. I always wanted a big car — I mean a *big* car — so I walk into the showroom and I'll never forget it — there's this burgundy and sand limousine. A Silver Shadow. I'm wearin' cowboy boots, jeans, a T-shirt and a jean jacket, long hair, moustache — look like a piece of shit, right? Here comes this little guy in a three-piece suit, got a watch chain, fob," Sanderson went through the motions of a person fingering the inside waist pockets of a vest.

" 'Can I help you,' the geek says, real snobby. A little English prick. I asked him how much for the car. 'I have no idea,' he says, like whatta stupid question."

I had to laugh at the thought of Turk being upstaged at his own game.

"You work here and you don't know how much the goddamn car is worth? How the hell do you sell 'em? He said, 'Sir, people usually order these automobiles over the phone.' 1–0 for the asshole. So I said, 'What do *you* do around here?' He said, 'I answer the phone.' 2–0. I try the car door. It's locked. I ask for the keys. I wanna sit in it. The little shit looks me over real good, but he gets the keys and we open her up. I sit down, try the steering wheel, step on the brake, open the ashtray. I said to him, 'not very comfortable.' He says, 'Excuse me, sir, but if you own one of these you normally sit in the back, which I can assure you is quite comfy.' 3–0. So I get out, start kicking the tires. 'How many miles to the gallon?' 'I'm sure I have no idea. I don't think any of the owners of this fine vehicle really care,' he said. 4–0.

"Now I'm really pissed off and I ask to see the boss. He comes out and I tell him I wanna buy the car and we go into his office. The price is $64,500. Hey, it's 1972. I tell him it's no problem. We call up my bank, who tell him they can send the money over by courier. He's impressed, so I tell him we have a deal, but he's gotta meet two conditions. I look at my watch. First condition, it's noon now, you have to have the car ready for me to drive off the lot at 5:00 p.m. He says it's no problem, we start shuffling paper, and call the bank. Walking out to the showroom, he asks me what's the second condition. I tell him it's a deal as long as that little shit doesn't get any commission." Sanderson pointed at our "host" who just happened to be waltzing by, surveying with a jaundiced eye the table covered in cups, cigarettes, ashtrays, notebooks, and ratty books of matches.

"Now it's 5–4. The Turk got him on an empty-netter," he said, adjusting the jacket lapels and craning his neck.

There was a trailer to the story. Sanderson, full of himself, was tooling down Broad Street at five o'clock and within two blocks of his hotel, the Latham, when the Silver Shadow ran out of gas in the rush-hour traffic. He abandoned it and walked to the hotel. "I told the doorman — the guy's wearin' jodhpurs fer Christ's sake — to pick it up and get the tank filled. Gave him 50 bucks and told him to keep the change." He waved at the air as if it was no big deal.

"Next day, I'm checkin' out. The guy brings the car up to the front door, gives me a look that'd kill. Goddamn car had two tanks, cost 48 dollars to fill." He got a chuckle out of the memory.

As we walked out of the café to the lobby, Sanderson introduced me to his "mentor," long-time Boston play-by-play man Fred Cusick, who probably wondered about my happy grin as we shook hands. I was remembering my pal Frenchy McFarlane, the Toronto comic, drawing a comparison between Cusick and Leafs' broadcaster Joe Bowen. "Cusick is such a homer, he makes Bowen look neutral."

As I picked up my bags at the concierge's desk and made my way out the revolving doors, I took one last glance around the lobby. Derek "Turk" Sanderson was signing autographs, Fred Cusick was waiting on the sidelines, and Tommy Johnson peeked out over the top of his book. Everything was back to normal.

90-SECOND ALL-STARS

G — **Gerry Cheevers** *". . . the best in this kind of situation. Forget goal-tending as a problem."*

D — **Bobby Orr** *". . . gotta love Bobby."*

D — **Bill White** *". . . couldn't be beaten, one-on-one."*

C — **Phil Esposito** *". . . great in front of the net, and never got credit for his defensive play."*

RW — **Gordie Howe** *". . . he never gave the puck away."*

LW — **Frank Mahovlich** *". . . he could win it all alone."*

Al Hamilton

The Barber Shop
Quartet

EVERY TIME AL HAMILTON'S NAME COMES UP, I immediately think of two things. Having a good laugh. And bad
haircuts.

I've always remembered Al Hamilton as one of those people
who enjoyed hockey more than others because it all seemed so natural. He
enjoyed the games, the practices, and most of all the heckling and banter, the
inside jokes that are a facet of the game that outsiders usually underestimate.

Sure, the greatest hecklers, comics, characters, and practical jokers cannot
save a bad team. They'll lose, laughing, but they'll still lose. A sullen, morose,
overly sensitive, humourless team can lose as well. But when the chips are
down, when the club has to reach down for something more than just talent,
when coaches can no longer browbeat, insult, and otherwise motivate, a
loosey-goosey team will have the fibre to pull on the same rope, going in the
same direction. Nobody on the team is excluded — not the muckers and not
the stars. The only ones left out are coaches and management. The last time
I checked, they were a source of common ground only for behind-doors
mimicking, which all players, and most school kids, can relate to.

Because this is a violent game played at top speed, frightening even for
those who appear to be comfortable on the pond, the fun part is a must. The
laughs have to be there. It's the side of the game that Al Hamilton loved best.

Al Hamilton: "...the WHA was offering three times *my Buffalo salary. Even I could figure it out."*

I met him as a member of the Buffalo Sabres way back in 1970, but like the rest of us in Buffalo, he had a prior life.

He started with the hometown Flin Flon Bombers as a permanent chattel of the New York Rangers. As a first-year junior he experienced what many never get a chance at. The Bombers won the west but lost to the Toronto Marlies in the Memorial Cup. Al then moved ever westward to the Detroit-owned Edmonton Oil Kings for two more junior seasons, losing the elusive Memorial Cup to Niagara Falls the second time around, then finally grabbing the Canadian junior crown in his last season. Who did they beat? Bobby Orr and the Oshawa Generals at Maple Leaf Gardens.

As they say in horse racing, the bloodlines were there. While he was slogging through the Memorial Cup trials, there was a three-game underage tryout with St. Paul of the Central League. The next year it was a four-game whirl with the New York Rangers, followed by the entire 66–67 season with Rangers' Omaha Knights of the Central League. He would alternate between the Rangers and the Buffalo Bisons of the American Hockey League for a couple of seasons, eventually making the big club for 59 games in 1969. On June 10, 1970, he was another of the kidnappings Punch Imlach perpetrated for the fledgling Sabres in the expansion draft.

Although he worked on the blue line, defence wasn't Big Al's trump card. Imlach, along with assistant Fred Hunt, a former player and GM of the Bisons, plus chief scout John Andersen, had seen enough of Hamilton's ability as the point man on power plays to fill the need for just such a player on their fledging defence. He had size — he was 6'1" and 200 pounds — and was an excellent skater. His puckhandling and passing rated well above average. In Buffalo he was most often paired with 5'9" Doug Barrie, and the two became the "Stapleton and White" of the Sabres, although not quite on the same frequency band.

The move to Buffalo was the long-awaited break he had been working toward for all those years in junior and the minors. The Rangers were loaded with defencemen, including Rod Seiling, Jim Neilson, Arnie Brown, and future Hall of Famers Brad Park and Tim Horton, all experienced, all unshakeable for the Rangers' clamouring horde of rookies looking for work. The chance to play with the Sabres and the bombastic Imlach was the stuff of dreams and he settled into Buffalo with an eye to the future there.

For the two seasons he was in Buffalo, once summer rolled around, Hammy and I could be found putting back a couple of cold ones at Mother's Bakery, or Gabe's Gate, or Coles up on Elmwood. I don't think Al ever went to my most frequent stop, The Place, on Lexington and Ashland, simply because it was considered a management spot, a place where you might run into Fred Hunt, maybe even Punch, and that was a no-no. For some reason I was able to walk the line between both factions.

In 1970 the Hamiltons bought a new home in Fort Erie, Ontario, where their first child was born, but after only two full, productive seasons with the fledgling Sabres he took the gamble and went back to the West to join the Edmonton Oilers of the World Hockey Association.

That's the way it was in 1972. While the rest of Canada was getting their TV sets up to speed for the coming "yawner" against the spoiled brats from Russia, who had never had to face the power of the NHL, Hamilton was starting out on a new venture. The new league had courted Hamilton and others tirelessly.

"When the showdown came, the Sabres only offered a contract worth a few grand more than I was getting in year one. The WHA was offering *three times* my Buffalo salary. Even I could figure it out," Big Al confided one day. No one could blame him for pulling up stakes. The money was good and getting better. But it was still risky, the kind of deal where you better have the money in your hand before you started spending it. I, among others, cautioned him in most of my counselling.

Late in the summer of 1972, my wife and I picked up the Hamiltons to drive them to Toronto, where they would stay with us overnight before heading to Alberta. I still remember getting a chuckle out of Al that warm August day as we drove away from their empty bungalow, a touching moment in the life of any young couple. His wife, Barb, took one last forlorn glance back at their first home and said wistfully, "I wonder if we'll ever see the house again."

Without even glancing back, Al snorted that snuffling laugh of his and said, "yeah — probably in October." That underlined the status of the new league at the time and did nothing to reassure his wife.

Yet, it's one thing to be able to make light of a domestic situation or otherwise chastise and sully the reputations of other players/management/fans as a humorous way to relieve the tensions of being a pro. It's another to be the *source* of the humour. The true test of a player is to be able to survive being the brunt of the joke, to withstand on fortitude and the humble acceptance of fate, using only your own rattlesnake wit as a counterpunch. Which leads me to the story of Big Al and the haircut.

It was in 1971, the opening of a fresh, unmarked training camp at the Garden City Arena in St. Catharines, a mere wind sprint from the Aud in Buffalo. A golf date involving the players and invited guests was the opening kickoff following the routine of medicals. Floyd Smith, Dick Duff, Phil Goyette, and Ed Shack were there to represent the old guard. The future consisted of players such as NHL Rookie of the Year Gil Perreault, Craig Ramsay, and an even younger kid (who also happened to be a scratch golfer) named Richard Martin. The golf course was in Fonthill, Ontario, and my partners were Al Hamilton and centre Gerry Meehan, plus an auto sales manager from Buffalo whom I won't name to protect the dealership.

I can distinctly remember driving to the course, anxious that I was running a little behind, but more concerned about how I'd play. My heaviest workload was in the off-season, summertime. I hadn't had a whole lot of opportunity to play, so I was worried about how much help I would be to my foursome. Having been to many of these matchups, I was even more apprehensive about the snide remarks and slanted asides I would have to endure.

As I suspected, there was the usual harping and carping taking place on the first tee, barely a squint away from an outdoor area crowded with other players sitting around awaiting their tee-off times. There were loaded comments about ratty-looking bags and equipment, and pointed aspersions about flamboyant dress and the colours of same.

"Where'd you get the sweater, Ron, the Loud Shoppe?"

"For Christ's sake, Larry, *all* your goddamn clubs are woods. Who whittled them, your old man?"

"Nice pants. I thought tweed was out this year."

"All you need with that shirt is long gloves and earrings."

"Hey, Ski. You look like a Polish sea cadet!"

Then each person had to step up on the tee, place a ball, and strike it, praying that nothing untoward or reputation-damaging would happen until at least the second hole.

Meehan and I paired off to watch and cringe at the rabble around the first tee. The mob scene reminded me of those people who gape up at some poor slob on a tenth-floor ledge, the ones who yell "*jump*." No one was spared.

"We're supposed to be playing the fairway straight in front of the tee, asshole."

"You really laid the lumber on that one. That's gotta be at least 60, maybe 70 feet out there."

"You only keep your head up in hockey, stupid."

"You shoot like that tomorrow and they'll cut your ass back to Cincinnati."

Inexorably, our time in the lion's den arrived.

Hamilton and our fourth man arrived about the time we were beginning to wonder if they were going to show at all. I think Hammie planned it that way, but the crowd at the first tee was ready for them anyway. Hamilton's partner was short, wore thick glasses, had a pronounced potbelly, and the worst pair of legs I had ever seen sticking out of plaid Bermuda shorts. He also sported oversize golf shoes, red ankle socks, and the fewest golf clubs in the biggest golf bag I had ever laid eyes on. Despite the side show, Hammy was the main attraction.

The moment he arrived on the scene, golf bag slung over his shoulder, the talk centred on Hamilton's haircut. From my vantage point he resembled Moe. Not Moe Norman either. He looked like a large Moe, one third of the Three Stooges. Whoever cut his hair was an out-and-out sadist. The style of the day was shaggy sideburns. Hammy's sideburns, usually a sight to behold, had been reduced to mere amputated shadows of themselves. The shearing had only served to enhance the size of his ears.

"Hammy! What happened to your head? Get it caught in a Lawn Boy?"

"Aw, shut up," Big Al grumbled incisively.

"Geez, I've heard of guys coming to camp trimmed down, but this is ridiculous."

"Kiss my ass," Hammy shot back.

"Lookin' at Hammy reminds me. Has a defenceman ever won the Lady Byng trophy?"

"Aw, shut up."

"Hambone, can you flap those buggers independently?"

"Up yours."

It continued like that until mercifully we got up on the tee. Meehan led off, to be followed by the auto dealer, who I had nicknamed "Bogs" — much to the delight of Hamilton, who was more than happy to have someone else get the heat.

"Bogs? What's Bogs?" Big Al inquired, pushing his glasses up on his nose with his ring finger, a familiar gesture that became his signature.

"Bucket of Guts," I said, giving Al his first smile of this rotten day.

That oversize bag contained a two-four of beer, a bottle of Canadian Club, a bottle of Cinzano sweet vermouth, a jar of marachino cherries, and a styrofoam cooler of ice cubes. Did I mention the cups? Did I mention the swizzle sticks?

The man was a Manhattan freak and had no intention of playing golf without his favourite drink. The beer was for us — a nice thought, but naive. Since this was a Sabre training-camp exercise, the suds were out of the question. Earlier in the year, the box of beer would have been insufficient.

Meehan, a practising golfer and a big guy to boot, smoked one off the elevated tee, which looked down into a valley landing area boasting a straight line of trees running down the left side. Meehan's ball fell to earth softly, good position, no problems, to the grudging admiration of the hecklers.

Next up was Bogs. He hit a drive in the most unorthodox fashion I have ever witnessed on a golf course, or in a swimming pool for that matter. The ball lofted high, sliced a bit, and landed inches short of a sand trap. So far so good. I was next.

As I went through the ritual of getting set, the boo-birds came out again.

"Hey, Hammy. Brewitt's got more hair than you have."

"Aw, shut up," Al fired back.

In my mind I went down a checklist for hitting a golf ball, drew the clubhead back slowly, in a straight line like it says in the book, then I blanked out. I don't remember actually swinging at the ball. The next thing I knew I was standing firmly on my left foot, looking down the fairway, my right heel turned upward pointing at the sky, hands just above my left shoulder, a classic pose worthy of a travel poster for Myrtle Beach. As my eyes picked up the ball it was on its way like a surface-to-air missile, splitting the fairway, nestling down on the sweet grass, about ten yards away from Meehan's ball.

Cries of "ringer, ringer," rang out behind me, but I was casually sliding the club back in the bag and was too engrossed in looking nonchalant to notice. Inside I was fervently mumbling a prayer of thanks to the Big Caddy in the sky. What a time to hit a career drive. Next came Al Hamilton.

"Hey Al. You should'a stopped shaving this morning while you were ahead."

"Hambone, you cold? Wanna borrow my golf touque?"

Whatever came over me on the tee completely missed Big Al. He jerked the club up like he was about to drive a stake through Drac's heart, lurched into the downswing, and thumped the ball into the turf, where it bounced lazily along the ground, over the edge of the tee, dribbling down the incline for a few feet until it nestled in a clump of scraggly grass. The laughter was raucous, and for Al it didn't get any better. Two more flailing shots were needed to get off the slope, and the second one found the fairway trap. The cackling followed us down the fairway after every stroke. It was cruel, more so when Hammy whacked his ball out of the trap and into another one across the fairway. Above and behind us, the PA system crackled on.

"Attention, Mr. Al Hamilton. The barbershop called. Your hair is ready."

Finally, mercifully out of eyeshot and earshot on the second tee, Meehan duck-hooked his drive into the bush. Bogs smacked one that went 300 feet. Straight up, and straight down. I hit one that corked a tree so hard people on other fairways were hitting the dirt, figuring a sniper was on the loose. Big Al drove one about 240 yards, dead centre. Nobody hooted, hollered, or laughed. They weren't watching. Justice is definitely blindfolded.

By the time we made the turn, the others were all out on the course, occasionally yelling at Al as we slid past each other on different fairways, but things seemed to have quieted down enough for me to ask about the haircut as we stood waiting for the group in front on a par three.

"Who the hell gnawed on your head?" I asked helpfully.

He glared at me for a second. "Kiss my ass," he said, turning to stare down the fairway. Shrugging off the rebuff I turned my attention to Bogs lolling woozily in the cart and another question that was bothering me. "What's with the red socks trick, Bogsy?" I queried. "Doesn't seem to be colour coordinated like the rest of your outfit."

"Aw, that's just in case I get tipped over in the rough, and am incapacitated," he answered, sloshing the ice around the bottom of his fourth

Manhattan. "This way they can spot the red socks a mile away." It somehow seemed logical, and I turned back to the stewing Hamilton. "Makes sense to me," I said to his back. He turned so quickly I was startled, and it all came out in a rush.

"Goddamn Dryden," he blurted, referring to Dave Dryden, the Sabre's goalie. "He told me about this place to get a real good haircut, cheap, too. He said the guy knew what he was doing." He pondered the point for a moment, frowning, visualizing his mangled hair, while I studied it. "So, I'm sittin' there and this guy is hackin' away so fast I couldn't believe it. I said, 'Hold on, pal, I ain't a goddamn recruit, I just want a trim,' and he says, 'I understand,' so I let the stupid bastard cut away. Now look at me."

With him glaring at me I couldn't. So I didn't. I just stood there sorting through which stupid bastard he was referring to.

As we walked down the 14th we met Richard Martin coming up 13. He took out an iron, hit the ball like a pro, and dropped the ball onto the green.

"Playin' pretty good, huh," Big Al said.

"Bullshit. I'm playing lousy," the rookie shot back emphatically. "I'm four over to here already."

Hammy rolled his eyes. "Yeah I know just how you feel, kid," he replied sarcastically. "I'm 26 over myself." Meehan laughed out loud. I turned away, biting my lip. Bogs plopped another marachino into his cup.

Finally, on the 18th, as we came into view of the early finishers camped on the veranda overlooking the last green like a gallery at a tour event, it was obvious the word on Hammy's haircut had preceded him. Other players were coming out of the clubhouse to gather in bunches, watching our progress. Meehan hit an eight iron within ten feet of the cup, to the appreciation of the crowd. Bogs wasn't playing anymore, just sitting in the cart babbling to himself in fits and starts, much like his cart driving. I hit my iron shot inside of Meehan's and almost went into a dead faint in relief over such a stroke of luck at that precise moment. Two flukes in one day was more than enough.

Hamilton hit his ball halfway up the hill behind the green, almost out of view of the mob on the veranda.

"Hambone. I thought when you got clipped like that, you're supposed to get weaker."

"How'd yuh like to weak this . . ." he muttered.

"Hey, Hammy. Ever notice that since you uncovered your ears you're more sensitive?"

"How'd yuh like to uncover this . . ."

"I can get you a great deal on a big helmet."

"Kiss my ass . . ."

Through the noise and the cat-calling, Al was calm and cool, taking only three shots to get off the hill and another three putts to hole out. By this time the boys on the veranda were collapsing on the floor, gasping, kicking chairs, cackling, and snorting.

As we walked up the hill together, I said, "Nice day, wasn't it?"

He absently fingered some prickly skin where sideburns used to flourish and said, "Super, just goddamn super."

But golf, haircuts, and the Fort Erie homestead aside, things worked out for Big Al. He never returned to Buffalo. Instead he suited up nine years with the Oilers, seven of them as captain, and many of those seasons injured. A collision with a goalpost shattered a kneecap. A deflected slapshot almost cost him an eye. When the Oilers joined the NHL in 1980 he was on a roll: 20 points in 19 games, and back in the "big" league. But as I said before, Justice is blind. A broken shoulder put the final cap on his career.

These days, he has his own successful promotion and marketing company in Edmonton, obviously a person with some smarts.

Still, I've often wondered if Hammy ever entertained the idea that the haircut, and even the barber, was a setup? It occurred to me the same day it happened. At about the fifth hole, as I recall. It was all too pat, too predictable, too blatantly obvious. Besides, whenever a goaltender is involved, even a "Mr. Straight Arrow" like Dave Dryden, I would have been suspicious. Then there's the other point. The stunt was so good Hammy would have loved it had it been pulled on someone else. He would have laughed the loudest.

Maybe Justice isn't blind, after all.

After all these years I still mull over the haircut inflicted on my old buddy, Hambone, and ask myself if I'm just a skeptic. Or have I stumbled across one of the all-time, all-cruel, great unknown scams in hockey?

90-SECOND ALL-STARS

G — **Terry Sawchuck**

D — **Bobby Orr**

D — **Denis Potvin**

C — **Wayne Gretzky**

RW — **Gordie Howe**

LW — **Bobby Hull**

". . . no one is gonna beat these six!"

Darryl Edestrand

Taking a Tumble

SITTING AT A WINDOW TABLE in the HoJo coffee shop on London's Wellington Street, I wait for an old pal, eyeballing the parking lot in time to see an exiting customer step off the curb into a water-filled pothole that could have used a sump pump. Although I can't hear him, the language, for a practised lip reader, is vile.

He stands there like a flamingo, one tasselled loafer held aloft, much the same as in a scene from *The Karate Kid*. Tough, I think to myself as the guy limps away in a snit, snarling at the inequity of the world.

There's a saying about being in the wrong place at the wrong time. It's usually reserved for hapless participants in accidents, those unfortunates who find themselves the victims of a senseless crime, or people who step in dog crap for no apparent reason other than it's there. Like this guy, I thought, watching him sitting inside the open door of a BMW wringing out a sock, still mouthing obscenities.

There are other terms to describe these poor souls. Innocent bystander comes to mind, but rarely does it apply in the game of hockey. Anyone who plays at the professional level is, generally speaking, far removed from innocent, and this was the case with Darryl Edestrand.

He came out of junior hockey a burgeoning defenceman who could

Darryl Edestrand with the Bruins: ". . . [Gary] Doak and I used to call ourselves the Acme defence. Just add ice and we could play, instantly."

contribute at both ends of the ice. He was a perfect match for the style the Toronto Maple Leafs expected from their prospects on the London Nationals, where future NHLers Walt McKechnie, Mike Corrigan, and goaltender Gerry Desjardins were Edestrand's teammates.

At 5'11" and 185 pounds he was mobile, had a great touch with the puck, and possessed something every scout looked for: skating speed. He could jump into the play on offence, maintain a defensive presence in front of his own net, and work the power play. All the earmarks were there, all the prerequisites were met, and the future looked bright.

Immediately following his final junior playoffs, there was a brief tail-end of a pro season with the Rochester Americans, Toronto's American Hockey League farm club, and then a fresh start with the Americans in the fall of 1966. Seven games into the schedule he broke his arm. The accident happened during an innocent skating drill, one of those mindless, assembly-line, end-to-end tongue draggers, the staple of a hockey player's drudgery. Something — possibly a sliver from stick, or a piece of a gum wrapper carelessly tossed onto the ice — pitched him into a freewheeling slide into a firmly fixed goalpost. His arm, instinctively thrown up to protect himself, was shattered. The surgery took out the fragments and left him with only one bone in his forearm above the wrist, and he was told his career was over. Despite the dire predictions, he managed to log 14 pro seasons.

The seasons were interrupted by sporadic visits to the NHL, and a list of minor-league cities that changed with unsettling regularity. There was Rochester in the 1960s, and again in the 1970s. Kansas City was followed by a brief stint with the St. Louis Blues, then came Quebec City, a cup of coffee with the Philadelphia Flyers, and back to Quebec, followed by a full season in Hershey. The Pittsburgh Penguins picked up his contract and he played there for two years before being traded to Boston, where he played three seasons and parts of two more with side trips to Rochester. In the Boston/Rochester season he was sold to the Los Angeles Kings, playing 13 games at the end of 1978, and 55 games in 78–79.

A roller-coaster career by anyone's standards but a significant one in that it took 14 pro seasons before he heeded the doctor's advice and hung them up. The seasons weren't empty ones, either.

Following the end of his final junior season, the broken wrist supposedly terminated another dream. But the NHL's first expansion saved his career when he was drafted by the St. Louis Blues after sitting on the shelf for almost a full season. Someone believed he could survive in the NHL.

"Scotty Bowman was the GM/coach back then, and the Blues sent me to KC," he told me on an Old Stars bus to Ottawa. "Doug Harvey was there as coach, and a real crazy bugger he was, too. I got to the rink one morning and the trainer is there saying Harvey called, said I was to pack my equipment and catch a plane to Detroit. So me and the trainer put all my shit into a bag, and he says there's a ticket waiting at the airport, that I'm leaving at 11:00 a.m. Hell, there wasn't time to even go home to pack some clothes, so away I go, make the goddamn plane, and walk into the hotel in Detroit just as the team is sitting down to their game meal.

"So here's me, jeans, boots, golf shirt, and a nylon jacket, freezing my ass off for two days in Detroit. You should have seen me going to the Olympia. Had to stick close to the boys or I couldn't get in the rink. I looked like the team janitor. When we got back to St. Louis I asked for time to get some clothes out of Kansas City, but Scotty said, 'No, buy some shit if you need it.' By this time I had borrowed a trenchcoat, but the golf shirt was starting to get high. After practice I bought my own ticket back to KC, picked up my stuff, and came back within a matter of hours."

"Did anyone ask you how you got the new wardrobe?" I inquired.

"Naw — and nobody reimbursed me either," he said with a sardonic grin, underlining once again how resolute you had to be to get by in the days before million-dollar contracts. Most players in the late '60s and early '70s were driven by the desire to play, to be in the NHL.

Another time I saw this ability to fend for himself was at an Old Stars game in Vernon, B.C. For some reason we were instructed to return to our bench earlier than necessary, with the result we had to watch the Zamboni make its final two laps. Some of our guys groused about the illegal tactics of the home team.

"Just like the goddamn Russians," said one who had been there.

"Good thing it wasn't between the second and third. That's when I usually take my dump," said another, wiping his brow in relief.

"Yep, and he's regular as clockwork," offered his roomie.

Turning on the bench, Edestrand asked, "You got a pen?"

"You gonna diagram a play?" I asked, wondering what a player in full uniform would need with a pen.

"Gotta take care of the boys," was all he said, scribbling a number on the wrist of his glove, before handing the pen back.

"What the hell is that all about?" I wondered aloud.

Darryl pointed at the Zamboni making its final pass in front of our bench, then pointed to his head, indicating a thinking man was inside. The large sign emblazoned along the side of the ice cleaner listed a pizza delivery place, open until 2:00 a.m., seven days a week.

"It'll save a lot of time back at the hotel. Remember how we got the nine of hearts in Kelowna?" I had to agree. By the time we returned to our hotel the whole town was shut down and though several of us frantically searched the Yellow Pages and called around, we were unable to rustle up any pizza, Chinese food, chicken, or subs. I pointed a "correct" finger at Darryl, and he replied with a wink. "Gotta get our priorities straight, girls," he said to the high-fives that were passed along the bench.

There was a touch of the ridiculous to his character, never more evident than the game we played in Rochester, New York, where Darryl was almost considered a native. We stayed at the Holiday Inn, and one of the events surrounding our game was a reception the night before in a banquet hall on the mezzanine floor. Darryl, for his own reasons, had perfected a way of falling down a flight of stairs with as much noise as a 200-pounder can muster without inflicting any actual harm. The trick was in the fact he never really let go of the hand rail, thumping along, legs flying, gripping it first with the left hand, rolling, then the right. To the novice it had all the earmarks of a serious accident. It had been awhile since I had first seen it, and most of us were unaware that it would happen at that place, at that time. The staircase leading down to the lobby was paralleled by escalators running in both directions. The people already travelling in both directions were in for a treat.

As he reached the top step the initial stumble began, accompanied by a drawn out "Jeeeeezzzzzuuussss Keeeeerrriissst . . ." and the flipping and flopping commenced. The horrified faces and gasps as he hurtled past those on the escalators was topped by the bug-eyed, ashen-faced woman in the lobby, hand to her mouth in terror as Edestrand finally came to ground and did a double arm-waving somersault before sitting spread-legged but upright in front of a cigarette machine. His trenchcoat was bunched over his shoulders and tangled in his armpits.

"Oh my Gawd . . . are you hurt?" she asked, approaching him with great car, tentative, a 911 look on her face.

"Yeah, yeah," Darryl said as if it were an hourly occurrence. "It's these goddamn new shoes," was all he offered her by way of explanation before dusting himself off, adjusting his pants, straightening his tie, and heading for the revolving door.

I don't know whether she was more surprised that he got up, or angry at the rest of us. We were scuffling, laughing, wiping tears from our eyes, as we threaded our way through the mob of hotel employees and guests who came a-runnin' to the accident scene.

But, between the fun and games Edestrand's career was a succession of stops, and a long line of coaches. Some he remembers better than others.

"My first coach in Rochester was Joe Crozier. I think he threatened Don Cherry, said I was gonna replace Grapes. I always thought that came back to haunt me in Boston. But the Americans had a hell of a team then. Cherry, Bronco Horvath, Gerry Ehman, Larry Hillman, Duane Rupp, Al Arbour, Dick Gamble — who had the best wrist shot I ever saw. That was the year I broke my arm. They won the Calder Cup. Mike Walton won the rookie of the year. A great team. Then Harvey, Scotty Bowman, and Vic Stasiuk in Quebec. Turk Broda followed him in Quebec City," he said, getting animated. "Whatta piece of work he was. Used to eat peanuts and popcorn on the bench during the game. Never knew when to take him seriously. I can honestly say I never really knew when he was giving me shit."

"Wasn't there a break in your time in Quebec?" I asked, trying to follow the patchwork of teams from memory.

"Two games is all," he said. "Played with Philadelphia on a weekend, thought I had made it and so did the other players, but Bud Poile sent me back, and the next year I went to Hershey. Got a break there," he enthused. "Frank Mathers was the GM/coach, and he told me Detroit was interested in me, to just go out and play my game until he told me to stop. Well, he never said stop, and the following season I was with Pittsburgh Penguins. There I met the best coach I ever had, Red Kelly. Taught me positional play, how to take the man out. He was great, and Pittsburgh was great. I got to play with my idol, Tim Horton, scored ten goals the first year, 15 the second. Hell, the second season with the Penguins I was tied in points with Bobby Orr and Brad Park at Christmas. Didn't get an invite to the All-Star game — they went for high draft choices. But I remember a game later in the season in Boston. I scored twice in nine seconds, got in a fight with Orr — yeah it was a big night. Wouldn't you know it, next year I was traded to Boston, for my old roomie in Hershey, Nick Beverly. Apparently the Bruins were getting a little edgy about waiting for Al Sims to pan out and they got me for insurance. The first year the coach was Bep Guidolin. Does that make you wonder?

"Don Cherry came in next year and I split my time between playing with Gary Doak and sitting on the bench, 'in reserve' is what they called it. Doak and I used to call ourselves the Acme Defence. Just add ice and we could play, instantly."

"I never heard that one," I muttered.

"Yeah, well we were the only ones who knew it," he muttered back. "Doakie used to always be saying, 'Get it up, get it up.'"

"Lot of guys say that to each other out there," I said. Edestrand fixed me with a stare.

"Gary used to say it to himself. When *he* was carrying the puck!" I nodded, agreeing that it was noteworthy.

"Then it was Rochester again. You know, it was ten years later and I was back where I had started. By the end of the 1978 season I had played one game with Boston, 64 with Rochester and had been sold to Los Angeles, where I played 13 games at the end of the year. L.A. had to be the most demoralized team I had ever seen. A good team, too. They had Charlie Simmer, Marcel Dionne, Mike Murphy, Dave Taylor, Tom Williams, Butch Goring, Glen Goldup — the makings of a good young team — but Ronnie Stewart, the coach, couldn't make out a goddamn line-up without checking first with the big guy upstairs."

"What big guy?" I asked, puzzled.

"Jack Kent Cooke, the goofy owner," he answered, irritated, as if I was the only one who didn't know.

"And then?" I prompted.

"Played my last year — 55 games with the Kings and it was over and out." Just like that.

We talked over a coffee refill until the lunch crowd had cleared out, and as often happens when the talk runs through a career, the best moments were saved for last.

"Did I ever tell you about our lawsuit with the cops?" I confessed I didn't know he had a rap sheet. "Oh yeah, it made the headlines: NUDE HOCKEY PLAYERS ASSAULT COPS. Honest to God. I was with Rochester, playing in Portland, Maine, against the Mariners. My roomie was a goalie named Jim "Seaweed" Pettie, a little guy, typical goaltender, stranger than a shithouse rat. We get back to the hotel and I'm sitting, bare-assed, wrapped in a towel reading the paper and watching the late TV sports. Seaweed is lying in the tub, door closed. He has the place all steamed up, soaking his ass in hot water. He's got a hamstring pull — or was it haemorrhoids?"

"How come you called him Seaweed?" I asked, not really interested in the diagnosis.

"If you saw him, you'd know. Didn't have much hair, but what was there was long and stringy. After a game, he'd take off the mask and it'd look like a bowl of dew worms. He'd get the dryer out, tease it and fluff it up. Well, like I say if you saw him . . ." I held up my hand, getting the picture.

"He has the tap running continual hot water and the door closed. Every time he thinks he hears something interestin' on the sports, he yells at me to repeat it. Now I gotta yell back. Pretty soon I say the hell with this and turn the TV up a bit. He's still yellin' at me, and I'm hollerin' back to shut the goddamn tap off and listen. The phone rings. It's the front desk, telling me our party is too loud. I'm tryin' to tell the asshole there is no party, and Seaweed starts yellin' again, wanting to know who's on the fuckin' phone. Next thing I know there's a rap on the door.

"By this time I'm in bed, so I get up, look through the peephole — it's the night manager — and open the door. I'm bare-ass naked, and he say's there have been complaints about our party. I said, 'there isn't any goddamn party,' and slam the door. Just as I get back into bed, Seaweed starts hollerin', asking who was it, and I'm yakkin' back and there's a knock on the door again. Same guy, but this time I grab my towel out of the bathroom and put it on. He starts up again about the party, so I invited him in. I said, 'Take a look. You see any fuckin' party?' We edge out into the hall, having this mild argument about keeping the noise down.

"Next thing I hear is Seaweed yellin', 'Who the hell is at the door?' and then I hear this scuffling on the stairs. About six cops come barrelling down the hallway, gonna break up this orgy, and in the meantime Seaweed has gotten out of the tub, into a towel, and comes out'ta the room. Me and the night manager jump aside, and two cops steamroll ol' Seaweed to the floor. But he's soaking wet and the first cop skidded off him like a greased pig, the second cop can't get the cuffs on him 'cause he's all soaped up or using bath gel or something. It was a fuckin' riot.

"The cop told the judge Seaweed was like a wiry peach-pit, couldn't find a place to grab onto him." Edestrand was wiping his eyes by this time. "We got off, but the best part was the cop who skidded into the wall sued Seaweed for $150,000, claiming that 'ever since the incident he could no longer perform his manly duties at home.' I think he settled for $1,500," Edestrand concluded, brushing back tears of laughter.

And that blustery afternoon as we went our separate ways through the HoJo parking lot, avoiding potholes, I wondered briefly about how hockey draws people together in strange ways.

It's nice to know, I thought, that after all the pain and suffering, the marks and scars from the wars of hockey, physical and mental, there's always a staircase to fall down, an all-night pizza house to discover, and people like Seaweed Pettie to make a player's day.

90-SECOND ALL-STARS

G — **Bernie Parent** *". . . he could beat you single-handed."*

D — **Bobby Orr** *". . . controlled the puck . . . and the game."*

D — **Larry Robinson** *". . . simply a great hockey talent."*

C — **Darryl Sittler** *". . . unbelievable drive. He kept coming at you, in either end of the ice."*

RW — **Mickey Redmond** *". . . all he'd need is one of those great shots. It would be over."*

LW — **Clark Gillies** *". . . under pressure, point A to point B, he'd get the job done."*

Tony McKegney

You Have the Right to Remain Silent

THE FIRST TIME I LAID EYES on Tony McKegney was in Kingston. He was playing for the Major A Junior Canadiens in that eastern Ontario city, and I was the newly appointed PR director for the Ontario Major Junior Hockey League on a familiarization visit to Oshawa, Peterborough, and Kingston. The OMJHL. Back before fax machines I had a Telex call sign that read OMJHLPR. It always struck me the initials looked like the name of a Czech hockey player looking to buy a vowel.

Nobody told me Tony was black. Not that anyone should have, but I remember thinking how unusual it was that the topic had never come up. Did it speak well for the OMJHL? Were we, as Canadians, in a sport and a country really and truly colour blind? Had the matter of race taken a hike here in the upper strata of amateur hockey? I don't think so. It was 1977 in Ontario. Not exactly 1955 in Selma, Alabama, but not the most liberal of times, either.

Kingston was a team of underachievers that year, but they had a great nucleus, and McKegney was one of the stars. Mike Gillis, Behn Wilson, Mike Simurda, and Tony went in the first two rounds of the 1978 draft. Ken "the Rat" Linseman was selected in the first round, too, but he had jumped the Kingston ship a year before and was being reclaimed from the outcast WHA.

Tony McKegney broke in with the Sabres: ". . . it takes some creativity and intelligence to score . . . in the NHL. I was able to do that, to prove myself."

As a junior, McKegney was one of the prototype wingers of the era. Big: 6′1″ and 192 pounds. He possessed speed and a great attitude. He thrived in the heavy going, and in his last season with the juniors began a pattern of point totals that would remain with him throughout his NHL career. In that final year he scored 43 goals, added 49 assists, and took only 19 minutes in penalties. Similarly, his goals and assists would never be far apart in the NHL. In a career spanning 13 seasons and eight teams, one of them twice, five times he had more goals than assists, once he was tied, and twice his goals were within three of his assists.

But back to his junior days for the moment. His close-out year with Kingston he was named to the Team Canada juniors for the World Championship. There in Montreal, chance would see him lined up with a kid centre from the Sault Ste. Marie Greyhounds named Gretzky. Tony's stock increased.

In the 1978 NHL draft he was picked 32nd, Buffalo's second selection behind defenceman Larry Playfair. McKegney spent 24 games in Hershey before the Sabres called him up to the parent club. Over 52 games he scored only eight times, but he had arrived. In the next four seasons he would go as high as 36 and never be below 23.

"Scotty Bowman was a great coach," he said with conviction. "But you could never get close to him as a friend. Maybe that's where I made a mistake, believing you could be a pal with any coach. The best you can hope for in this game is to be able to understand what the hell it is they want from you. Some coaches don't articulate the plan very well, you know," he added, twisting a napkin, making the remark more as a comment than a criticism.

Tony McKegney is qualified to have a valid opinion about coaches in the NHL. He had more than his share, and though it has never been easy, hockey has been good. Looking around me, it showed.

We are in Amherst, New York, sitting at the dining-room table of a beautiful two-storey brick-and-glass house, with enough tall fir trees in the front and backyards to keep a couple of lumberjacks busy for a week. On this spring day in 1993, the NHL is over for Tony McKegney. After 13 years there will be only one more trip to training camp. Tampa Bay Lightning have offered him a contract as a free agent. He will be home before their training camp ends.

In 1978, coming out of junior, his resumé for the NHL was impeccable. The statistics were the kind GMs squabble over. His demeanour was a coach's dream, and he was above all a team player, ready to shoulder any responsibility. So why did he get to wear eight NHL sweaters?

The man he admired as a coach, Scotty Bowman, packaged him off to Quebec in 1983. A season and a half later he was on his way to Minnesota for another two seasons, then he was pushed along to the New York Rangers for 64 games. He kept scoring in New York, totalling 29 goals, but in 1987 it was on to St. Louis. A full 80 games and career highs in goals (40), assists (38), and points (78) were followed by another complete season with the Blues. But it wasn't enough to circle the trade wagons and he moved off to Detroit for a quick stint, a hotel for an address, before returning to Quebec, finally finishing with the Blackhawks.

But team results were more important to him than personal marks. He took pride in recalling for me the days of the 79–80 Sabres, the best team he ever played on.

"Gil Perreault finished fourth in the scoring, Bob Sauve and Don Edwards won the Vezina Trophy, we won the division, finished second overall in the NHL behind Philadelphia. Hell, the Flyers went 35 games without a loss that year.

"But the Islanders won their first Stanley Cup," he said resignedly. There is always something in hockey to stabilize euphoria. The thought took him back to another disappointment in that final year of junior.

The Canadian team stayed at La Cité and I remember checking in, wading through the couches and potted plants of the spacious foyer, seeing Rob Ramage and his defence partner from the London Knights, Brad Marsh, practising their lobby-watching act. They weren't alone, because the best of the country's juniors were assembled for this international series. Stan Smyl, Wayne Babych, Ryan Walter, Richard David, Willy Huber, Bobby Smith, Pat Riggin, Craig Hartsburg, Gaston Gingras, McKegney, and Gretzky. On the other side, the names that come to mind were Sweden's Pelle Lindberg, Anton Stasny with the Czechs, and a Soviet defenceman named Fetisov.

"The first time we played the Russians, it was a lesson, believe me," he said from across the table. "For the first ten minutes they were all over us, then they suddenly backed off. We beat them 7–3, I got a hat trick, but there was a sneaking suspicion they hadn't shown us everything. In the final they beat us by one goal. It was a totally different game."

I asked about playing with the Great One, the skinny, geeky-looking kid named Gretzky.

"Easiest hockey I ever played. Just get in the open and — bang! — the puck was on the tape," he said, enthused for a moment. "You know he wasn't even supposed to be there? Bill Derlago from the Brandon Wheat Kings was the centre they named to the team, but he broke his leg and Wayne was brought in as a replacement. How does that grab you!" We agreed everyone had to start somewhere, even Gretzky. Then we got into Tony's start in the NHL.

"Imlach sent me to Hershey. I wasn't unhappy because Buffalo was a pretty good team at the time, and it would have been a stretch to make it, even though I gave it my best shot. See, some of the guys I played with went to clubs in last place. There was room for them. After 24 games the Sabres called me up.

"Billy Inglis was the coach," he said, looking up at the chandelier for guidance. "Did the guys tell you about the rape case?" he asked, a smile starting to crease his face, as if I was in on the story. To me even the word "rape" is no cause to smile so I just gave it my best stern look and shook my head.

"I had just joined the team. It was the Christmas break and I had invited my girlfriend from Kingston down for the holidays. I was 20, she was 17. After a practice at the Aud, I'm about half undressed, and these two big bastards in coats come in asking, 'Which one is McKegney?' like it was a tough pick." Unfazed, I remained concerned, stern, and troubled.

"The whole room went silent when they walked over to me. These guys weren't bullshittin'. Both of them took out leather folders with ID and big police badges and stuck them in front of my face. 'You Tony McKegney? Do you live at . . .' whatever the address was, and I said 'Yes.' 'Do you have a girl named —— in your apartment?' I said yes again and they started, 'You are under arrest, you have the right to remain silent, you have the right —.'

"Richard Martin started to protest and the cop who wasn't reading me my rights glared at him and said, 'Keep the hell out of it, pal, or you'll be goin' with him.' Meanwhile I'm in shock, asking 'for what, for what, what the hell am I in trouble for?' The big one right in front of me puts the card away and says, 'Get dressed. No shower, just get dressed. You're goin' downtown.'

"By this time Inglis is in on it, demanding to know who the hell they are, who the hell let them in, and what the hell do they think they're doing. He's yelling at the trainer to call up to the office, 'and get Swados down here.'

"You know Swados?" Tony asks, and I nod solemnly, remembering the Sabre's member of the Board of Directors, team counsel, and a partner in the heavy-duty, well-placed law firm of Cohen, Swados, Wright, Hanifin, and Bradford. As if that wasn't enough, Swados was also a politically correct bigwig on the local scene.

"Everybody is asking the same question as me, what did I do, and the cop says, 'You ain't in Canada no more. Down here relations with any female under 18 is statutory rape.' *Rape.* Honest, Ross, I know we've all heard the expression many times but I almost shit myself then and there. Now the room is in an uproar, guys are cursing, the ones coming out of the shower are being filled in by the others and everybody is looking at me like I'm goin' to the chair.

"Inglis comes roaring back just as the cops are puttin' the cuffs on me. Now I'm really ready to piss my pants as well, and Inglis is telling me they got a hold of Bob Swados. He's got a guy on it already, not to worry, I have the support of the organization, we'll get you out, shit like that. He asks me what can he do for me right now. I say call my dad, call —— and tell her. Martin says he'll look after my car in the parking lot. Somebody said they'll deport my ass back to Canada, if I ever get out. Another asks when visiting hours are. One of the boys even asked if the charges were serious enough to get a last supper. Yeah, there were some assholes in the room, as usual. Meanwhile, I'm ready to burst into tears. The two cops throw my coat over my shoulders, grab me by the arms and hustle me out of the dressing room and out the back door of the Auditorium to the parking lot, and straight for a marked police car. When we get to the cruiser they take off the cuffs and say "Welcome to Buffalo,' laughing their asses off as they drive away."

After we got through chuckling I asked him if he ever found out who the instigators were.

"Naw, but I have my suspicions. It was Rick Martin and probably René Robert." What made him think those two would be the culprits?

"When I had a chance to go over the events, they were the most concerned, the most shocked in the dressing room. When they were taking me away, Ricky offered to water my plants, whatever the hell that was supposed to mean." We had another good laugh.

After the cloud-nine feeling of a rookie year, the game becomes what it really is, a business, a job of goals and points, wins and losses, you-against-them all season, and in competition with management at contract time.

McKegney began to experience the pitfalls of a good player who can always help a team. He seemed interchangeable and played more than adequately wherever he was sent, usually moving along having gained something, picking up a trick or two. In Quebec he did the job assigned to him, confessing that he liked the fiery, arbitrary Michel Bergeron. "He was a motivator, a good one, and treated the players fairly."

He scored well in New York, claiming Roger Neilson was "the best coach I ever had," but 29 goals in 64 games for the Rangers wasn't enough to keep him around. He moved on to St. Louis and scored 40 in 80 games, posting 78 total points, his best in the NHL. The following season he slipped to 25 goals and skidded into Detroit, back to Quebec, and finally to nine brief appearances at the end of the 1991 season with the Blackhawks. It was the last minute of play for McKegney. There was a 24-game season in Italy the next year, which brought us to the dining-room table in the spacious house in Amherst. There was still the possibility of the Tampa Bay job at the time, and when I left that day, he followed me out of the driveway on his way to a fitness club, and another of the never-ending workouts that make up an aging athlete's life.

A year later, we met at Sabreland, the rink where the Sabres alumni, the 1990s euphemism for "old farts," hold their weekly skate and do-or-die pickup game.

The alumni weren't well represented on this afternoon, and neither were the pickups. Only three ex-Sabres suited up: Freddy Stanfield, Wilf Paiement, and McKegney. Four if you count Porky Palmer, the Sabre's equipment man, in goal. He's been with Buffalo pro hockey longer than Clifford Olsen will spend in jail.

The nets were moved inward to the blue lines, making play behind the net something Wayne Gretzky could only dream of, to accommodate the four-aside teams the luxury of a calorie-saving mini neutral zone. Paiement and Stanfield, plus a local car dealer as a rover and a masked man disguised as a goaltender, were on one side. On side B you had McKegney with the professionally attired Palmer in net, plus three teammates who served the same purpose as orange practice pylons. You *do* have to go around them. Tony, the most recent retiree, turned it on in spurts, the bowed legs churning into high gear whenever necessary. Stanfield, older and perhaps a tad more hockey-wise, also showed flashes of speed he'll probably have into the next century. Paiement, big, like a bus shelter on skates, intimidated the pickups as the need arose, much as he did in the NHL.

The pros did what pros do to amateurs. They breezed in, made a move. Goal. Next time they wheeled in, no move, just the threat of one. Goal. They shot one off the wrong foot. Goal. They looked off, faking a pass. Instead it zipped through the goalie's feet. Paiement fired a slapshot from a long way out. It thudded into the pads like a billiard ball with top spin and rolled forward anyway. Goal. Stanfield coasted in like a seagull riding an updraft, stuffed it into the top of the net on the short side. The goalie looked behind in wonder, because he had only given him a puck width at best. McKegney swooped in, moved left, parallel to the goalmouth and held, held, held while the netminder crawled along like a pull toy, before dropping it over him, end-over-end like a field goal. The only spontaneous laugh from all nine players came when one of the pickups, his back to the net, was feathered a beautiful between-the-skates pass, right on the stick blade, and was so startled he hooked a backhand into the corner rafters.

"Straighten out that backhand, Boomer, and you're goin' places," Stanfield heckled Mike the auto-person after the game as they peeled off their soggy uniforms.

"It's hard going all-out for 60 minutes," said another of the civilians.

"We only have the ice for 50," McKegney said, snorting.

"What the fuck do you call this — coasting?" puffed the red-faced, sweating first speaker, a headlock on one foot, leg contorted sideways and upward, trying mightily to tug off a skate.

"How come you wear two jocks?" Porky Palmer asked his counterpart.

"Because I care," answered the other.

That's what it's all about, why the "boys" keep coming out, playing in scruffy arenas in uniforms made up from teams and places long gone. But the next day it's back to the business of making your way in the real world, and McKegney is no exception. He has his hands full with a bustling new venture.

As I drive into the parking lot of the Caddyshack Golf Dome at 9:00 a.m. sharp, I wondered if the workers didn't have the best-looking cars I'd ever seen on a construction site. It was Friday and the April air was still cold surrounding the huge white bubble, which is fronted by a long one-storey building. Entering, I found one of the largest pro shops I've ever seen. A little farther up the hallway a big bar and restaurant spread out to the right. Through the revolving doors at the top of the hall I stepped into what must be an inspiring sight for the first-time visitor.

An eight-storey-high soft roof allows bright daylight to illuminate the interior, occasionally turning skied balls back to the green-carpeted floor below. Deep-turfed mats, bag stands at the ready, circle an arc of 27 golf stations on ground level, with the same number a flight of stairs overhead. A hundred yards away the draped wall stifles golf balls hit into it by the early crowd, the ones that own the nice cars outside. The familiar sound of clubs cutting the air and crack or ping of golf balls being struck is pleasant, the sharpness eaten up by the yawning void between ceiling and floor.

A line of golfers included women in skirts, women in slacks, even one in a nurse's uniform and white nylons. The dress code for men ranged from track suits, white shirts, with ties hanging down, to a guy in safety boots and coveralls who had doffed his hard hat for the occasion. There was a dad with a video camera shooting a 12-year-old with a swing that would make Tom Kite envious. An old gentleman with a jerky, short, flat swing, got the same results as an overly practised hacker with an expensive bag and clubs he didn't deserve. A fat man did everything wrong: arms bent, elbows flying, set up like a guy walking through hot coals. He hit one arrow-straight sweet five iron after another, repeatedly dimpling the drapery in the same area with aggravating accuracy. The place was humming with golfers and it wasn't even 10:00 a.m.

"This is actually slow," Tony said as we sipped coffee in the office. "Wait until later today. Top and bottom, full tilt," he said, indicating the two tiers outside the window. Later we took a tour, and he pointed out some of the things I had missed. Like a white sand trap, netting draped against a side wall. A fake landscaper was putting the finishing touches on the fake plants bordering a mini-putt course, just right of the revolving doors. Outside we looked down the real grass fairway and real sandtraps of the outdoor driving range being readied for the warmer weather.

Before a scheduled meeting with some important investors from Boston, people intrigued by the development ideas of Tony and his partners, I asked some questions to finish off the interview. How does he look at his career, from this distance, and to what does he attribute his many moves?

"First off, I think it takes some creativity and intelligence to score 40 goals — or for that matter over 300 — in the NHL. I was able to do that, to prove myself. Sometimes it's hard to live up to other people's standards. I was picked in the second round in one of the best draft years the NHL ever saw. I was expected to do well, and I think I did. As for the travel, the moves, I'm not kidding myself. It's harder on the wives than the players. Sue stuck it out, just like I did. Another wife may have crumbled." He studied his coffee cup seriously for a moment. "On the hockey side, let's just say I was never an ass-kisser, but I was talented, and leave it at that," he said as we walked out to the parking lot. An anxious golfer slammed on his brakes as I took the key out of my pocket, content to wait for such a choice spot.

"I think back to Gretzky quite often. The guy is a tireless worker, with a will to prove people who knock him that they are wrong. He has to face shadows every day, every game. He's an incredible competitor. I like to think I was a good one, too."

A pair of acquaintances and regular golf customers walked up. After exchanging greetings and introductions, one of them bemoaned the fact he had to take his young son to a hockey tryout for assignment to next year's team. Tony agreed that it's a dumb practice, since he was taking one of his boys, too. We shook our heads at the mysteries of minor hockey.

"Kids at that age can sprout four inches between now and October," the man said.

"Yeah, and they can get taller, too," the other answered deadpan.

The man in the waiting car sits stolidly behind the wheel as we say our goodbyes, and McKegney confides that whatever it was he was trying to remember to mention has escaped him again.

"Touch of Alzheimer's," he says, nodding in agreement with himself.

"Shackie calls it All-Timers," I corrected, and we said our wishes for good golfing. Backing out, Tony suddenly appeared at my side window. I stopped again, and the window dropped down.

"Remember the cop that arrested me on the "rape" charge? I see him every once in a while."

"No kidding," I replied.

"He comes in here to hit golf balls, and we get a real kick out of the improbable odds of that happening."

The only guy not laughing is the man in the other car. He finally loses it, leaning on his horn.

90-SECOND ALL-STARS

G — **Grant Fuhr** *". . . big in big games, used to a lot of shots."*

D — **Ray Bourque**

D — **Chris Chelios** *". . . both of these guys combine offence and defence."*

C — **Wayne Gretzky** *". . . he can play it both ways."*

RW — **Mark Messier** *". . . another gifted scorer, and not bad defensively either."*

LW — **Mike Bossy** *". . . a pure scorer."*

Dennis Hull

Follow the Rented Hair

LADIES AND GENTLEMEN! *Our featured speaker is a 14-year veteran of the National Hockey League, playing in over 1,000 games and bringing a wealth of stories to our head table tonight.*

He possessed a shot that rivalled his brother Bobby's, and his inclusion in the select group of pros who have scored over 300 goals attests to those skills.

Following his retirement in 1979, he returned to school and received his degree from Brock University in St. Catharines, the scene of his successful junior hockey career. After graduation he took up a position at the prestigious Ridley College as a history teacher and hockey coach. Four years later he became the athletic director at the Illinois Institute of Technology in Chicago, moving up to director of development. In addition he hosts a popular hockey-talk show on radio in the Windy City.

His hockey career brought considerable recognition, including six All-Star selections, and his play with Team Canada '72 in the great summit series with the Russians. Today, he splits his time between business interests in Chicago and his Chrysler dealership in Welland, Ontario. Ladies and gentlemen, would you welcome one of the most sought-after speakers on the banquet circuit: DENNIS HULL.

Dennis Hull (10) splits Rangers Ed Ciacomin in goal and Gordie Howe: "get out there and watch Gordie Howe" . . . "I can see him fine from here."

That's been Dennis Hull's introduction for a lot of years and while it capsulizes a story, it's not the whole story.

I've always said there's nothing a player can do about his "black and white," meaning those final statistics that make up the one-liner in the *NHL Guide*. Every player must live with it when his career is over. Changes, cosmetic or otherwise, are too late and padding the numbers is only wishful thinking. But between what the figures say and what they mean is a world of difference.

Take Dennis Hull. The brother of Bobby.

I know lots of brothers who have played in the NHL. The Espositos, Tony and Phil. The Richards, Rocket and Pocket. The Mahovlichs, Frank and Peter. The Dillons, Wayne and Gary. The Drydens and the Gardners, a Ken, a Paul, and two Daves. Then there's the Busniaks! Ron and Mike are from Thunder Bay, so I usually don't go around telling everybody that bit of hockey trivia. Besides, I didn't say they were all superstars. But Dennis Hull is unique. I have a bonus in working with Dennis Hull. It's in the laughs.

There isn't a subject, an incident, a news item, or a conversation that doesn't trigger a memorable reflection, a humorous comment, or a gut-busting response. Fortunately, I've only had to withstand this avalanche of funny retorts and giggling comebacks for 15 years. The family and friends of Dennis Hull, the fellow hockey players and lifelong associates, have absorbed a lot more than their share of the unique sense of humour he brings to the table. And table, as in "head table," where the after-dinner speakers perch, is as good a reference point as any, for it's in this arena, the place where a podium is the only protective equipment allowed, that Dennis Hull is a Hall of Famer. Let's start with a typical opening.

"Thank you. First, I'd like to apologize for my appearance tonight. Since my brother Bobby and I no longer play in the NHL and don't make those big dollars, we only have the one set of hair. *(pause for mild laughter)* Bobby has it tonight. *(laughter rising)* He has it for weekends and weddings, and I usually have it for banquets. Since there's no one here in a white dress, this must be a banquet. *(laughter level rises again)* Come to think of it, there wasn't anybody in a white dress at any of Bobby's weddings either. *(room erupts)*

So it goes for about 30 minutes, a tour through fables and insight, myth and partial facts about life in hockey, all leading to one of the two closers he is most comfortable with. The one I enjoy the most is this memorable story.

"Ask any player who has ever played in the NHL, and he can relate every detail about his first game. Who they were playing, where, the line-up on both sides, everything. My first game was against the Detroit Red Wings at the old Olympia. It was only the second NHL game I had ever seen, it was the first time I got in for free, and it was the best seat I ever had. I mean, there I was on the bench, on the wrong side of the player's door, and out on the ice are Normie Ullman, Alex Delvecchio, Gordie Howe. Gordie's picture was still up on my bedroom wall in Pointe Anne. No kidding! I'm sittin' there with my arm like this, you know, hand over the boards. If I want, when they line up for a face-off at the blue line, I can touch them." He always lays his forearm across the lectern and flicks his hand gently.

"In the third period I get this persistent tapping on my back. I brush it away a couple of times, then I realize it's my coach, Billy Reay. 'Whadda *you* want?' I ask." Hull takes on a gruff voice, something never done by a rookie to a head coach, and the audience giggles. "Reay says, 'Get out there and watch number 9.' I say, 'Which one, ours or theirs?'" Again the laughter begins to swell as two of the three most famous number 9's in Canada are bandied about. "'Not ours,' Ray says, 'get out there and watch Gordie Howe.' I say, 'I can see him fine from here,' and Reay says, 'Just get out there.' So I hop over the boards and on the way to the corner I decide I'm gonna score the fastest goal ever by a rookie. My centreman is Red Hay, the other winger is Eric Nesterenko, and I figure if Hay gets it to Eric, I'm up the centre and in on goal. It'll either be in the top corner of the net, or in some lady's bra in the second balcony.

"But I find myself shoulder to shoulder with Gordie Howe, and he's winkin' and blinkin' like a toad eatin' fireflies," Hull states, screwing up his face in a series of twitches and grimaces. "Sure enough, when the puck drops Hay wins the draw, gets the puck to Nesterenko, and I'm busting up centre just like it was planned. Suddenly my skates are off the ice, and there's Mr. Howe holding me up by the back of the pants sayin', 'Where do you think yer goin', sonny?' *(pause for laughter)* And I say, 'Wherever you are, sir.'"

The appreciative audience response has been the same for years, yet back in 1979 the applause was a surprise. I didn't know there was this talent lying under the surface, a hockey player who could take serious situations, turn them into humour, and deliver them like a stand-up philosopher, nor was I given any indication the first time we met. He joined us with the ProStars in St. Catharines, through Dale Tallon who tipped me to the availability of another active NHLer living where we were playing a game. Dennis Hull? Goddamn right, I remember saying when the name came up and there he was, driving a vintage car up to the ball park. He hung around long enough to play some outfield, have a couple of beers, and then he was gone. Not exactly the funniest guy I'd ever met. But it would all come together.

Several years later, 1979, we crossed paths again with the Old Stars. He had just retired from the NHL. And in those days he and his family had a small farm outside of St. Catharines. He was intending to return to school to get his degree, a piece of paper he needed to do some of the things that were uppermost on his priority list as an ex-hockey player. Namely to find work.

As I have mentioned earlier, the Old Stars were much like an organization tree, with the principals on the depth chart sprouting fingers and tentacles, branching and splitting in all directions. Shack opened the door to Nevin, Nevin to Pappin, Pappin to Hull, Hull to Pit Martin, Martin to Tom Williams. It sounded much like a play-by-play of an actual game, and indeed the grapevine and old-boys network has always been the easiest route to go, especially when you're selling something good.

Back then, Dennis drove from St. Catharines to our practices in Rexdale, not often, but frequently enough to show his interest, and played in our inaugural game in Thunder Bay. Did I know he was going to become the best sports speaker in Canada? Did I realize he would rank in the top five sports speakers in North America? Of course not. My interest at the time was in his hockey skills, and to be honest, my first impression was of a wisecracker, a gifted one who had the attention of the other players. It always reminded me of the old adage that a comedian was very, very good if he could make the band laugh. Believe me, with the likes of Ed Shack, Jim McKenny, Pat Stapleton, and Bill White, you had to do something bizarre to get their attention.

But as our time with the Old Stars progressed, it became abundantly evident that his forte was up at the mike. The speaking odyssey began, modestly at first.

Although he was already known to be an entertainer, I recall booking his first "pro" engagement in this country in front of a group of electrical engineers at their whoop-de-doo in Hamilton. Since we were trying to find a starting point, we both spoke that night under the premise I could make notes on material used and the reaction to it. I opened, Dennis followed.

The mood in the room was the equivalent of a herd of disgruntled in-laws. In other words, this group wasn't your usual "Evening at the Improv." They weren't up on sports, current events, or even the wattage of your basic, run-of-the-mill boom-box. At the time, after 15 years of speaking at everything from weddings to IBM coffee breaks to Moose Lodge "Call-yer-Mate" baked-bean cookoffs, I had to admit they had me unsettled. We have a saying in the after-dinner business: If they're listening, but squinting, it's over.

I would have slipped quietly back to my seat, except for a table of six on the far right who seemed to be the only ones buying the lines that night and having a good time. Plunging ahead, part of my job was to introduce Dennis, which I did, and as we exchanged places I muttered "go to your right" and wished him the best.

After the first few minutes of squinting and desultory laughter, Dennis told a little blurb he'd been saving for just such an occasion.

"Everybody wonders about my brother Bobby, how he's doing, and I can tell you he's doin' real good. Has a nice new little business. It's a combination taxidermist and veterinary shop," he said deadpan through the first groans of the night. Then, chuckling, shaking his head in mock honesty, he held up his hand for patience. "Yeah. He has these little cards made up. They say, 'Either way you get your dog back.'"

There was a moment of silence then the laughter started and grew until the whole room was cackling and hands banged on tables, and a strange thing happened. Dennis stood there, looking wryly back at the audience. As the crowd's laughter began to subside, Dennis appeared unable to hold his composure any longer and let go with a burst of laughter of his own. A Dennis Hull laugh shows a lot of teeth, and is infectious, to say the least. Without another word being said, he and the audience went through this routine two more times in succession, much like a private group in a bar who have just heard a good one. As one side began to gain control, the other side busted up once more. It broke the ice and saved the night. The table of six to the right who were with us from the start? The band, "Jeffrey and the Juniors," who knocked 'em dead after we finished.

While looking through my notes from dinners past I came across my sheet for that particular evening and there on the upper right corner I had jotted in bold letters, "LEAVE THE LAUGHING IN," and it's been part of the delivery for years, timed and perfected, and now it has a trailer. Somewhere in the chase of laughing, Dennis sneaks in, "That's the first time I've heard that," then he and the audience are off on another fit of table-thumping and guffaws.

If anything, that story, and the fact he can laugh at his own joke, indicates a guy who enjoys speaking — and the audience knows it. Were a lesser speaker to try such a ploy the result would be something contrived, if not downright corny. For the most part he is a storyteller, rather than a one-liner or a quipster. He plays masterfully against the backdrop of being cast as a "poor soul," the guy who gets no respect, the kid picked last when choosing up sides. But every once in a while the "poor soul" gets a good one off at his tormentors. As in the story about the basketball broadcaster.

"You know, living in Chicago and being a hockey player means you are playing the same time as the NBA, the Bulls, and there was a time when they weren't very good. They have an ex-Bull, John "Red" Kerr, a 6'10" Irishman, who does colour for the broadcast. All the time I lived there I had to listen to him run down hockey players. You know, bragging how basketball players were the smartest athletes, then came football players, baseball players, bowlers, jockeys, wrestlers, and on down the list to hockey players, who he said were the dumbest. Well, every year they have a big sports affair in Chicago, organized and emceed by Red Kerr. One year he ran out of speaker candidates and was forced to ask me. At the luncheon, he's popping off about the superior athletes in the NBA then introduces me. As usual I said the wrong thing when I got up. I offered my thanks for having me there, and further, added that I agreed with him, there really was a place in the world for the NBA. Otherwise we'd be up to our asses in seven-foot janitors."

Audiences in Canada usually give a collective "touché."

One time his penchant for outrageous self-deprecating humour backfired, big-time, catching an innocent man in a crossfire. It happened at a celebrity dinner in Thunder Bay.

In the Canadian sports speaking field, the Thunder Bay dinner is the equivalent of playing the Palladium, or Broadway, or the seventh game of the Stanley Cup final. In the quality of speakers it's the cutting edge, having all of the best in the business before the other major dinners catch on. It traces its roots back to the first dinner in 1955, and if it isn't the longest running consecutive event on the sports circuit, I would be surprised. Sponsored from inception by the combined branches of the Royal Canadian Legion, it's a clockwork example of minute-by-minute scheduling for cocktails, dinner, awards, four prominent sports figures as guest speakers, and an emcee. In terms of organization, execution, and community fund-raising it's a dinner I hold up to other events as the prototype, the ultimate success story, evolved and fine-tuned into the state-of-the-art model all the rest should emulate.

Dennis, unavailable for many years when dates didn't coincide, finally appeared at the 1988 event along with American League umpire Marty Springstad, boxer Jake LaMotta (making his second appearance, the first being in 1967), and ex-Miami Dolphins fullback Larry Csonka. The emcee was a veteran of many years, Lloyd Gilbart, a local Mercury dealer, who like most things connected with the Thunder Bay dinner was a more-than-capable fixture. He is one of the best master of ceremonies in the business. Gilbart is never one to be satisfied with introductions sent out in publicity packages for the hordes of superstars he has made welcome over the years. Instead, he does his own research, writes his own material, and delivers it with humour, amity, feeling, a heartfelt sense of responsibility, and a lot of class. It is another facet of the dinner most of the illustrious guests appreciate.

Dennis was no exception, but he slipped up just the same. You see, fate had put Hull's opening remark in the wrong place at the wrong time.

The tuxedoed Gilbart wears a toupe. Not a startling thing in this day and age. So does the craggy, hulking, menacing Csonka, and although not present there was the inference to Bobby Hull, the subject matter of Dennis Hull's patented opening and the man seen on TV across the country who had "lost his hair in front of the whole world."

Doing his usual superlative job, Gilbart got up after Csonka had completed his talk, thanked him in the proper manner, adding a couple of barbs of his own to the delight of the hometown crowd. He then introduced Dennis with a tribute to his hockey ability, and how the younger brother had faced adversity struggling to shine in the brilliance of his more famous brother. Dennis rose to his feet, looked forlornly at the crowd of 600, and said, "I guess it's my lot in life to follow an asshole in rented hair!" The explosion of laughter was one of the loudest in dinner history, but everybody wasn't laughing at the same thing. There was Lloyd Gilbart looking stricken on Hull's one side, Csonka glowering dangerously on the other. Dennis was left on his own, attempting to placate both gentlemen while trying in vain to explain over the din of laughter that he had really meant his brother Bobby.

That kind of faux pas is exactly the grist for Dennis Hull's mill, because it's the kind of spur-of-the-moment remark that adds to the growing legend, perpetuating an image of a bumbling, ramshackle kind of speaker who plods on in spite of self-inflicted injury. Nothing could be further from the truth. He is quick-witted, an opportunist when it comes to injecting a humorous line, and creative as well, registering with the crowd almost from the moment he steps up to the microphone.

As a result, Dennis escapes backlash simply by coming off as acceptable, much like Eddie Shack, who often says things at dinners that most of us, uttering the same remark, would be stoned for.

Case in point. Hull was speaking at the Harold Ballard Roast at the Royal York Canadian ballroom in Toronto. He was a head-table partner with Normie Kwong, the great "China Clipper" of the Calgary Stampeders and Canadian Football League Hall of Fame.

"I really want to thank the organizers for sitting me beside Normie Kwong, one of my childhood football heroes — he said he'd have my shirts back by Friday," Hull said, straight-faced. Last we heard, Kwong was still using the line himself.

Which is one of the pitfalls of public speaking. It's a bit disconcerting when you are up there and can see dinner guests, and sometimes even those at the head table, scribbling down the lines that get the best laughs. Invariably the quote appears in the scribbler's next speech, usually done badly, missing some of the key words or phrases, leaving the originator's work expendable. It's an unwritten law in the trade that you don't use other people's material. If you do, you at least give them the credit. Some guys don't go by the rules, unwritten or otherwise, nor do the "line rustlers" give credit. It has been my distinct displeasure to hear speakers blatantly usurp fellow-speakers' text on the very next night, prattling on without a clue as to where this line or two came from. The secret is to be up first, but rarely will a dinner chair lead off with his best. Which brings us back to a Dennis Hull closing story about the first game he ever played.

We were at a Southern Ontario dinner that will go unnamed so as to cause the least embarrassment to the organizers, or the perpetrators: fellow speakers we had both worked with many times. Before the evening was out we had counted, by signalling to each other with fingers held aloft, how many times the rule was being broken. The worst was when the speaker ahead of Dennis, a good friend and respected hockey player, got up and said to the audience, "My old pal Dennis is sitting on the dais. I remember his first hockey game in the NHL." He proceeded to do the rookie story from start — "He was on the ice goin' around touchin' everybody . . ." — to the "bein' dragged around the ice sayin' I'll go anywhere you want me to go" finish. Everything he said was bent and, needless to say, the anecdote lost so much in the translation it was burned for a while.

Being at the top in any business or sport doesn't mean it gets any easier. In fact the reverse is true. In that regard Dennis Hull has handled everything with a laid-back grace that would have looked good on a saint. Through the burden of playing in the shadow of one of the greatest players of all time, to the Blackhawks' growing reputation of being a "close-but-no-cigar" team with great potential but no tangible results, to the people who filched his original material.

Therefore, the opportunity to line up with Team Canada '72 has to be his crowning achievement. Even then he knew he was a replacement, that had his brother not been ineligible to play because of the jump to the World Hockey Association, he may well have been watching the series of the century on television with the rest of us.

"At first I turned down the chance to go to training camp when they called," he told me one sunny June morning as we drove along the Queen Elizabeth Way toward St. Catharines. "I was upset about the situation. I thought Bobby was one of the greatest players in the game, then and now, and here he was, left off the team because of politics and business that has nothing to do with being a Canadian hockey player. When I talked to Bobby, he encouraged me to go to the training camp, said it was the chance of a lifetime, that even if he couldn't join the team that I should."

As it turned out, Dennis was no shrinking violet on the Canadian team, scoring twice and assisting twice in the four games he played.

In fact the venerable Jacques Plante, feeling a kindred spirit with young Vladislav Tretiak, advised the Soviet goaltender on some of the Canadian shooters. "Keep your eye on number ten, Dennis Hull. He's the only one who can score on you from the red line."

Despite reaching traumatic lows, and the delirious highs that were the essence of the Canada-Russia series in 1972, Dennis emerged unscathed with a flood of new stories and anecdotes. In signature style he tells the audiences about Paul Henderson.

"I suppose the most important achievement in my career was being named to play for my country. Back in 1972 we played the Russians and in that series Paul Henderson became a true hockey hero. Not only did he score the winning goal in the eighth game with only 30 seconds or so remaining, but he scored the winning goal in all three games we won over there, and he became a Canadian hockey legend. He and I were ordinary players when we went over and became ordinary again when we got back, but for 27 days in September 1972 he was a folk hero — and rightfully so. But Paul Henderson believed he was placed on this earth to score those three goals, and after hockey became a born-again Christian, and has since become a minister in the church. . . .*(pause)* . . . Some mornings when I wake up with a hangover, I thank God I didn't score those three goals."

After the roller coaster of Team Canada, Dennis came back to reality and had his career year in the NHL. In the 72–73 season, Dennis scored 39 times, totalled 90 points, and was the second All-Star team selection at left wing. The Blackhawks finished atop the West and battled their way into the Stanley Cup finals against Montreal.

It would be the third time facing the Canadiens for Dennis Hull and the Blackhawks. In his rookie season, 64–65, the Habs beat the Hawks in seven, and seven games were needed in 70–71 to again crown Montreal over Chicago. In the Cup finals of 72–73 Dennis played in 16 games scored nine goals, and had a playoff-leading 15 assists for 24 total points. On the other side, Team Canada teammate Yvan Cournoyer was scoring 15 goals and 10 assists for 25 points. Everyone on press row knew the MVP of the playoffs was between the Roadrunner and Hull, but it would depend on what team came out victorious. Montreal prevailed, this time in six games, Cournoyer skating off with the Conn Smythe trophy as the MVP, and driving away in the luxury car that went with it.

When the exhibition season rolled around next fall, the Habs and Hawks squared off in an Ottawa exhibition match. During the warm-up Cournoyer beckoned Dennis over and said, "Denee, I want you to know, your car, she run real good."

Dennis always tells that story, ending with a groaning "oh noooo" mouth pulled down and a look that sits the fence between a grin and a facial plea for help.

But it's all sham, simply one in a long list of eye-watering stories delivered in restaurants, bars, waiting rooms, and cars whizzing down the highway between 100 km-h and the speedometer redline. It's only another good-humoured slur in an even longer list of indignities that are the lot of the guy who'd like everyone to know how tough it is out there.

Being Dennis Hull.

90-SECOND ALL-STARS

G — **Glenn Hall** *". . . like a cat, the quickest I ever saw."*

D — **Bobby Orr** *". . . he was literally unstoppable."*

D — **Serge Savard** *". . . the most underrated defenceman, second only to Orr."*

C — **Jean Beliveau** *". . . so many great centres, but he dominated the game, did more than the fans ever saw."*

RW — **Gordie Howe** *". . . the most feared player in the game."*

LW — **Bobby Hull** *". . . unquestionably the best player in our family. Even ahead of Maxine."*

Tim Horton

Strong-Arm Tactics

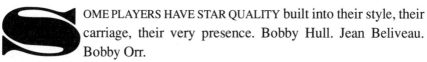OME PLAYERS HAVE STAR QUALITY built into their style, their carriage, their very presence. Bobby Hull. Jean Beliveau. Bobby Orr.

Others become legends through their accomplishments, and when the hockey playing is done, take on a mantle of graciousness and controlled modesty that sets them apart in the world of professional sport. Gordie Howe. Henri Richard. Alex Delvecchio. Dave Keon.

Some names ring out brassy, feisty, and ever combative. The brothers Esposito, Tony and Phil. Ted Lindsay. Stan Mikita.

Still others, also enshrined proudly in the Hall of Fame, fade into the background, blend into civilian life to emerge on only rare public occasions, almost curiosity pieces from the past, names that might as well be trivia questions for present fans. Who is Leo Boivin? What kind of a name is Teeder Kennedy? Who are Bert Olmstead, Fern Flaman, Harry Lumley? What about this Miles Gilbert Horton?

I once overheard two teenage fans discussing a picture hanging in the halls of Maple Leaf Gardens.

"Tim Horton? Did he play hockey?" one backward baseball hat said to the other.

"Yeah. Then he invented the doughnut shop," replied the one in a blue

Tim Horton, captured in the last game he ever played, February 20, 1974, by photographer Bob Shaver. George Armstrong, Toronto Maple Leaf captain, said of him: ". . . he used his strength as a deterrent, like a mechanic using a wrench. It was only a tool."

Potvin sweater. The first one laughed, while the second shook his head and giggled at the wonder of it all.

How typical, I thought, of a generation that can't even tie their sneakers. Then I cautioned myself about how things change, and how time marches on. But I was saddened by the irreverence, plus the fact that on this day Tim Horton was nothing more than a fast-food memory.

If that's the case among the newest generation of fans, rightfully caught up in their own era, it sure as hell isn't among those who played the game with, and against, Tim Horton. It isn't that way for even those players who followed years after his tragic passing in a 1974 auto accident. The respect and regard still linger.

Hang around the places where the hockey people gather and the stories about Tim Horton occasionally resemble tales of the fabled Paul Bunyan, or the steel-driving John Henry celebrated in song. Or Superman.

If any athlete resembled the mild-mannered Clark Kent, studious reporter on the *Daily Planet* who became the Man of Steel by simply ducking into a phone booth and shrugging off his suit, Timmy was the guy.

Why? There are no asterisks beside his statistics because he never led the league in any department. The NHL doesn't have a category for respect. Plus or minus.

Pit Martin, the nifty little centre who broke in with the Wings in 63–64, just in time to see Timmy and the boys of Toronto win their third straight Stanley Cup, is representative of two generations of NHLers in his remarks.

"He was a quiet, unassuming guy. Did his job," he said recently after I asked him what came to mind first about Horton, sounding like those TV bits they use when interviewing neighbours about the guy next door discovered to be an axe murderer. "He was a quiet man," is their stock answer. Then Martin smiled, that all-encompassing smile of one who has been there and survived. "But God, he could sure whack you!" That, too, in hockey parlance at least, is a stock answer.

Tim Horton was a fearfully strong man, *the* strongest, according to most first-hand observers. There were bigger players than Tim Horton. At 5'10" and 185 pounds, there were a hell of a lot of players bigger than him. Certainly, there were meaner players, ones who went around looking for trouble, and who made their way in the game by starting trouble. That type of player was in the league then, and they're still with us today, but they come and go, an endless string of forgettable butt ends and fists. Horton was far removed from that group.

Studying Tim Horton we are led back to the respect he was accorded, not as a result of intimidation or threat of being punched out (because by all reports Timmy never fought, couldn't fight). The word was don't mess with him. It was an attitude that was acceptable to most players but Timmy wasn't beyond explaining in his own way when some Young Turk would come along to try him out. Anyone who strayed over Horton's line could expect to get "whacked," as Pit Martin put it. Today the word has a more terminal meaning, but back when Timmy played, it referred to a treatment known to get your attention, and keep you on the straight and narrow.

Tim came out of high school in Sudbury, a product of the Falconbridge Mine Company kids' recreation program. It was a prudent move by the corporation. Top-notch recreation facilities kept the good miners and their families around. The hockey league, called the "Little NHL" was run by Bob Wilson, a gardener by trade at the Falconbridge headquarters. It was there many of the future prospects of the area got their start. Horton and teammate George "Chief" Armstrong were two of the kids who found their way through the system up to the Coppercliff Juniors. Armstrong, the future captain of the Toronto Maple Leafs and fellow Hall of Fame member, recalled the circumstances of the day.

"We were in the same high-school class, 16 years old," he said over a coffee in the restaurant at the Westbury Hotel down the street from Maple Leaf Gardens. "There was a tryout, a practice for the junior club. I said to Timmy, 'Let's go, we'll get some ice time.' That was the primary purpose, just to get some skating in with the big guys. Surprise! Timmy and I made it, with another kid, Red McCarthy, and signed C forms, which made us part of the Toronto chain.

"Next year, Wilson thought we were ready to recommend for St. Michael's, but he had a small reservation on Tim. He said Horton was OK, except he couldn't see very well, but added that if he couldn't play hockey, he was willing to recommend him for football, so sign him. See, even then Timmy's strength and force were beginning to show."

Coming out of junior, they were part-time with the Pittsburgh Hornets of the AHL and the Leafs, arriving to full-season status in the 52–53 season.

Horton and Armstrong spent over 20 years together as professionals, 19 of those seasons wearing the blue and white of Toronto. Armstrong would total 21 years, all with the same club, Horton 24, with Toronto, New York, Pittsburgh, and Buffalo. Armstrong captained the Leafs from 1957 to 1969, while Horton put together four All-Star selections and was twice runner-up in the Norris trophy ballotting as the NHL's top defenceman — the first time in 1964 behind Pierre Pilote's second of three straight, and again in 1969, trailing Bobby Orr's second trophy out of eight consecutive wins. But the two kids from the "Little NHL" won four Stanley Cups together and checked into the Hockey Hall of Fame, Armstrong in 1975 and Horton posthumously in 1977. Not bad for a couple of teenagers looking for some extra ice time back in the years following the Second World War.

"Timmy was one of the first guys to wear contacts in the league," Armstrong continued, as we watched the College and Yonge Street crowd file past our window booth, earrings on the guys, brush cuts on the girls, and army boots on both. "They were huge in those days and had to be dead centre or they lost focus. They were the cause of a hit that would have put a lesser man out for good," he commented, referring to the devastating check defence-man Bill Gadsby laid on Horton. "Caught him coming through the neutral zone. Tim's contact moved and he had to look down at the puck. Gadsby nailed him dead centre. Broke his jaw, his leg, and separated his shoulder, all in one shot. He was out for 35 games I think, yet he came back and played a couple of games in the playoffs that year, too."

And so the legend of Tim Horton was set in motion. The stories about his strength, his character, his unflappable performance in the toughest moments the game had to offer became the kind of example other players looked for in order to shore up their own waning reserves. He was the ultimate team man, the one who preached togetherness on the ice, the one who delivered a solid check of his own, and the player who led by example.

Dennis Hull once told me about his first on-ice encounter with Horton, making sure I was aware that it was much the same through their 20th and 100th meetings as well.

"He was so strong, just arming me out of the way like I was a rag doll. I always thought there were categories in the league, you know, guys who played in the NHL, players who were pretty good in the NHL, then you had your stars, next came your superstars, up to the people who had no equal. Timmy was up there at the top. I never thought anyone else in hockey was built like my brother Bobby until I ran into Timmy."

He wasn't alone in his evaluation.

The words strong and strength are used incessantly to describe Tim Horton. The fact that he used it in a restrained way might belie the claim he had no idea of how strong he was. According to old school chum and teammate George Armstrong, who should know, he was truly unaware of his strength, but sure knew how to use it.

"He had class, and was a gentle person," Armstrong reflected. "He was also mischievous. Geez, I'd like to pick a better word but that fits the situation exactly," he added, wincing at the term.

"Yeah, there was Doctor Horton, ready to shave a rookie at the most opportune time. When Timmy got you down, it was all over, they'd only struggle for a bit, then the rest of us would be able to wrap them up after Timmy had taken the starch out of them." The Chief snickered at the memory. "But he'd get them together, the rookies I mean, and tell them straight that they were expected to look after themselves, that frightened guys were gonna be run out of the league, that they had to pull their own weight if they wanted to stay.

"You have to remember teams were only carrying 18 players then. There were no floaters around, and if there were, the Leafs had a lot of hungry guys in a big farm system waiting to step in. Timmy always set the kids straight. He also had a sense of team, a concern for the order of things. For instance, we were on the train on our way to New York, and I was tired, headed straight to the rack. Horton and a few other guys went to the Pullman smoker to have a couple of beers when one of them suggested it was time to shave the captain, meaning me. Timmy said, 'Nobody touches the captain on this team,' planted himself in the doorway and kept Pete Stemkowski, Bobby Pulford, and Mike Walton penned up until they got tired and quit. You should have seen them. Lumps, rug burns, bruises, even Timmy's finger marks were showing up a few days later. The three of them never got out of the room.

"You'd think they'd know better," he said shaking his head, grinning from ear to ear. "Once in Boston we decided to have a team wrestling match in the hotel room — me and Todd Sloan, against Horton. He beat the livin' snot out of us. Sloanie stretched knee ligaments and had to tell Imlach it must have happened in the game the night before. Not a very bright move on our part, eh? *We* should have known better.

"Another time we were up north at his cottage, supposedly on a work detail to build a retaining wall, or somethin' like that. He's out in the sun all morning, tossing railway ties around like they were two-by-fours, while the rest of us were luggin' them with a man on either end. When we broke for lunch, Timmy went for a little sleep, but the noise of the guys going up to the beer fridge on the porch kept him awake. He came stormin' out of the cottage, put those arms around the refrigerator, walked it down the stairs, and dropped it on the front lawn. The fuckin' thing was full of beer, too. Then he went back to lie down. He'd scare the crap outta you. He didn't have a clue as to how strong he was."

But then Armstrong drifted away from the comical stories and zeroed in on Horton's character. "He was a leader, did it quietly, too. We only had a couple of team meetings a year back then, and when we were going good — the Imlach era I guess they call it — we had a common enemy: Imlach. Soon as we'd get together, some of the guys would start carping about Punch and his methods, the way he was at practice, behind the bench, you know, snarky. That's when Tim would say, 'We're not here to challenge Imlach, we're here to help ourselves. Shut up, Stemmer,' or whoever it happened to be, and they shut up, and paid attention. When Timmy talked, they listened." He bobbed his head for emphasis, as I wondered where else I'd heard this play on the tag line for E.F. Hutton's commercial.

"I don't know if he was the strongest guy in the league, but I never saw him outdone. He used his strength as a deterrant. Like a mechanic using a wrench, it was only a tool. He could do so many other things well, it was nothing but an extra bonus. Timmy was never aggressive, never went around hacking and chopping, looking for trouble. And very little came his way. Most guys would think twice before getting him pissed off, because it was too goddamn dangerous. He never had any enemies that I know of. He had all kinds of respect around the league. If he didn't respect another player, he never said so, not that I ever heard.

"On the other hand, you didn't have to be afraid of him," Armstrong said flippantly, as if to say it was obvious. "Of course, we were the only guys who knew that," he added, breaking into another fit of laughing.

Walking down Wood Street behind the Gardens that sunny, late fall afternoon, we spoke briefly about Armstrong's scouting job with the Leafs and the way the game has evolved. Some retired players have a penchant for living in the past, tending to their memories like a gardener prunes and primps a rose garden, cutting out the bad, sprucing up the good. Not the Chief. He is every bit as caustic, abrasive, and tongue-in-cheek sarcastic as I remember him.

"Some people say the game is going backwards, Chief," I said as we approached our cars.

"Some people are full of shit," he answered with a snort. "If hockey is going backwards, it's the only thing that's going backwards. In my day the biggest forwards were Beliveau, Howe, and Frank Mahovlich. Now there's 200 guys that size. Jesse Owens couldn't win a goddamn ladies' race with his best time these days."

The Chief added one final note of tribute to the Horton file before he left. "As far as I'm concerned Tim Horton was a better person than he was a player — and that ought'a say something about him."

The sincere remark took me back to another conversation, with Dave Keon, riding in a van between speaking dates in Ontario. Keon, like other Hall of Famers, often slipped back to the glory days with little or no prodding. His recollections of Horton, a man he called the "glue" of the 1960s Leafs, were detailed and delivered with respect.

"He was powerful, in every sense of the word. Sheer power, and a leader, not rahrah but a leader all the same. One time a coach remarked how well he skated and I remember George Armstrong saying, 'You should have seen him before the hit.' You know about the Gadsby check," and I nodded, while Keon broke into a grin at some returning memory. "When he had to turn on the speed his ass would go down. He had a great work ethic, regarded it as a part of his job, just like injuries. He considered them an inconvenience, an interruption, like rain, or a late subway, just part of the territory.

"Course it was easy for him," Keon grinned. "He had a high pain threshold, too. He wasn't a creative passer, like an Orr, Pilote or Harvey, but he was a defensive defenceman who was rarely out of position, quick enough to cover up any mistakes, and he played the body. He had a sense of fair play and he'd get into it if he saw a dirty move. If a bigger guy ran me or Billy Harris, then watch out. If they ran a guy like Ron Stewart, OK, but not the Singer Midgets. That's what he used to call us. I think he referred to the little sewing machines they used to make." Keon threw his head back and laughed, prompting another thought outlining the man.

"We were on the ice at practice and Timmy was late. Imlach had just gathered us at centre ice to chew our ass like he always did, and Horton comes out all suited up, ready to go, but still late. So we start snickering and heckling and Timmy just skated up to Imlach and handed him a piece of paper, a note from Tim's wife Lori. Imlach read it, put it in his pocket and said, 'All right, let's go. Don't any of *you* assholes try this, it's already been done."

From Keon's descriptions of places and incidents it was evident Horton took his strength in stride, alternately using it to advantage on the ice, then employing it to bring those around him, friend or foe, into his way of thinking. "He assumed everyone else could perform to his level, couldn't fathom why others weren't as strong as him, and wasn't beyond taking some leeway when dealing with his teammates," Keon explained.

"You never knew what you were gonna get — Superman or Clark Kent. It was the mild-mannered reporter most of the time, but you never knew, he might go into a phone booth." Keon chuckled, stifling a cough at the same time. "He had this thing about knockin' down doors. You see that kind of stuff in the movies or on TV, but believe me it's no easy thing to knock down a door. See those cops on TV? They use those steel ramrods to batter doors down. Timmy used to do it for goddamn laughs.

"Once we were in Boston," he said, leaning forward as if there might be someone overhearing us. "In the playoffs, Frank Mahovlich and I are room-ies, and the telephone rings. It's Tim and he wants to know where are we going. He never asked, he'd just say, 'Where we goin?' In other words we're going out, whether you like it or not, but we're still going . . . the question is where. So I told him Frank and I are bushed and we'll pass. I hang up. He calls back insisting that we're going out. Now it's gettin' into dangerous territory, because when Timmy wants to go out, you're going' out. But Frank shakes his head. Timmy says, 'Do I have to come down there and get you two sissy bastards?' Now we got problems. Once he sets his mind, it's all over, but we agree, no matter what happens, we're gonna stay in bed. Sure enough, Tim comes down and starts banging on the door. 'C'mon you chickenshits, let's go, open the door or I'm gonna take 'er down.' By this time Frank and I are gettin' worried and sure enough, *Ba-boom,* the whole goddamn room jiggled. *Ba-boom,* and we can hear nails givin' way. *Ba-boom* — and in he comes with a cloud of plaster dust. All right you Singer Midget, let's go!' Honest to God, Ross, he grabbed the footboard with one hand and fired it up against the wall, like a goddamn pulldown bed. Good thing I bailed out half way up or he'd have crunched me into the wall.

"By this time we've gathered a crowd of players in the hall. Frank and I are pissin' our pants, terrified, I mean this ain't funny, yuh know. Just then somebody says, 'Imlach's coming,' and of course everybody splits, including Horton. Punch always stayed one floor above the team, for personal safety reasons I suppose. So here's Imlach, in his underwear and socks, walking around with hands on his hips as usual, all he needed was the damn fedora. We're still trying to straighten up my bed. You should have seen the wreckage. The door is fine, and still locked, but Timmy had knocked the whole door frame off the wall, and pushed it backward into the room. Honest to God, the freakin' door is still locked.

"Now Punch starts in. 'What's all the goddamn ruckus about? You two are gonna pay for this. Who did the door?' That's when I lost it. 'Who do you know, on this goddamn team, could pull this little stunt off?' I yelled at him. Still cost Frank and me $325 dollars. Next morning on the bus to the Boston Garden there's ol' Clark Kent sittin' by himself, glasses on, reading the paper." We share a laugh over that one.

"You know, in practice we'd have these one-on-ones, and the first thing you learned was never get too close to those arms. He had this trick of putting his stick handle down on the ice to stop pucks. I'd seen him do it a hundred times, but I thought I was faster than he was. I'd come roaring down on him, make about three moves, and try to push the puck out either side of him. No dice. I never could get it past him before he reacted. He was a master." Keon said it wistfully, drifting off to another recollection.

"Clothes were nothing to Tim — just a requirement. It wasn't until he got older that he became conscious of what he wore. When we went to Montreal the guys used to get suits and stuff from Tony the Tailor. Tony conned Timmy into buying this humungous winter top coat. Must have been made for

Beliveau, weighed about 100 pounds. I guess Tony figured Horton was the only one who could carry it.

"Same thing with his hair. Wasn't until the late 1960s that he let it grow. Usually he looked like a boot-camp drill sergeant on leave. And he was different from the rest of us, in that hockey never took anything out of him. We'd all head home for a sandwich, a beer, and bed down after practice. Timmy would be going to an auction or something like that. He was fascinated by the car business, or for that matter any business. But he never let it interfere with his game.

"In the 1964 Stanley Cup playoffs, we had gotten past Montreal and we're facing Detroit. Down 3–2 in games and heading back to the Olympia, the news hit about a strike at Texas Gulf in Timmins. Lot of the guys on our team had shares in the company and all the talk in the dressing room at practice centred on the business. During the game meal at the hotel, Timmy got up and said we were letting too many distractions into the room, that we had to deal with the Red Wings first. Just the way he said it got your attention, and there wasn't a word said about stocks and bonds, about losin' money or business dealings again. We went out that night and Boomer Baun, broken leg and all, got the 4–3 winner in overtime and we went back to Toronto and beat them 4–0 in the seventh game for the Cup.

"When Timmy talked, everybody listened," Dave said, leaning forward once again, and it came to me where I'd heard the phrase from the E.F. Hutton commercial before.

"Hockey took up about three hours of his day, and that was it," Keon continued. "He handled winning and losing the same way, keeping it to himself, never letting it show. He was tough, not just physically, either. I recall him joking one day at practice, saying 'we're gonna move the Gardens. I'll take this end, don't drop yours,' so I suppose he wasn't as blind to his strength as we thought. One time when Elmer Vasko belted Bert Olmstead in the corner, Timmy took exception and came rushing in, pissed about the cheap shot I guess. Elmer turned just in time to see him coming. Timmy didn't punch him — he couldn't punch anything, strong as he was — but they locked arms, and Timmy was on the bottom for just an instant. The next moment Vasko was on his back on the ice in a death grip and the fight was over. Like I said he was tough every way. Did you know he never wore contacts again after *the hit?* That's why he didn't like practices where they only used the black pucks, made it tough for him to see them. In games, they used the other pucks. Orange NHL logo on one side, team logo on the other — a lot easier for him to pick it up."

Keon, Baun, Horton, and the other great Leafs of the era nailed down Toronto's last Stanley Cup in 1967 when Keon won the Conn Smythe Trophy as the most valuable player of the playoffs. "I had three goals and five assists. So did Tim, but I guess his didn't count," Keon said as we got ready to pull into London, Ontario, in time for lunch.

Though Toronto nose-dived in the next two seasons, Horton was named to the first All-Star defence alongside Bobby Orr as his age crept through 38 and 39, when he had his "career" year point-wise, with 11 goals, 29 assists, 40 points in 74 games.

Why then, I wondered that day as the countryside went by, did the Leafs trade away as good a player and person as Tim Horton to the New York Rangers in March 1970 for Guy Trottier and Denis Dupere? Age was the governing factor. Trottier at 29 was a triggerman from the Rangers' minor-league team in Buffalo. He had just come off a 55-goal season. Dupere was a big 21-year-old winger and centre playing in Tulsa. Horton was 41.

Before the trade, Leaf general manager Jim Gregory told Horton he had a choice, that he could refuse the trade, but Horton accepted his fate and moved on, although as George Armstrong said, Horton considered himself to be a Maple Leaf forever.

"We were in Oakland when the word came down," Keon said sadly. "Timmy never even came to the dressing room before he left."

The two would cross paths on the ice, and occasionally in the summer. Horton toiled in New York for the following season. Ready to retire, he was picked up by the Pittsburgh Penguins for the 71–72 season. The effects of further expansion still lingered in the new NHL and, ready to retire all over again, he was lured to Buffalo by his old mentor, and tormentor, Punch Imlach, to suit up with the experience-short Sabres.

Keon recalled their phone call after Horton signed with the Sabres. "I asked why he'd consented to go to Buffalo. 'Punch offered me a contract I couldn't refuse. He's probably trying to make up for all the times he screwed us before. Whatever his reasons, I can't turn it down.'"

Then came February 20, 1974, at Maple Leaf Gardens. Horton played only the first two periods of a 4–2 loss to the Leafs, sitting on the bench throughout the third, a victim of a growing, gnawing pain in his face, the result of what is now suspected to be a broken jaw suffered a couple of nights earlier in Detroit.

"After the game I walked up to the parking lot north of the Gardens with my sister, Patricia, and we ran into Punch and Do Imlach and Timmy. He looked beat up, ragged around the edges, you know, and he was on painkillers. We talked for a while, I told him to get to the doctor in Buffalo, and he left. Never saw him again. Later that morning he was killed. He didn't play one shift in the last period and he was still picked third star."

As many times as I've heard the story, with its nuances and assumptions, I've never failed to be chilled by the series of events. After his talk with Keon and Imlach, Horton had stopped in to the Oakville corporate offices of his burgeoning doughnut company, and they say he had something to drink. It was well known that Timmy liked to drive fast, and he had just the machine to do it. Later, as he hurtled along the Queen Elizabeth Way, the Pantera sailed into oblivion near the Lake Street cutoff in St. Catharines. Six weeks after turning 44, on February 21, 1974, the greatest of the pure defencemen was gone.

I still remember vividly the game against the Atlanta Flames the next night at the Memorial Auditorium and the pre-game ceremony, black armbands on the uniforms, and a long moment of unbroken silence among 16,000 fans while Jim Schoenfeld, the large Sabre defenceman, wept openly, his blue line partner snatched away. He wasn't alone.

Over lunch I asked Dave Keon about how Horton would fare trying to defend against "gang-checking," the modern habit that sometimes finds three players from one team against two players from the other, all in the same corner. Or how would Tim handle the latest offensive zone gambit of "cycling," where players twist and turn, reversing inside-out against the boards, using their stick and feet to control the puck.

Keon gave me a dubious look, advising he was well aware of the present-day practice.

"First guy who tried to wheel-and-deal with Timmy would be one-armed and pasted face-first up on the glass, with his skates about six inches off the ice," Keon said emphatically. "Try 'cycling' from that position."

In the course of writing this book I continually asked the players and hockey notables to offer an opinion on Tim Horton. In a regular, monotonous parade, the comments about his strength and his universal respect by team-mate and opponent alike were repeated. But a few stick out in my mind.

Frank Selke Jr., the long-time broadcaster with *Hockey Night in Canada* in Montreal, GM of the California Seals, and later VP of HNIC, said, "He was never flamboyant or flashy, he just did it right, routinely, reliably, again and again. At the end of a game, even though he had played great, his name seldom came to mind. Maybe that's a comment on his entire career. He was so great, so steady, for so long, we began to take him for granted."

I called Jim Schoenfeld just as he became coach of the Washington Capitals. He answered quickly, almost as if he had been waiting for the question. "When I was a kid I pulled for the Leafs. Tim was an idol of mine. What are the odds on making the NHL, then being paired with your idol? It's the stuff dreams are made of. Timmy did everything to the nth degree, playing hard on the ice and chasing life just as hard off it. To a lot of us, the young Sabres, we knew he was 40-some but we couldn't see it. It didn't seem right to us to picture him as a grandfather, or even that he'd grow older, stuff like that. He used to say to me, 'Kid, the hard way is the easy way,' when I'd get tired of practice. He was right. I can still remember seeing him at the Statler Hilton in Buffalo. We went up to his room, he had just been told his new Pantera was ready, and he was so excited. He was forever young."

I was barrelling along the 401 on the way to Brockville with Dennis Hull when a thought struck him out of the blue. "I was an instructor at Allan Stanley's hockey school in Fenelon Falls back in the 1960s when Timmy came in to the camp with a big bag of doughnuts, samples for the guys to try. He said he was thinking about a new venture. We ate the doughnuts, but I distinctly remember telling him *nobody* is ever gonna make a go of a place that only sells doughnuts!" That one kept us laughing for several miles.

And I too, thought back to Tim Horton, a latter day Sir Galahad in a hockey uniform, a player who protected the less able, who stood for excellence, a player who played the game much bigger than his physical presence.

Each time I hear Tim's name come up in conversation over the years I'm reminded of the American policeman who, to this day, may never be aware of what happened to Timmy.

I had travelled on the Leaf team charter to St. Louis. We stayed at the Chase Park Plaza and after the game a few of us had gone to a small corner bar called Culpepper's not far from the hotel. We had only just arrived when a large policeman came in, took the shot of Southern Comfort proffered by the tavern owner, knocked it back and stared suspiciously at me, Dave Keon, Bruce Gamble, and Jim McKenny. After a second shot, he looked even more leery, finally asking aloud, "Haven't I seen you guys somewheres before?" It was explained who he was talking to and after a few more questions of Dave Keon he loosened up considerably, thereby loosening us up in turn.

"Where's the big guy?" he asked.

As soon as we determined the big guy was Timmy, it fell to Davey once again to explain how Horton had been traded to New York. Then we heard the story as seen from the other side.

The previous year, there had been a bit of a post-game beer party put on by a few of the Leafs in their hotel rooms. During the discussions about the noise between hotel management, the police, and the Leaf players reluctant to go to bed, Tim Horton apparently had come out of his room, a non-participant in the affair but a part of the team to the end.

"My partner looks up and spots this big dude coming down the hallway, and he ain't got on nothin' but skivvies, and muscles. He's ankle to eyeball in muscles. I said, 'What the *hell* is this, and my ol' partner Jerome says, 'Ah truly don't know, but I do hope t' fuck he's in a good mood.'" It was such an upbeat story we bought him a couple of Jim Beam chasers.

There are those who say Horton would have stayed in hockey, as a coach. Some say he'd have been an excellent NHL coach. But the people who knew best believe he would have gone straight into business with nary a look back at the game. Dave Keon remembers Horton this way: "He never came on as best anything, but he sure as hell was. He was very humble and the marvellous thing about Timmy was that he never changed. He knew what he was, what he wanted to do . . ." The thought trails off. "Yep, he would have gone into business," Keon says as if a decision was required.

It's logical. Hockey only took three hours out of Tim Horton's day.

The shame of it is, we'll never know.

Epilogue

THE LAST TIME I WAS BACK in Thunder Bay was in mid-May, 1994. The Fort William Country Club was "almost" open, which afforded the luxury of a golf game where we played the nine holes available, twice around. It's always nice to get home, rent a car, and amaze myself at how little has changed, how I can still find my way around even though they have things like expressways and advanced turning greens these days.

I can still find the Fort William Gardens, but just like the thousands that flock to the Senator games there, I can't find a parking spot. The FW Gardens is home to the Thunder Bay Senators, a pro farm club of the NHL's version of *Let's Make a Deal.* They are in the Colonial League, and although they lead in everything from attendance to real money, the rest of the league would like very much if they went west, south, or anywhere else. It's been the lot of any sports team from the Lakehead since I was a kid, this problem of distance, proximity to the population corridors, and the fact that it's a butt-numbing eight-hour bus ride from anywhere of any significance. Any place farther is airplane time, and that's expensive. It's ironic that when they finally get a successful team, one that wins the league championship, strains the capabilities of the 40-year-plus building, there's no room at the inn. But that's life in northwestern Ontario. Nobody can guarantee a golf game on May 15, and nobody wants you when you're a winner.

I can also find the ball park. The Port Arthur Stadium had a face-lift of sorts last year, expanded fences, new turf, a paint job, and a beer and wine counter. The Whiskey Jacks of the Northern League put 6,500 in a 2,500-seat stadium for opening day in their inaugural game. And the honeymoon with the fans continued until the end. This season it started all over again, with a new rival in the resurrected Winnipeg Goldeyes. They made TSN. Twice.

As the park was being readied by a horde of workmen in June of that first year, I parked and wandered onto the playing field, standing where the new mound would be. It was skinned out, just a bare circle surrounded by new sod, but looking toward home plate it brought back a flood of memories for me, a left-handed pitcher who lived and died on two breaking balls and the occasional "heat" I laughingly called a fastball. The theory and strategy I employed was to not throw too long, vary my speeds from slow to slower, and zip in the "heat" any time after a loud foul ball. I may have been the only sore-armed pitcher who used a fastball as a change-up.

Back then, a lot of hockey players in Thunder Bay played baseball. Alex "Fats" Delvecchio was a teammate, as was Larry "Hank" Cahan, and we had opponents like Bruce Gamble, and Rudy Migay, all NHLers with a host of other minor-league hockey hopefuls strung out through the four teams.

I had stopped in unannounced and unescorted through the army of sod-layers, electricians, and painters on that June day, knowing full well that 40 years before I had won a game on the same date right here on this non-mound I stood on. As I was lost in the recollection of those "good ol' days" days, a guy in a hard hat was able to sneak up and scare the crap out of me.

"You need some help, pal?" he barked, an official-looking drawing in his hand, a tape measure, plus the all-important ring of keys hanging from a heavy leather belt.

"The only help I could have used from here was a good fastball," I chuckled, but stifled it quickly, looking into his unsmiling face. "Actually I was just reminiscing," I said, collected now, but still a little dreamy from the memories.

"Yeah, well how'dja like to reminisce yerself a pair of safety boots, and a hat," he said looking at my loafers, now messed up with grey muck on the sides. "You a politician?" he threw in as an afterthought. I shook my head, introduced myself, using my nickname in the middle in case it might ring a bell, and tried to explain.

"I'm in from Toronto, just driving by and — well, I used to play, years ago, in fact I won a game here against the Port Arthur Giants 40 years ago today. I was just 16, thought I was pretty good, too," I added with a big smile, all designed to impress him.

He stood there stone-faced. "You ain't from the Workers' Comp are you?" he said, direct and to the point. I could only shake my head, and realized I might *need* a hard hat before this inquisition ended.

"Forty years ago I was three," he said, finally taking the edge out of his voice.

"Guess you weren't at the game then," I replied, snappy and on top of things.

"That's right, Lefty, and if we don't get this grass down I won't be seeing the next one here either."

But he was nice enough to take me on a tour of the reconstructed field and the new dressing rooms. Then he walked me out to the parking lot, where we shook hands.

"You here to throw out the first ball or somethin'?" he asked as I turned to leave.

"Naw. Nobody asked me. Besides I don't think I could reach home plate on the fly," I said, and he laughed, which caused me to wonder if he *had* seen me pitch before.

The encounter started me wondering about the great life I had as a kid growing up in the Twin Cities, and I realized it was the reason I had always wanted to write about people like Alex Delvecchio and Larry Cahan. Not about their hockey-playing days so much as the people they were when they were in their hometown, walking down the streets of the old neighbourhood, about how they were all like us, and we in turn were just like them. It's where the idea for . . . *Last Minute of Play* came from, the Bruce Gambles, Pete Goegans, Lou Marcons, Bob McCammons, and all the others who followed, and the fact that except for geography they could be from anywhere in Canada.

I eventually got to write about Delvecchio, and a certain baseball game, in . . . *Last Minute of Play,* but sadly, the complete story on Larry Cahan, one of the all-time funny people to ever play in the NHL, sits unpolished in a file folder. He passed away much too soon, in Vancouver a week before our scheduled get-together.

It took awhile for me to realize that Fort William, Port Arthur, Thunder Bay, whatever, is identical to every other city in the country. Only the nicknames change. Through all the trips, all the late-night discussions with players, the only differences were the nicknames.

And after that golf game on a chilly May day in the shadow of Mount McKay, I travelled across the city with "Chinky." We headed up to Hodder Avenue and a little store with a house attached to the back. Here I run into the owner, a guy called "3D" — or sometimes "Nipper," although that handle has apparently fallen to his son. 3D is busily making hamburger patties. The nondescript store is the answer to an ex–Fort William boy's dream. French fries in brown bags, hamburgers with real beef, and hot dogs, the world's best hot dogs in soft, steamed buns, garnished with finely diced onions, a chili sauce to top it off, with mustard added to choice. The former World Champion Montreal Forum version just fell four dogs out of first place.

The "boys" begin to stop in, some for the conversation, others on their way to cottages along Lake Superior. There's Chubby already there, followed by Hammer, then Sniper stops in to pick up lunch. I thank him for the loan of his golf clubs. "Might as well use 'em, Lefty, they don't do a goddamn thing for me," he complains.

Sitting around munching our hot dogs, I can't help but go over the nicknames again. At the golf course it was Mañana, Chili, Fuzz, Corn, and Honeycomb. Then came the nicknames from the past, spattered through our conversation about the days of fastball, baseball, and hockey. Fats, Hank, Beaver, Juicer, Bates, Quack, Chucker, Scoots, Scratchy, Tinker, Kayo, and Bullet. Not to forget the present company of 3D, Chubby, Hammer, Sniper, and my driver, Chinky, who made it to the NHL's St. Louis Blues. Lefty was there, too.

We all played in Thunder Bay. Looking down the halls of my memory then around the room, I asked a question that I'd personally gone over thousands of times. "You guys ever wonder what would have happened if we hadn't been involved in sports?"

"Yeah. We could've formed our own chain gang." Solemnly, we toasted each other with hot dogs.

One extra thing writing these stories has taught me is that we're all the same, no matter what the locale or the nicknames. From the late-blooming Jim "The Bird" Pappin to the carefully articulate Gil "le Gros" Perreault. Pete Mahovlich isn't much different from Pat "Whitey" Stapleton, give or take a foot in height and a missing nickname. There are the unique ones in this edition, like Tim "Thrifty" Horton, Jean "Le Gros Bill" Beliveau, and Derek "Turk" Sanderson, but even the regal Beliveau and the irreverent Sanderson are a similar species, with relative bloodlines. One was a race horse, the other was a mustang. Horton had the strength of a Clydesdale.

Then there's Dennis "Buster" Hull, and a little story to make a point. Where did the blazing shot come from, the one Plante told Tretiak to watch for?

"I saw Ralph Backstrom slap a puck from the red line into the empty net once, and that was my inspiration. I went home that summer and paced off a hundred feet from the concrete wall of the garage. Everything in Point Anne is concrete," Dennis notes, a reference to the Canada Cement Company, father Bob Senior's employer for a lifetime. "I had one puck, and a piece of linoleum to shoot off. So I'd blast one, run down then back, and I'd shoot again. I was forever losing the puck in the damn rhubarb, but by the end of the summer I could hit the roof." That's where one of the most feared shots in the NHL was developed, by a 12-year-old in a rural yard, against a concrete wall.

"Years later in Chicago we were leaving a practice and somebody said I couldn't slap the puck from behind the goal line, make it go around the other end glass, and come back behind the goal line again. I said 'Gimme my stick' and went out there and cranked one, like a rocket. What I didn't see was this guy on a stepladder cleaning the glass at the blue line on the opposite side. The puck hit at the far end in the corner, came rattling around the glass and clipped him on the ankle. 'Oh noooo,' I moaned, one hand over my eyes."

"Bet he was really pissed about it," I said, imagining the pain and wincing.

"Naw. Saw him a couple of days after he got the cast on and he came up and thanked me. Six months off at full pay."

What about the nickname, Buster?

"We came back to O'Hare airport one day and at the baggage claim one of the guys spotted "Dear Abby" and her manager. The boys pushed me into going over and talking to her. So I walked up, stuck out my hand and said, 'Hi, I'm Dennis Hull with the Blackhawks.' She glared at me like I was handing her a rattlesnake and said, 'Write me a letter, Buster!' My wife's called me Buster ever since."

It's what's known in the business as an empty-netter.